The Man No

The Life and Legacy of B. Traven

Roy Pateman

University Press of America,® Inc.
Lanham · Boulder · New York · Toronto · Oxford

Copyright © 2005 by
University Press of America,® Inc.
4501 Forbes Boulevard
Suite 200
Lanham, Maryland 20706
UPA Acquisitions Department (301) 459-3366

PO Box 317
Oxford
OX2 9RU, UK

All rights reserved
Printed in the United States of America
British Library Cataloging in Publication Information Available

Library of Congress Control Number: 2004109771
ISBN 0-7618-2973-3 (paperback : alk. ppr.)

∞™ The paper used in this publication meets the minimum
requirements of American National Standard for Information
Sciences—Permanence of Paper for Printed Library Materials,
ANSI Z39.48—1984

Dedicated to my lifelong friends John and Anne Shelley

Contents

Preface and Acknowledgments	vii
1. Who Was B. Traven?	1
2. The Red Thread: Major Influences on Traven's Life and Work	21
3. Traven's Life, Work and Times	37
4. Traven's American Alter Ego	51
5. Tierra y Libertad	83
6. Traven's Legacy	123
Epilogue: A Tale of Two or More Men	159
Glossary and Acronyms	167
Bibliography	175
Index	213
Author's Biography	240

Preface and Acknowledgments

I first heard of B. Traven through occasional articles in the British anarchist weekly *Freedom* and from hearing a broadcast on BBC radio in England in 1972. I was immediately drawn to the man and his writing possibly because I shared his wish that, "I will for my part contribute to the disappearance of all authorities and veneration for authority" (cited Georg 1929, 484). Over the past thirty years I have read and reread all of his novels and collections of short stories available in English, all of the biographies and most of the secondary literature in English, as well as some of the voluminous material in German, French, and Spanish (as may be seen by looking at my end notes, bibliography and index).

I have made generous use of translations - even though I take heed of Richard Wagner's warning, "he who has not made himself thoroughly at home with a foreign, unaccustomed tongue, must pay heed to its idiosyncrasies in everything he says" (Wagner 1966 I, 363). But I am also encouraged by Emerson's comments about translation "what is really best in any book is translatable" (Emerson 1904, 204). After all, one does not usually wade through a river if you can use a bridge.

I have drawn upon my discussion notes on *The Death Ship* published by the Council of Adult Education in Victoria in 1977.[1] I started collecting Traveniana in the 1970s, and while browsing through Princeton's library in 1985 I came across Traven's hard-to-find travel book *Land des Frühlings* (1926). I copied it with good intentions of making the first translation into English, but it has languished in my file drawers to this day.[2]

Throughout the 1980s and early 1990s I had been promising David Goodway the convener of the anarchist strain of the annual History Workshop Conference held in Britain, a paper on Traven to supplement the ones I had already given on "How Libertarian is the EPLF?" and "Wagner: Anarchism and National Socialism". Here, at last David is the rather long paper along with my appreciation for many years of unfortunately intermittent communication between us. I would also like to thank Carole Pateman for the many decades of illuminating conversations and comments about Traven, the wobblies and many other matters.

The book is dedicated to my cousin John who was born five hours before me, and who has been my dearest friend since that day. And also to his wife Anne with whom for forty years or more I have spent many a happy hour sharing our mutual love of books and malt whisky.

I have done most of the research at my home base in Westwood Village in Los Angeles. The librarians at the University of California Los Angeles (UCLA) were as always friendly and helpful, and I am particularly indebted to the Special Collections where I was able to see the Lawrence Clark Powell boxes on Traven ephemera. Here it was fascinating to read of the correspondence between some of my predecessors: William Weber Johnson, Herbert and Mina Klein, John Fraser, E. R. Hagemann and Robert Goss, and benefit from their more esoteric research work. I also came across humorists such as Anthony West who clearly is somewhat ambivalent at times about Traven and his admirers whom he dubs the: "marginally literate inhabitants of the vast empty spaces of the Southwest" (West 1967, 82). Another collection at University California Riverside (UCR) yielded a useful haul of theses, and hard-to-find secondary materials.

The most significant and useful works that I have found in writing this book include: Edward Treverton, *B. Traven: A Bibliography* (1999); Michael Baumann, *B. Traven: An Introduction* (1976); Karl Guthke, *B. Traven: The Life behind the Legends* (1991); Rolf Recknagel, *B. Traven: Beiträge zur Biografie* (1983); Ernst Schürer, and Philip Jenkins, eds. *B. Traven: Life and Work* (1987); Heidi Zogbaum, *B. Traven: a Vision of Mexico* (1992); and Charles Humphrey's Ph. D. dissertation, University of Texas, 1965.

This is not a conventional biography. I take to heart Traven's views that the creative person should have no other biography than his works. Instead this book follows the schemata of my earlier book on Wagner: *Chaos and Dancing Star* (2002). There is a brief discussion of Traven's alternative histories, followed by an attempt to find out what were the major influences on this elusive man. I then deal with his politics and his life of humanist anarchism. I discuss all of his works with most of my emphasis on *The Death Ship*, *The Treasure of the Sierra Madre* and the "Jungle Sextet".

I do not give a detailed long analysis of any of the works. I assume that readers of this book have either read Traven or will be galvanized to do so; you can make up your own mind. All I will do is to highlight some phrases, sentences and passages that are relevant to my main argument. However, I have managed to track down, read, and digest more reviews of his work than any other scholar writing in English. I have also seen many reviews in German, Spanish, French and Italian and cite them where appropriate. I attach a glossary of words, abbreviations and common phrases, mainly in Mexican Spanish, that you will run across in reading Traven and my bibliographic entries. I also give a chronology of his life, work and times which is fuller than that to be found in any other study of Traven, and is I hope more reader-friendly and accurate than they often are.

One of my most substantial chapters is "Traven's Legacy" where I look at what some significant writers, artists, activists and musicians, among other vocations, have thought of Traven. I follow the approach I adopted in my recent book *Chaos and Dancing Star*. I discuss some promising candidates who so far in my research turn out not to have been interested in Traven either as a writer or a man. But the bulk of the chapter consists of a solid core of very diverse people who could be classed as fans of Traven. It is I think a more substantial and scholarly account of Traven's legacy than most others in the literature.

I am very aware of the dangers of drifting into the *post hoc ergo propter hoc* fallacy. Resemblance, affinities of minds and analogies may indicate a common source, rather than a strong influence on Traven or by Traven (Thatcher 1970, 13). As Gide said so trenchantly, "nothing is so absurd as that accusation of *influence* (in which certain critics excel every time they note a resemblance)" (cited Thatcher, 15). Much of what we shall consider falls properly under the heading of *Zeitgeist* and is a matter of general sympathies (Martin 1982, x). Cicora makes an apt comment, "what goes on in the mind of an artist can never be exactly described by anyone" (Cicora 1992, 66).

I will also try to avoid the "intentional fallacy" that eminently fruitless exercise in literary criticism, the trying to determine an artist's intention, and using this as the final criterion to be used in judging his [or her] work (Shattuck 1972, 80). Tanner also alerts us to the "fallacy of origins;" this is the erroneous line of argument that the most completed form of the work of art is nothing more than its elementary form "cosmeticised" (Tanner 1996, 35). I will also certainly watch out for "over-determinism"- the belief that a web of social and cultural conditions and dominant values imposed unavoidable choices that Traven (or any other artist) was compelled to make (Hutton 1994, 6).

César Vallejo wrote very aptly that it is, "for the illiterate for whom I write" (cited Garland 1982, 126). But Traven is also a man whose readership probably spreads across broader class, race and language divides than anyone else writing in the twentieth century. So the main innovation on my part compared with the other critics is the account of some of the most important and interesting people over the years who have enjoyed the books or been influenced by Traven. I end with a modest proposal, my attempts to emulate Swift in finding a solution to the intractable problem of who Traven really was and where he was born and raised.[3]

The book is not an exercise in literary scholarship or polemical broadsides; Traven said that literary scholars were "that class of men for whom a special hell ought to be created" (cited Baumann 1987, 25). I also remind myself of Donald Chankin's warning that this special place is in circle seven, round three of Dante's *Inferno* where we find the "violent against art" (Chankin 1988, 234).

Neither is it an attempt to claim Traven as a "proletarian writer"; I regard him rather as a man who more than any other has shown throughout his adult life a compassion for the proletariat and the dispossessed, and an ability to write about them more entertainingly and movingly than any other person I have encountered in my sixty four years reading.

One of the affinities I have with Traven is that we are both philosophical anarchists who were activists in our early years, and who closely identified ourselves with revolutionary movements in the Third World; in his case with the Mexican Indians and the Mexican Revolution after 1910, and in my case with the Eritrean liberation struggle of 1961 to 1991. I like to think that with him (or Gales) that I became something of a philosopher by living with people of a different race speaking a different language (Raskin 1980, 178). In both our cases we lived to see the Revolution hijacked by dictators and the *peones* exchanging one master for another, but neither of us ever lost faith in the people.

I also feel that Traven and I would agree on the whole with the good Doctor Johnson who in his robust way said: "I would not give half a guinea to live under one form of government rather than another. It is of no moment to the happiness of an individual" (Birbeck 1934, 170).

Roy Pateman
Los Angeles CA
30 April 2004

Notes

1. They are usually 4,000 words in length and take the form of a critical review essay, and up to ten searching questions and comments for discussion. Over an eleven year period I contributed some thirty-two reviews each of 4,000 words and two of 12,000 words. Topics covered a wide range of disciplines including, politics, history, economics and poetry, as well as fiction.
2. I was drawn to the book because even with my rudimentary German I felt empathy with its combination of detailed, eclectic, objective analysis and the subjective opinion of an individualist anarchist – rather like me.
3. Jonathan, Swift. *A Modest Proposal: for Preventing the Children of Poor People from being a Burden to Their Parents, or the Country, and for Making Them Beneficial to the Public.* First published in England in 1729.

Chapter 1

Who Was B. Traven?

A name unoccupied by an identity. (Wyatt 1980, 1)

Travens - one to five and counting

It is admittedly debatable whether it is entirely appropriate to say as does my title, an edition of his short stories, and the blurb to an American edition of *The Death Ship*, that: "Traven is the man nobody knows". It is problematic whether a man whose novels are available in some thirty languages, about 250 editions, and of which some thirty-two million copies have been printed is unknown.[1]

Some of the languages in which one can read Traven are as follows: Arabic, Bulgarian, Catalan, Czech, Danish, Dutch, English, Estonian, Finnish, Flemish, French, German, Greek, Hebrew, Hungarian, Icelandic, Italian, Japanese, Latvian, Lithuanian, Norwegian, Polish, Portuguese, Romanian, Russian, Serbo-Croat, Slovak, Slovenian, Spanish, Swedish, Turkish and Yiddish. Edward Treverton found no trace of Chinese language editions but is sure that they exist, both on the mainland and Taiwan, in pirated editions (Treverton 1999, 17).

He has been read and appreciated by some of the finest minds and writers of his and succeeding generations, and I deal with a number of these men and women in my final chapter. The distinguished poet Kenneth Rexroth made an extremely penetrating and influential observation when he said of Traven: "the first, and still the greatest, novelist of total disengagement is not a young man at all, but an elderly former I.W.W. of German ancestry" (Rexroth 1957, 35).

Traven for many years deliberately shunned publicity; the only contact his publishers had with him was via a post office in an obscure town in a remote and impoverished Mexican state. I received a letter from Traven's literary agent in America and Europe in 1971 (in response to a request for information about films made from Traven's books or scripts) and was told that they had never contacted Traven personally but only through another agent – probably his wife Señora Rosa Elena Luján (born 1915) - who negotiated deals: "in a most clandestine manner".[2]

Traven rarely gave interviews - or so at least some stories go. In the mid 1960s he is supposed to have approved of an article appearing in the Mexico City paper *Excelsior* but such cooperation was rare (Nichols 1967, 51). His first and most brilliant English editor Bernard Smith says that Traven's insistence on anonymity was not primarily because of principle but was just another example of his shrewdness. For publisher and author alike: "publicizing the no-publicity aspect of our relationship with him proved to be excellent publicity" (Smith 1994, 71).

He remained adamant on anonymity sticking to a view he made when he was writing in 1919 as Ret Marut "I shall always and at all times prefer to be pissed on by dogs than reveal who I am" (Baumann 1976, 17). When he agreed to let his books be published in the USA he stipulated that there should be no blurb on the jacket and that they should be advertised only in three "liberal" weeklies (Powell nd, 3). One ingenious and plausible psychological reason suggested for his desire for utter privacy is maybe because "the gratification that comes from being able to praise yourself publicly without false humility is unsurpassable" (Le Boutillier 1948, 15).

In later life Traven became ever more eccentric and adopted the habit of referring to "Traven" in the third person. In his *alter egos* as Torsvan and Croves, Traven often criticized Traven. When Croves/Torsvan went to Berlin in 1959 to help put the finishing touches to the movie made from *The Death Ship* he even went through the charade of placing a phone call to Traven in Mexico claiming that he wanted Traven's opinion on the filming of a scene where Croves and the Director did not see eye to eye; naturally Traven concurred with Croves (Guthke 1993, 116).

On at least one occasion Croves dismissed Marut (an anarchist journalist and actor, and Traven's persona in Germany prior to 1924) as a political charlatan (Kirsch 1977, 11). The journalist Luís Spota claims that Traven as Torsvan rated *The Bridge in the Jungle* as Traven's best novel, but thought *La Rosa Blanca* to be a detestable melodrama (Spota 1948, 25-26).[3] To muddy the waters further, Traven/Croves' wife told Croves in the presence of Judy Stone that *La Rosa Blanca* was her favorite novel (Stone October 1967, 59). According to Lawrence Hill,

Mrs. Rosa Elena Luján Traven under Traven's direction was primarily responsible for the English version published in London in 1965 (cited Ponick 1976, 14n30). It is generally regarded as being much inferior to other versions.

Some of this hyperbole arises from the fact that Croves/Torsvan could have been in exasperation and eventual exhaustion at the continuing quest for the real Traven. He wrote in *The Death Ship* "yet who is he that could stand a hundred questions and answer none?" (Kirsch, 11). Baumann points out interestingly that Traven did begin to promote his books and their author from 1951 until 1960. His Zurich agent, Josef Weider at Traven's request brought out the *BT-Mitteilungen* (the *BT Newsletter*) that gave German readers random information about his books, Traven ephemera, and denouncement of imposters – but no clue as to his identity or whereabouts (Baumann 1971, 49n26).

The Mexican journalist Antonio Rodríguez claims that Traven writing as Traven Torsvan said "I am sure that B. Traven has not written his books by himself ... there are passages in them which only a very intelligent woman could have written." And Traven reputedly rejected the "Order of the Aztec" saying that he was not the writer, merely, one of three people who could identify the man or men who were hiding behind the pseudonym B, Traven (Rodríguez, cited by Humphrey 1965, 125-126). One reason why I am skeptical about this is that the article was published on 1 April 1964 – All Fool's Day.[4]

There has been endless and pointless speculation on what "B." stands for. Traven denied on several occasions that he was called: Ben, Benno, Bruno, Ber(r)ick, Benito, Bernard or Bendrich. Karl Guthke thinks that "B" may be a way of paying homage to Berthold, the name given to Stansilaus in the handwritten first English draft of *The Death Ship*. Traven claimed that the sailor who was the inspiration for Stansilaus had saved his life (Guthke 1991, 74).

The derivation of his pseudonym "Traven" has also been the subject of much ingenious wrangling. In Swedish, *Traven* apparently means a pile of sticks or books (Braybrooke 1963, 141). In German, *Traven* is a nautical term meaning to "stow in a hold or press into a bale" (Hagemann 1960, 370). And for those interested in anagrams, Marut becomes *traum* or dream. Manfred Georg(e) claims that the first story that Traven sent to a German paper was signed "Traum." Karl Doescher being interested in anagrams rearranged the letters to read Marut and gratuitously added a "B" as a given name (Georg 1947, 35). To complicate matters an undated Dutch translation of *Das Totenschiff* dubs the author, "Trave" (Treverton, 20).

A fairly convincing explanation for the name may be as follows. Traven had a picture in his study in Mexico City of the River *Trave* in Lübeck, Germany (Stone 1977, 85). Wyatt also tells us that Traven may have seen a German vessel called the *Trave* which was docked in London in April 1924 as he was preparing to board the *Hegre* taking him to the New World (Wyatt, 218-219). This could have been the spur behind his choice of the new pen name.

Woodcock plays along with this anagram and word substitution game: Traum – Trauen – Traven. *Trauen* in German means "to dare". He also says (correctly of course) that Croves is an anagram of Covers and that Hal Covers is an apt description of what Traven's *alter ego* did so well (Woodcock 1976, 1053). Chankin rather fancifully argues that B. Traven if spoken out suggests "betrayed" (Chankin 1975, 123n42).

Understandably, Traven's identity was the subject of conjecture and legend for almost fifty years; a high point of interest followed the making of the very successful movie *The Treasure of the Sierra Madre* (from Traven's third book) in 1948.[5] Just as he was constantly reworking his books and stories so he continually rewrote his life. The books have been translated many times into many languages; each time this is done the book is in essence, rewritten and we have a fresh text. And each time a researcher or particularly intelligent Ph. D. student comes up with a new approach to Traven or another candidate for the mantle of the famous writer, so interest in the books is rekindled and someone else is moved to buy one or read one.

Of the many attempts to find Traven's "true" identity that of Luís Spota was the most theatrical (Spota 1948, 12-26). In 1948, Spota claimed that Traven was Berick Traven Torsvan who was born in Chicago in 1890 and entered Mexico through Ciudad Juárez in June 1914. Torsvan had lived with the Mexican Indian schoolteacher María de la Luz Martínez as man and wife for sixteen years – Martinez said she had three children all of whom died young; Torsvan typically made no mention of them or ever admitted to a marriage with their mother.

Spota found out that Torsvan had possessed a safe deposit box in a bank in Mexico City since 1934. He got the address of the owner and tracked Torsvan down to his home in Acapulco. He claims to have had several lengthy and productive talks with him. Traven's attitude to him is summed up in the fact that he told Spota that the real Traven was in a sanatorium in Switzerland, and the meal he prepared for him with considerable care was appropriately enough - cooked Goose. Spota remained convinced that Torsvan was Traven, used some very questionable tactics in finding evidence; in print he robbed Traven of the anonymity he had nurtured so neurotically for years (Humphrey 1965, 47).

Traven was an energetic correspondent but he always asked the recipients to send back his letters. Traven exchanged ten letters with his editor Bernard Smith in 1936; Smith kept them even though Traven asked for them back. They were offered for sale after Traven's death (Howard, 1987).

One of the main planks of Traven's philosophy is that while the work was important, the man who wrote it was unimportant (Baumann 1976, 11). He did not regard himself as an author or writer, but as a worker. His work he considered to be the writing of books (*Die Büchergilde*, 1931).

He was such a confirmed recluse that conflicting stories became current as to his accent and his ability to speak German, English or Spanish correctly. In September 1967, an American journalist, Judy Stone announced that she had met and spoken several times with Traven, by then a very frail and deaf man of at least seventy-seven years of age.[6] Curiously, the publisher Lawrence Hill who also met Traven in the same year says that he looked younger than his seventy-seven years (Hill 1970, 10). This discrepancy fuelled further speculation that "Traven" masked the identity of two men.

Stone said that Traven spoke English accented by a trace of German (Stone 1977, 3). One of his neighbors said he did not have a German accent (Raskin 1980, 55-56). Lawrence Hill states he had a slight German accent whilst Traven's widow claims he spoke beautiful British-English (Hill 1970, 10; Baumann 1976, 167n4). It is interesting that no one has ever claimed that he spoke with an American accent as surely he would if he had been educated for any length of time in the USA – everybody else learns quickly to do so (Guthke 1993, 125).

Bill Johnson also met Traven for the first time in 1967, and said that he was a "slight frail old man who spoke Spanish and English fluently with what I took to be a German accent" (Johnson 1983, 168). Evelyn Keyes who at the time was married to the Film Director John Huston spent a lot of time in his presence in 1948 (both in Mexico and Los Angeles) says that his accent was "hard to define". Of course not all of them can be right unless we accept the two or three Traven hypothesis.

In a letter to Harry Schwarz Traven said that he is "not even of German race or blood" (Schwarz 1937, 80). Traven went to great lengths to put enquirers off the track. M. L. Martinez, his "agent in Mexico" apparently had a long and fluent correspondence in English with Mina Klein in 1943. She/he asserted that Traven "knows no German at all" (Mina Klein 8 April 1943, Folio 8). Although Recknagel reproduces a certified photograph of M. L. (Maria de la Luz) Martinez taken in Acapulco in 1963, Herbert Klein continued to maintain that Martinez and Traven were the same person (Recknagel 1983, 282; Klein, Folio 12).

When Stone interviewed Traven in 1967 he was living in Mexico City and still insisting vehemently that he was Hal Croves, Traven's agent (and/or his cousin). She was not convinced and subsequently published the results of her researches into Traven's life and an interview with him, first in *Ramparts* and then in a monograph (1980). Traven went on with his life as a recluse and continued to assert that he was in fact Hal Croves. He maintained that it was Croves who had negotiated with John Huston (1906-1987), the director of *The Treasure of the Sierra Madre*. Huston was never completely convinced that Croves was Traven; he thought the bumbling, reticent personality of Croves was inconsistent with the wonderful vivid writer he had read in 1934, and the "generous" man he had known through the letters they exchanged (cited Naremore 1979, 15-16). He said that Croves spoke English with a decided Scandinavian accent (Pratley 1977, 61).

Stone's interview stimulated another round of interest in Traven's work and in *Traveniana:* interest which has never faded, and has only became stronger with the birth and growth of the internet.[7] As "Gary Snyder, among others, has pointed out that we are the first generation ever to have access to all the world's cultures" (Garland 1982, vii). This has given us a heavy burden to carry, but since Traven's death in 1969 it has been possible to collect together more information about this mysterious and magnetic writer. I give here a brief account of what might be his long and exciting life/lives. In my epilogue I try to reconcile the lives and come up with an original idea to throw any readers and potential researchers further off the scent.

Traven was firmly of the belief that children should be allowed to choose their own names or change those imposed upon them (Johnson 1976, 8). He followed this policy with great assiduity throughout his life. Baumann raises the intriguing possibility that Traven was simply an orphan who did not know who his parents were (Baumann 1971, xvi). He may have had no idea where he was born, or he may have known his mother but not his father.

At a number of times he claimed to be Traven Torsvan Croves, born on 4 March 1890 in Chicago, the son of working-class parents – Burton Torsvan who was probably Scandinavian (Norwegian), and Dorothy Croves who was possibly of Irish/Scottish extraction. Traven's death certificate certainly corroborates this legend even though a search of Cook County records in Chicago could not confirm the birth (Wyatt 1980, 292). At one time in his life he told his wife that he was born in Chicago and that his parents were well-to-do (Cheuse 1974, 30). He also told her that the name Croves came from that of his mother's Scottish family (Johnson 1980, 3).

We do not know whether or not these putative parents were married but are informed by Traven that soon after his birth the family moved to Germany, possibly via England.[8] Traven specialized and enjoyed in giving out false or conflicting information on almost every aspect of his life. At some times, he claimed to have attended a seminary in Germany but had been thrown out apparently for asking "indecent questions". This assertion has not been verified.

With this marked passion for disguise and acting a part, it is not surprising that he was drawn to the stage and retained a fascination with movies throughout a very long life. In 1907, he (as Ret Marut) became an actor playing minor roles and later was employed as a stage manager at various German theaters until 1916. He can be placed in Essen, Thuringia, Chemnitz, Danzig, Berlin, Prussia and Düsseldorf (Treverton, 3). From 1910 he was also writing for the theatrical magazine *Masken* (Tschörtner 1987, 56-57). In 1966, after years of denial, he reluctantly admitted to having spent some time in Germany (Miller 1966, 84).[9]

He wrote many short stories; some forty-four different titles being submitted to various publishers from 1924-1926, a number were published at the time in German, and some of them much later in English in the collection: *The Kidnapped Saint and other Stories*, edited by Rosa Elena Luján, Mina C. Klein and H. Arthur Klein (1981). I give a complete list of these stories in chapter five.

Others were published in *To the Honourable Miss S., and Other Stories* (1981). In order of appearance they are: "The Story of a Nun", (*Die Klosterfrau* 1918); "The Silk Scarf", (*Das Seidentuch* 1917); "The Actor and the King", (*Der Schausspieler und der König* 1919); "A Writer of Serpentine Shrewdness", (*Die Geschichte vom schlangenklugen Dichter* 1919); "The BLue Speckled SParroW", (*Der BLaugertupfte SPerlinG* 1919); "Deceivers", (*Der Bertrüger* 1919); "Titles", (*Titel* 1919); "My Visit to the Writer Pguwlhkschrj Rnfajbzxlquy", (*Mein Besuch bei dem Dichter Pguwlhkschrj Rnfajbzxlquy* 1919); "The Art of the Painter", (*Malkunst*: 1919); "The Kind of Thing That Can Happen in France", (*Was in Frankreich alles geshehen kann* 1919); "Mother Beleke", (*Mutter Beleke* 1915); "In the Fog", (*Nebel* 1916); "The Unknown Soldier", (*Der fremde Soldat* 1915); "To the Honourable Miss S.", (*An das Fräulein S* 1916). The last one was penned under the name Richard Maurhut.[10]

Traven went to great lengths throughout his life to hide his tracks; he spent an enormous amount of time and effort into putting reporters, researchers, publishers and such like off the scent. Consequently there are at least two other plausible biographies other than "born in Chicago".

Will Wyatt energetically with the aid of BBC and British taxpayers' money pursued the claim that Traven was Otto (Herman Albert Maximilian) Feige born in 1882 on 23rd February in Schwiebus (Zwiebodzin) near Posen (Poznan) – then in Germany but incorporated into Poland after the First World War. This indeed is the identity Traven claimed when he was questioned by Special Branch police in England in 1923 (Wyatt, 264). That Traven knew all four Christian names of Feige lends some credence to the Feige/Marut hypothesis. However, Guthke explains this away by positing that Marut met Feige in Brixton "nick" and borrowed his identity as he was prone to do so.

In this life he was the son of a potter (or *ziegelbrenner*) in a brick works, Adolf Rudolf Feige, and a mill-hand Hormina Wienecke. He was first an apprentice locksmith, and later a soldier and political agitator. It is not surprising that Traven would hide the fact of being called *Feige* which in its adjectival form translates from the German as cowardly (Johnson 1980, 3). One of the aliases later used by Marut was Albert Otto Max Wienecke - presumably a putative cousin of Otto Feige. Traven also told the London police in 1924 that his mother had been a mill hand as indeed Hormina was (Berman 1981, 25).

This biography has been accepted by many other scholars and researchers and has been enshrined in a number of official biographical dictionaries even though its credibility mainly hinges on an identification made in front of television cameras by putative siblings who had not seen their "brother" for nearly sixty years (Wyatt, 323). One further drawback to accepting this life is that it was never proved that Feige had been to sea – apart from the necessary passage to Mexico. Throughout his life Traven was passionately devoted to the sea and retained many memories of his life at sea. It is also unknown where Feige would have learnt English to the level of expertise that Traven possessed.

Once Traven had landed in Mexico there is no record of his ever again claiming to have been Feige. Not even on his death bed did he "confess" this past to his wife even though he did admit he had been Ret Marut the revolutionary in the Bavarian Revolution of 1919. Baumann seems to be right when he says that Wyatt established that a man called Otto Feige existed but not that he had categorically been identified with Marut (Baumann, 1982, 32).

Photographs of Feige and Marut/Torsvan/Traven/Croves viewed side by side in the view of many people show a very good fit. I have studied the photographs of Feige closely and compared them with those of Croves, Marut and Torsvan. I concentrated on the nose and ears, and while those of Croves/Marut/Torsvan are a very good match and I am assured they are the same man, Feige is the odd man out. See the photographs in Wyatt (Wyatt, plates between 226-227).

Evelyn Keyes was certain that Traven was a small man; even with lifts he just reached just 5' 6" (1.68 meters) in height (Keyes 1977, 116). All of Will Wyatt's researches agree at least on Traven's somewhat diminutive stature – possibly only 1.65 meters).[11] It is interesting though that Wyatt does not tell us how tall Feige was; this could be very supportive evidence for his hypothesis, or of course if Feige was of medium height or above he could not be Traven.

When Traven applied for American papers in London in 1924 he claimed a third life. He wrote that he was born in San Francisco also in 1882 (but two days later than Otto Feige on 25 February) as Ret Marut: his parents being William and Helene Marut (née Ottarent) and his father's occupation declared as "impresario". He claimed that he couldn't confirm these facts as his papers had all been destroyed in the San Francisco earthquake of 1906 (Guthke 1991, 160).[12] Raskin looked at the birth records for 1881-1883 in *The San Francisco Chronicle* but found no trace of a Marut being born in the area (Raskin 1978, 159).

A fourth identity claimed by Traven from 1926 until the 1930s was the photographer/engineer, archaeologist and anthropologist Ber(r)ick Traven Torsvan. He now said that he was born on 5 March 1890 in Chicago and first entered Mexico via Ciudad Juárez in 1914 (Guthke 1991, 335-336). In this life he claims to have been an active wobbly in the USA around 1910, encountered the wrath of the FBI and was forced to flee his homeland (Hagemann 1960, 372). A later embellishment to this story is his claim that well before he became a Wobbly, after a checkered twenty six days of schooling, he ran away from home at the age of ten and enlisted as a cabin boy. He spent at least six weeks in French Indo-China and also visited the ports of Sydney, Singapore, Rotterdam, Hamburg, Rio de Janeiro, New York, San Francisco and Mazatalán.[13] He jumped a Dutch ship at this last port of call aged twelve and spent the rest of his life in Mexico apart from several spells as a merchant seaman (Johnson 1947, 14). Later on we will see that it is difficult to imagine that a largely illiterate nomad could have written unaided such literary masterpieces as *The Death Ship* and *The Treasure of the Sierra Madre*.

The widow of the archeologist Frans Blom says that Blom met Torsvan in Chiapas in 1926 and Croves on the set on the film *The Rebellion of the Hanged* in 1953 and in spite of some ravages over the years was sure they were the same man. On the later occasion Blom said "goodbye Mr. Traven" much to the chagrin of our hero (Raskin 1978, 213).[14] When Humphrey Bogart was shown a photo of Croves taken on the set of the *Treasure of the Sierra Madre* alongside one of Torsvan as he was setting out on the Chiapas expedition over twenty years before he also said that it was the same man (Whitney 1948, 66).

A further (fifth) proven identity was "Richard Maurhut", the author in 1916 of one of the most memorable and biting stories of the First World War "To the Honorable Miss S". Re-reading this it seems to me almost impossible not to believe that Traven fought in the war – or at least had some infantry experience. His protagonist wins a couple of Iron Crosses and promotions for selfless heroism when all he wants to do is to die, and end the ghastly life in the trenches. It is an astounding work on a par with that of Robert Graves, Erich Maria Remarque and Siegfried Sassoon, and the many memorable and poignant poems by poets from both sides of the war - but it is still fiction. Leopold Spitzegger, the biographer of Erich Mühsam, a fellow member with Traven in the Bavarian Soviet argues that Maurhut is probably Traven's given name (Spitzegger 1946, 671). But he gives no convincing evidence to back up this claim.

Some More Unlikely Candidates

Recknagel who has been one of the most assiduous and meticulous of Traven researchers suggested that Traven was born Charles Trefny in St. Louis on 2 July 1880. He studied theology (I assume Protestant theology) at the University of Freiberg but was expelled in 1903 for an "immoral act" (Recknagel 1983, 44-47). This assertion has never been proved and has not been accepted by most other "authorities" on Traven.[15] But because Traven showed such a pronounced persisting dislike of the Roman Catholic Church I can see why some researchers are intrigued by this lead.

A British writer William McAlpine raised a further hare by claiming that the English magazine *Picture Post* of 28 September 1940 had a story about a German national, Captain Hugo Baruch (pseudonym - Captain Jack Bilbo) who had been interned on the Isle of Man as an enemy alien and who maintained he was the famous writer B. Traven. McAlpine further stated that the U.S. West Coast English/German journal *Die Westküste* ran this story under the title "Der Falsche Traven" on 19 March 1943 with further elaboration by a fellow internee, Emil Rameau (Guthke 1991, 46). Reputedly Traven wrote to the editor of *Die Westküste* Hans Kafka, denying the story and claiming not to have crossed the Atlantic during the past thirty years (McAlpine 1948, 43).

In the 1950s, the normally assiduous bibliographer E. R. Hagemann was unable to find the references or even confirm the existence of the

"West Coast Journal" (Powell Collection, folio 12). However, with the help of modern advances I was able to ascertain that from 1941 *Die Westküste* was a fortnightly section of the New York journal *Aufbau* designed for the three pacific states. McAlpine is right. The journal was in German and English and originally aimed at Jewish immigrants. Current issues can be accessed online.

Many other names and identities have been advanced. A Czech writer posits the theory that the Bohemian writer Arthur Breisky (1885-1910) faked his death in New York and assumed the identity of Traven (Vápeník 1987, 272-273). This cannot be substantiated.

Wyatt refers to an article by Ernst Fallen de Droog in the September 1967 issue of the German Magazine *Der Monat*. He claims to have met in Spain in the spring of 1937 a new volunteer (August Bibeljé) who joined the Republican army. He went by the name of *Ziegelbrenner*, said he had been in the Bavarian Revolution, was a writer and referred to *Die Weisse Rose* (1929) and *Die Baumwollpflücker* (1928) as his books. He was killed on New Year's Eve 1937 in the battle for Teruel.[16] Wyatt tried and failed to find de Droog (Wyatt, 206-207).

P. I. Travin *aka* Sletov was a Russian born radical labor organizer who worked in America for a number of years until the Russian Revolution. He returned to Russia and was asked by Lenin to deliver his "Letter to American Workers" to the USA in August 1918. John Reed was instrumental in arranging the letter's publication in a number of radical and liberal papers. He is another man suspected of being Traven. It seems clear that he was not.

Judy Stone had second (or third) thoughts about Traven's identity after being approached in 1987 by Ursula Beckmann de Bourba who claimed that her husband (Wladislac de Bourba, son of a lady-in-waiting to the last Czarina of Russia) who died when his ship went down on August 12 1942 had given her a great deal of circumstantial evidence that he was Traven – or at last part of the Traven syndicate (Stone 1987, 66-72). There is almost no evidence to corroborate this story all of whose details could have been found out by a careful reading of for instance, Guthke (1987) or Recknagel (1966). However, Stone repeated her doubts in an after word written for a 2001 online version of her pioneering work on Traven *The Mystery of B. Traven* (1977).

A further and very interesting twist is given by Michael Baumann who explores the existence of an American *Erlebensträger* (carrier of experience, or "Ur-Traven") as a man (a seaman and wobbly) who furnished Traven with the material for some of his early books (Baumann 1976, 27-37).[17] This theory stems from a doubt that Traven could have produced by himself such a formidable body of work for publication in Germany only a few years after his arrival in Mexico in 1924. Nine books were published in a space of six years some in English and some in German. Guthke however, plausibly points out that Marut was an experienced journalist used to writing at speed (Guthke 1987, 15).[18] Guthke also makes a very shrewd point that Traven was the first person to raise the possibility that the identity "Traven" covered more than one man; he did this in 1948 when cornered by Luís Spota (Guthke 1991, 122). The existence of this mystery man has never been proved, but I explore and amplify this suggestion in my epilogue as well as raising a red herring of my very own.

Baumann does not present any documentary evidence for his opinion that "Traven" covered a dual or split personality nor give a satisfactory explanation of why the carrier should have done what he did. At the same time, Baumann makes a great deal of the fact that as Marut and Traven used many English and American expressions in their German prose there must have been at least two different writers involved. Surely this fact is perfectly explainable if one accepts the hypothesis that Traven was born in the USA of German speaking parents and learnt German as well as English as a child (Baumann 1976, 84).[19]

Traven also claimed on occasions through his life to be the illegitimate son of Kaiser Wilhelm II (1859-1941) - or sometimes Frederick III - and the Irish actress Helene Marut or Mareth (Recknagel, 39), or Frau Von Sternwaldt an opera singer. For this incarnation he claimed to have been born in early 1882 (Raskin 1978, 47; Cook, 11). There is no record of the birth, marriage, career or death of either of these putative mothers. If the Kaiser had any illegitimate children he hid them well enough to fool all subsequent historians (Wyatt, 263). Traven's widow repeated this story to the reporter Judy Stone on the day of Traven's funeral (Stone 1973, 11).[20] Gerd Heidemann wrote a couple of stories in the German magazine *Stern* in the 1960s saying that Traven's widow had categorically said to him that Traven had claimed to her that he was a son of the Kaiser (Heidemann 1963, 1967). Predictably Mrs. Traven then denied that she had even spoken to Heidemann.

Heidemann seems a very unreliable source. According to the anthropologist Gertrude Duby Blom, (unlike her husband she never met Traven) Heidemann told her that Traven never worked as a sailor but got the tale for *The Death Ship* from his homosexual lover Anton Biglier (Raskin 1980, 210). There is no other evidence that this story is true; no other Traven researcher believes it, and neither do I. Neither is there any other evidence or firm suggestion that Traven was gay.

In 1993 Guthke followed up on the Von Sternwaldt lead. It seems that it was the stage name of a number of German actors and actresses in the later half of the nineteenth century who performed in the USA as well as in Germany. Traven sent a play bill from 1840 to be put in the Library of Congress archives in Washington and drew attention to "a noble actress" Frau von Sternwaldt. Guthke pursues the possibility of her being an ancestor of Traven but also explodes the myth that she was of noble birth. However, he plays around with the name and comes up with the anagram: L. Warnstedt. Someone with this name came from a fairly prosperous German family with Scandinavian branches (Traven often claimed this sort of background) which lived in Schleswig-Holstein in a place called Traventhal which is not far from Marutendorf (Guthke 1993, 129-130).

There are other even more unlikely histories; I will allude to some of these later on. Some support for the multiple or split personality of Traven is that throughout much of his long life Traven showed what can only be called abnormal behavior patterns and evidence that he was suffering from many demons. At several periods he seemed to have a tenuous or non-existent grasp of reality to such an extent that he could be a diagnosed as a schizophrenic.

Publishing History

Bernard Smith the American publisher's (Alfred Knopf) editor gave Traven's first three novels a rigorous editing before they were published in the USA (Stone 1977, 92).[21] Although Hubert Jannach appears to be unaware both of Smith's role and the fact that it was Traven himself who retranslated the first three books from German into English he does present a convincing case that they were all written by a man who had a German background. Inge Kutt also presses the case that German is Traven's most versatile, controlled and expressive language (Kutt 1979, 327).

Hill maintains that when Alfred Knopf started to publish many of Traven's other novels in English in 1967 the English manuscripts all needed extensive editing (Hill 1970, 10). This can be explained by the common phenomenon that if one moves into another country and starts to function and write in the local tongue, one over time gets rusty in the mother tongue, and uses outdated colloquial expressions. Guthke points out that as Traven's spoken English improved after 1924 so his written German deteriorated (Guthke 1987, 18-19).

According to one scholar, the American quotations in the first German editions do not read as though they were by an American (Jannach 1963, 468).[22] In another article Jannach says the German writer of "Traven" used a number of regionally limited German words that would indicate he was from Southern Germany or Austria/Hungary – or at least very familiar with the area (Jannach 1961, 29). Woodcock argues that Traven's accent in German was not that of a foreigner but of a provincial (Woodcock 1976, 1053).

Siegfied Bernfeld who was a *lektor* (foreign language assistant) for Traven's publisher, *Büchergilde Gutenberg* says that all Traven's manuscripts submitted to the press were in German, and that he had no reason to doubt that the writer's mother tongue was German. He adds an interesting gloss that in a letter to Oskar Maria Graf (1894-1967) after the failure of the Bavarian Soviet, Traven says that "I'm going to learn English, just in case" (*New York Times Book Review* 1970, 10).

But I most add an important *caveat* that we do not often really know whether the polished German we see is from the pen of Traven, his translators or editors. Neither are we totally sure what was his handwriting. There is a distinct difference between the handwriting of Marut in his letters penned whilst he was in Germany from 1907 until 1924 and that to be found in a diary Traven started to keep after he landed in Mexico in July 1924 and manuscripts written after then.

Ret Marut, Munich and Mexico

In 1915 Traven appeared in Munich as Ret Marut, and on 1 September 1917 with the assistance of his girl friend, Irene Mermet alias Mennet (1893-1956), published the first edition of an occasional political magazine, *Der Ziegelbrenner – the Brick Maker* (alternatively *Brickburner*). I prefer the first translation as the title is an obvious allusion to a man who makes bricks that he hopes will be the foundation of a better world.[23] He continued an elaborate and intricate practice of concealing his name, parentage, age, date, and place of birth, and even his nationality from friends as well as policemen, bureaucrats registering aliens, and customs officials. Like his alter ego, Gerard (Gerry) Gales in *The Death Ship* who automatically gives wrong names to policemen and the skipper of the *Yorikke*, Traven never wanted to be classified, regulated or pigeon-holed.[24]

In a move that his individualist anarchist mentor, Stirner would not have approved of, Traven became a member of the first (anarchist) Soviet Republic of Workers' Soldiers' and Farmers' Councils in Bavaria in 1918. This was the formative event in Traven's life and I spend some time on this later on. Traven (as Ret Marut) became a member of the propaganda committee of the Soviet that was in charge of the censorship of bourgeois newspapers. Traven clearly enjoyed the job; in later years he still referred to the press as the "public whore".[25]

He is in the long tradition of cynical hard boiled press men such as James Regler a scribbler for W. R. Hearst, who declared that "a Hearst newspaper is like a screaming woman running down the street with her throat cut" (cited Sanciprián 1991, 62n3). Traven was also elected to the Preparatory Commission for the Formation of the Revolutionary Tribunal (Garland, 129).

Marut was arrested (by his own account) on May Day 1919 outside the Café Maria Theresa in *Augustenstraße* in Munich by White Guards, who acting under orders of a social democratic government in Berlin overthrew the Bavarian republic. The guards massacred thousands of people, radicals, intellectuals and workers and from this bloody Bavarian base Hitler eventually rose to power (*The Death Ship*, 285). Marut was sentenced to death by a court martial, but escaped from custody while two of his guards looked the other way.

It is because of this miraculous escape from almost certain death, as well as the strange fact that Marut, a pacifist (and possibly an alien) was able to publish several issues of a virulent anti-war journal throughout Germany's most bellicose period to that date, that rumors began to circulate that Traven was protected by a very high figure in Imperial Germany. However, *Der Ziegelbrenner* was censored heavily and export outside Germany forbidden.[26] It is possible that an army officer sympathetic to the anarchists protected Traven (Stone 1977, 27). It is also possible that Marut manufactured the story of his miraculous escape (Wyatt, 284).

Marut remained in hiding in Austria and Germany until 1921 sporadically publishing *Der Ziegelbrenner*. Losing faith in any progressive revolutionary change in Germany and fearful for his life he wandered through Germany and Czechoslovakia reduced to the most abject poverty and trying to sell rag dolls and toys for a living. However, he never lost his faith that somewhere conditions were ripe for a genuine revolution. He eventually became a sailor, a sailor on death ships.

In what is the most generally accepted version of his life, Traven came to Mexico from Germany via England in 1924 and lived the rest of his life in that country. He first settled in Tampico on the Atlantic Coast, a city where there were almost as many foreigners as Mexicans. In the 1920s Tampico was an anarcho-syndicalist Industrial Worker's of the World (I.W.W.) wobbly stronghold, while in Mexico City the American Radical Linn A. E. Gale published *Gale's International Monthly for Revolutionary Communism* from 1919-1921.[27] The Wobblies were still active in 1927 (Guthke 1991, 184-185).

The anarcho-syndicalist labor organization, *Casa del Obrero Mundial* was formed in Mexico in 1909 and its program of direct action made it the dominant labor organization by early 1913 (Hart 1987, 109, 118). In 1911 the anarchist revolutionary Flores Magón brothers (Ricardo, Jesús and Enrique) from bases in the USA mounted strikes, reprisals and armed raids into Baja California. Joe Hill (Joseph Hillstron, 1882-1915) the wobbly song writer took part in one of the battles (Gunn 1974A, 55-56).

Many Mexicans who went to find work in the USA were wobblies. One of the most important was Primo Tapia who lived there for most of 1907-1920 and became a wobbly about 1911. After his return to Mexico he was accepted as a rural revolutionary leader of the Tarascan people in central Michoacán, and led a struggle which successfully led to one of the largest land grants in Mexican history. He was assassinated by government troops on the night of 26-27 April 1926 (Friedrich 1970, 130).

Traven shared the Wobbly principles of personal secrecy, self-sacrifice and public direct action for most of his active life (Miller 1967, 59). For a sympathetic account of the methods used by the I.W.W. to achieve their ends there is in my view little better to read than *The Cotton-Pickers* Traven's second book (called *Der Wobbly* in the first German edition). In it Gales says: I was forced to become a rebel and a revolutionary, a revolutionary out of love of justice, out of a desire to help out the wretched and the ragged.[28]

But while Traven was a revolutionary he was no supporter of state socialism. When the Spanish Civil War broke out in 1936 Traven gave his full support to the Republican cause and corresponded regularly with Pedro Herrera, the editor of the anarcho-syndicalist monthly *Timón* but pointedly did not deal with the Spanish government (Zogbaum 1992, 133). In 1936, four anarchists joined the Republican Spanish Government.[29] Traven certainly opposed this and would agree with Emma Goldman (1869-1940):

> is the abstention from participation in elections for Anarchists a matter of principle? I certainly think it is ... After all, participation in election means the transfer of one's will and decisions to another, which is contrary to the fundamental principles of anarchism. Secondly since Anarchists do not believe in the Jesuitical formulas of the Bolsheviks that the end justifies the means it is but logical for Anarchists not to consider political participation as a "simple question of tactics." Such tactics are not only incompatible with Anarchist thought and principles, but they also injure the stand of anarchism as the one and only truly revolutionary social philosophy. (Emma Goldman *Vanguard*, 1969)

He helped the veterans of the International Brigades, like Bill Miller who settled in Mexico after 1938 (Raskin 1978, 29). In 1966 he gave his first interview to the press in forty-one years, and said that in 1936 he had been if necessary prepared to sell every book in his library to aid the loyalists (Miller 1966, 84).

Many other European writers visited Mexico and some settled there for a significant time. For most of them as Woodcock aptly remarks: "Mexico became the state of mind of its observers" (Woodcock 1956, 32). Traven remains the most important. He also went the whole hog and became a Mexican citizen in 1951 (Johnson 1969A, 9).

Traven married Rosa Elena Luján in 1957, and according to his wife in the last twelve years of his life never again directly involved himself in politics although he remained as sympathetic to the anarchists and anarcho-syndicalists as he had been throughout the century. In 1968 at the end of his life he walked to the Reforma hotel in Mexico City to listen to speeches and watch the student demonstration that was quelled with such brutality (Raskin 1977, 76).[30]

Notes

1. One bizarre example of this is that the entire printing (5,000 copies) of the first edition of *Ein General Kommt aus dem Dschungel – The General from the Jungle*, was purchased by occupying German troops when they took Amsterdam in 1940. What they made of such a biting indictment of Fascism is anybody's guess (Stone 1973, 13).
2. She is as much a mystery as is Traven. Raskin shows that after Traven's death she was continuing to weave a shroud of mystery around the writer (Raskin, 1980).
3. Luís Spota was not a negligible or contemptible personality; he enjoyed an astounding success both as a newspaper columnist on *Mañana* magazine and as a best selling novelist from 1948 onwards. *Casi el paraíso* (1956) a condemnation of café society in Mexico City was his most popular tale (Brushwood 1966, 28).
4. I am aware though that Mexicans do not usually recognize this celebration of gullibility.
5. *The Treasure of the Sierra Madre* directed by John Huston (who also wrote the screen play) in 1948 is frequently shown on late night TV and is always worth watching for Bogart and Walton Huston giving the performances of their lives. John Huston was a character much larger than life whose formative years were filled with as much action as Traven's (Agee 2000, 389). Huston had read *The Treasure of the Sierra Madre* in 1936 and was impressed with how it conjured up memories of his own life in the Mexican cavalry (Kaminsky 1978, 48). I say much more about the book and the film in chapters four and six.
6. Judy Stone, the sister of another renowned journalist I. F. (Izzy) Stone was the film critic of the *San Francisco Chronicle* for some fifty years.

7. Croves was hired as a technical adviser but his name does not appear in the production credits; this perhaps intentional sheltering of Traven's treasured anonymity is one of the many ironies of his life. As indeed was the fact that the film did not turn a profit for Warner Brothers (Kaminsky 1978A, 64). Traven is actually on the screen in the film for about two seconds as one of the extras in the Oso Negro Hotel listening to Walter Huston talking about prospecting for gold. Raskin carelessly claims that the clip lasts five seconds (Raskin 1978, 156).

8. Recknagel found among Traven's possessions the birth certificate of Johann Christof Friedrich Gale born in Lübeck in 1884. However, other researchers have established that he lived for only five months (Wyatt, 74).

9. Charles H. Miller (1913-1992) was a foremost devotee of Traven's work. He was a Thoreauvian in spirit and like Traven knocked about a bit, being stone mason, farmer, seller of encyclopedias and a documentary film maker at different periods of his life. At the time of his death he was working on an essay on Traven. He is not the "Bill" Miller who lived in Mexico and also turns up in the literature.

10. *Malkunst* appeared first as *Roter Mohn* ("Red Poppy") in *Vorwärts* 1913. "The BLue-Speckled SParroW" also appeared first in the same journal with the title: *Die grungesprenkelte Eule* ("The Green-spotted Owl") (Guthke 1991, 119).

11. As the author of these pages is at most 1.70 meters tall whilst his uncles and grandfathers were six footers I can empathize with Traven's desire for deliberate confusion about his height.

12. It has been observed that Marut is the name of the Hindu storm God. Torsvan is derived from the Norse god, Thor, the bringer of lightning and thunder. Hindu literature was popular in Germany ever since Schopenhauer and Wagner's time. It cannot be a coincidence that one (or several) of Traven's most memorable characters is called Gerry Gales – as in storm-bringer. Just as Marut is the anarchist stirrer-upper so, wherever Gales alights, trouble begins - but hopefully a better world arises from the upheavals.

13. In an unpublished letter of 1914 he claimed to a publisher to have been in Indochina for an extended period of time in 1899 (Guthke 1993, 119).

14. Traven would have been very amused to learn that Blom was just one of the many people suspected (or accused) of being Traven (Guthke 1993, 117).

15. I was intrigued to learn that a young American Charles Frey turned up in the jungles of Chiapas in the early years of the Second World War, taught himself archaeology and made a significant contribution to our knowledge (Cordan 1964, 30). He drowned in 1949. He had a mixed background (Swiss father and German Mother) like the main characters in *The Death Ship* and his name to me at least is a strange echo of Trefny.

16. It is almost impossible to underestimate the effect of the Spanish Civil War on the left of the period. One of my earliest memories is being awakened in my cot in the fall of 1936 at the age of one and being shown to my uncle and two of his friends, John Cornford and David Haden-Guest before they went off to join the International Brigades in Spain. Cornford and Haden-Guest were both

killed. I survived the German air raids of 1940-1944, and my uncle some years as a Major in the Parachute Regiment.
17. Baumann developed this notion after reading Max Schmid (writing under the pseudonym of Gerard Gale) in the Zurich journal *Tages-Anzeiger* (1963-1964).
18. Not everyone works at the leisurely pace customary among a number of American graduate students. During the last two years I have published three books, made extensive revisions and additions to the third edition of my most successful book, virtually written half of this one and a quarter of another. I am not surprised at Traven's speed - merely envious.
19. In spite of Zogbaum's claims; to have German as your mother tongue by no means precludes you from being born in the USA (Zogbaum, xviii).
20. Of course it may be a completely false trail, even though Traven believed it. In my own family there is a legend that because my great grandmother (a not insignificant actress in her day) had briefly been one of Edward Prince of Wales - later Edward VII - countless mistresses we were related to the British Royal Family. Apart from mentioning that like the related Romanov dynasty and other descendants of Queen Victoria I have a tendency to bleed profusely when I scratch myself, I make no further claims.
21. To some people it is somewhat puzzling that Traven allowed Smith such freedom when he refused to have a word omitted from his German manuscripts (Kutt 1979, 315). Smith in his very engaging autobiography says that after he had edited (rewrote) the first twenty-five pages of *The Death Ship* he sent it off with some trepidation to Traven. A couple of weeks later Traven returned the pages with a warm and enthusiastic letter approving everything he had done (Smith 1994, 69). Later on we will see that Traven was very cooperative with Harlan Ellison when he rewrote parts of three stories.
22. Indeed Jannach rather stridently describes the translations as "inferior" and "incompetent" (Jannach 1963, 459, 464).
23. *Der Ziegelbrennen* means the man who burns or bakes bricks or tiles.
24. This is very reminiscent of Proudon:

> to be GOVERNED is to be kept in sight, inspected, spied upon, directed, law-driven, numbered, enrolled, indoctrinated, preached at, controlled, estimated, valued, censured, commanded, by creatures who have neither the right nor the wisdom nor the virtue to do so. To be GOVERNED is to be at every operation, at every transaction, noted, registered, enrolled, taxed, stamped, measured, numbered, assessed, licensed, authorized, admonished, for-bidden, reformed, corrected, punished. It is under pretext of the public utility, and in the name of general interest, trained, ransomed, exploited, monopolized, extorted, squeezed, mystified, robbed; then at the slightest resistance, the first word of complaint, to be repressed, fined, despised, harassed, trailed, abused, clubbed, disarmed, choked, imprisoned, judged, condemned, deported, scarified, sold, betrayed, and to crown all mocked, ridiculed, outraged, dishonored. That is government that is its justice that is its morality. (Proudhon 1923, 294)

25. Another writer Oskar Maria Graf (1893-1959) was also involved in censorship for the Bavarian Soviet. He describes his harrowing physical and mental experiences during the war, the revolution, and its aftermath in *Wir sind Gefangene-Prisoners All* (Graf, 1928).

26. One example of his skill in evading censorship is his twenty-seven "Death Songs of Hyotamore of Kyrene" where his aphorisms opposing war, the state and capitalism are disguised as ancient Indian poetry (Traven 2003, 7).

27. However, one source says that this was an official communist publication (Britton 1987, 19-20). For more details and a photograph of the cover see (Recknagel, 138). Both researchers might be correct as many wobblies crossed over to the Communist Party after 1918 and hearing of the success of the Bolshevik Revolution in Russia (Friedrich 1970, 128n28).

28. At their first conference held in Chicago in 1906 the wobblies coined their slogan "building a new world within the shell of the old". The name wobbly possibly derives from the way Chinese waiters would pronounce IWW "I Wobbleoo Wobbleoo" (Wyatt, 21). However, I must add a caveat, that the world wide web - www, is invariably pronounced on Italian rock radio stations as "wu wu wu".

29. Garcia Oliver, Minister of Justice, Juan Peiro, Industry, Juan Lopez, Commerce, and Federica Montseny, Health.

30. General José Hernández, who led the troops in the massacre, later commanded the Mexican army in Chiapas during the decades of terror before and during the Zapatista uprising from 1994 onwards.

Chapter 2

The Red Thread: Major Influences on Traven's Life and Work

We don't want to build up a state or a church or an army. Just men.
(Malraux 1941, *Man's Hope*)

Der Ziegelbrenner the subtitle of which is: "Criticism of Current Conditions and Disgusting Contemporaries", is understandably full of passionate attacks on militarism, as well as national and religious hypocrisy. A vicious war was being waged in Europe and was entering its fourth year when the first issue came out in 1917.[1]

Traven was at this time an outspoken individualist anarchist and his main concern was, as he saw it, the waste of the world's goods in capitalist world economies. Throughout his books and articles Traven constantly emphasizes the need for work that will make men feel useful and enrich their lives; these are themes to which he returns time and time again in his novels – he leaves us to draw the conclusion (if we so wish) that this will not be until workers take full control of their lives.

Did Traven read Pierre Joseph Proudhon (1809-1865)? Proudhon's most famous dictum is, "property is theft": this is a belief that Traven shared. He would also have agreed with Proudhon's dictum that "the men who are most completely ignorant of the state of the country are almost always those who represent it" (cited Marshall 1993, 244).

At the same time, Traven would surely also have agreed with the views expressed in Proudhon's pamphlet to Mazzini on Italian unity, "to govern twenty-six million people who have been robbed of all dominion over themselves calls for a gigantic machine; then to set this machine in motion, a monstrous bureaucracy, a legion of officials" (cited Rocker 1937, 426).

> *Property is the right of increase.* To us this axiom shall be like the name of the beast in the Apocalypse. It was known that he who should solve the mystery of this name would succeed in mastering the beast. We shall pursue the old serpent through his coils. It requires something more than courage to subdue this monster. It was written that it should not die until a proletarian armed with a magic wand, had fought with it. (Proudhon 1969, 161)

Proudhon was convinced of, "man's ineradicable tendency toward evil. All that could be done to remedy this was to seek to create a social order in which men's evil inclinations would be held in check" (cited Edwards 1970, 27).

Traven was a fervent follower of the individualist anarchist Max Stirner (1806-1856) - the *nom de plume* of Johann Caspar Schmidt - and he lived as far as possible according to Stirner's dictum that in order to become the unique one - *der Einzige* – one must shed all limitations of one's former life in order to realize one's inherent powers (Zogbaum, xxi). In fact throughout his life Traven devoted much of his energy to shedding all traces of his real, ascribed or given identity.

Stirner was one of his five favorite authors – the others being Percy Bysshe Shelley (1792-1822), Walt Whitman (1819-1892), Jack London (1876-1916), and Herman Bang – a Danish novelist. Bang (1857-1912) seems to have had a significant influence on Traven; in his novel, *De Uden Fædreland - Denied a Country* (1906) Bang says that "a man without a country is the free man" (Bang 1927, 134). This is one of the main themes running through Traven's first and probably best regarded book *The Death Ship.* A life of Jack London along with Shelley's *Complete Works* was in Traven's library at his death (Recknagel 1983, 329).

Marut/Traven is very indebted to Stirner's philosophy (Baumann 1976, 66-67, 163n11). The biographer of Stirner and fellow individualist anarchist John Henry Mackay (1864-1935) also worked with Marut during the Bavarian Revolution (Recknagel, 36).

Stirner - wrote that a man "cannot let himself be embraced and taken up by the party".[2] He is still important, even though Marx and Engels dismissed him contemptuously as, "Saint Max" and fellow-traveling Marxists routinely parrot the great men's jibes. His extremely influential book, *Der Einzige und sein Eigentum - The Ego and His Own*, was published in late 1844; it remains a vital text for the individualist school of anarchism to this day. He wrote:

for the State it is indispensable that nobody have an *own will*; if one had, the State would have to exclude (lock up, banish) him; if all had, they would do away with the State. (Stirner 1963, 195-196)

Stirner also had an influence on the anarchist terrorists of the 1880s-1890s, as well as the diverse and growing opposition to Hegel, (cited Jay 1974, 115). Stirner stressed the will and instincts rather than the reason. He anticipates Alfred Adler (1870-1937) in his description of the will as the highest faculty of the ego (Marshall 1993, 225). Stirner believed that we have proof of nothing but our own existence, and that self-interest was the basis of morality. His ideal was the Egoist, a man in conflict with other individuals, and using force if necessary to change the authoritarian and anti-individual nature of society. An individualist is not limited to sole action, but is able to unite with others for the arrangements of matters of convenience. The state is the greatest enemy of the individual and individuals must rebel to overthrow it.

Very importantly, Stirner also stresses, "the need for each person to realize himself in the mastery of his craft" (Carroll 1974, 141-142). Such arguments - in particular the latter would have appealed to Traven. Certainly, Stirner anticipates Friedrich Wilhelm Nietzsche (1844-1900) with his call for the self-exaltation of the whole individual, and his attack on Christian morality (Marshall 1993, 220).[3] This would also strike a chord with Traven. In *The Treasure of the Sierra Madre* he refers to the Catholic Church in Mexico as the powers of darkness (113). And in a number of his other novels and short stories he shows Indians losing their Christian faith.

And Stirner's remarks that, "a man expressed himself in what he owned" are as damning a case against the fetish of property, as Proudhon and Wagner made (Janik and Toulmin 1973, 42). At Traven's death a copy of *Der Einzige und sein Eigentum* was still in his library (Guthke 1991, 374). Traven to the end believed with Stirner that the state is the deadliest of man-conceived powers.

Some scholars spend a deal of time trying to slot Traven into a political slot. Discussion ranges over the question of whether the Stirnerite individualist anarchist became a syndicalist in his early years in Mexico, and then a communist anarchist as he learnt more about traditional Indian society and lived through the degeneration of the Mexican Revolution. Patrick Murphy calls the anarchism in the later books "anarcho-primitivism", and says it is a far cry from Stirner's individualism (Murphy 1987, 216). Of course such is the elasticity of anarchism that Traven would enjoy being all three types of anarchist at once. He would agree with Peter Marshall that is acceptable to call oneself an individualist in everyday life, a syndicalist in wanting self-management at work, and a communist in looking forward to a society in which goods are shared in common (Marshall, 11).

At his death Traven still possessed a copy of Nietzsche's *Also Sprach Zarathustra* (Recknagel 1983, 328). Not all anarchists are attracted to Nietzsche; Kropotkin called him, "a philosopher in carpet slippers" (Woodcock and Avakumovic 1971, 282). Nietzsche is not an anarchist in the historical sense of this term, although Zarathustra's *Doppelgänger* quotes the famous anarchist dictum, "nothing is true, all is permitted" (Hollinrake 1982, 116). He also says that "whatever the State speaks is falsehood, and whatever it possesses it has stolen" (cited, Brooks 1994, 237). Benjamin Tucker is right: "Nietzsche says splendid things, - often, indeed, Anarchistic things, - but he is no anarchist" (cited Brooks, 224). But, Nietzsche's tenet, that art is the only justification for life: this, "simultaneously despairing and ecstatic conviction" (Dahlhaus and Deathridge 1984, 4) is profoundly anarchistic.

Nietzsche is certainly a revolutionary, "a magnificent disdainer of both the past and the present" (Mencken 1921, xvi). Marshall gives a very convincing picture of the libertarian, Nietzsche, a man with much to offer present day libertarians and post-modernists; the ideal individual being someone who, "makes a work of art out of himself", along with the belief, that the struggle to achieve freedom is more important than its attainment (Marshall, 159). Jürgen Habermas sees the relationship, between Wagner and Nietzsche, which led to Nietzsche writing *The Birth of Tragedy out of the Spirit of Music* (1872) as responsible for the diversion of philosophy, "away from rationalism on to the slippery subjectivist path towards so-called postmodernity" (cited Deathridge 1991, 387).[4] In chapter six I briefly discuss the "post-modern" Traven.

Nietzsche's aphorism; "who will attain anything great if he does not possess the strength and will to inflict great suffering", seems apt here (Nietzsche 1969, 195). However, we must take regard of Walter Kaufmann's warning not to, "rashly take a well-phrased point for Nietzsche's ultimate position" (Kaufmann 1971, 1) before we decide whether such a writer belongs in a university, mental asylum or prison. Nietzsche intended to annoy us. There are other extremely contentious moments. For instance, what do we make of Nietzsche's comment, that woman is the source of, "outbreaks of infinite pity" (Nietzsche 1982, 679). Ernest Newman has an apt remark "the trouble with Nietzsche his whole life long was that he combined the modesty of the peacock with the consistency of the weathercock" (Newman 1946, 347).[5] Nietzsche's influence on Traven does not seem to have been examined very closely by English language scholars; unfortunately in this short monograph I cannot pursue this and other fascinating trails.[6]

Traven was influenced by a number of anarchists, by no means all of whom were Stirnerites. He was for instance a close friend of Gustav Landauer (1870-1919), the most important anarchist thinker to emerge in Germany after the death of Max Stirner. In all of his novels and stories set in Mexico there are parallels between Traven's thinking and that of Landauer (Goss 1987, 53). Landauer's *Aufruf aum Sozialismus – Call to Socialism* - seems the most seminal influence on Traven. His comment that the "struggle for Socialism is a struggle for the soil" resounds with Traven's own writings (Seibert 1987, 160; 167). The Indian struggle and Zapata's struggle was for "*tierra y libertad*". This is so familiar and resonant a term it hardly needs translation as "land and liberty".

Landauer viewed the German *Völk* in terms of German language, customs, and culture rather than the state. In his advocacy of a left-wing form of the *völkisch* movement, he was as eloquent a spokesman for a German community as Wagner; but at the same time he was the only Jewish leader of the Bavarian revolution who did not renounce his Jewish heritage.

It was from his reading of his contemporary, the sociologist, Ferdinand Tönnies (1855-1946) that Landauer developed the idea that a nation could exist without a state (Marshall, 412). He founded the *Sozialistischer-Bund - Socialist League*, in 1908; this was dedicated to the creation of producer/consumer cooperatives that were designed to free the working class from all forms of authority (McCloskey 1997, 29). During his early adolescent years, he was an admirer of Schopenhauer, and while a student at Heidelberg University he was absorbed in the study of Ibsen and Nietzsche (Lunn 1973, 17). These are passions that he shared with Traven.

At fifteen, "he fell victim to the magic of Wagner" (Maurer 1971, 25); Wagner had nourished the "romantic longing of my heart" (cited Lunn, 22). He was very much drawn to the theater, "as an art form of communal experience" (Lunn, 286). He was an authority on Shakespeare; this love of the theater is another bond he shared with Traven. (Bruno Wille (1860-1928) was also a member of *Die Jungen* and a founder of the *Volksbühnenbewegung* - the Movement for a People's Theatre - where he may well have come into contact with Marut/Traven.) Marut escaped Landauer's fate. This brave and brilliant man was kicked almost to death by Bavarian and Württemberg infantry before they shot him. But Traven would have remembered Landauer's last words to his killers, "I've not betrayed you; you don't know yourselves how terribly you've been betrayed" (Coper 1955, 256).

Marut dedicated *Der Ziegelbrenner's* issue of 20 March 1920 to Landauer's memory (Guthke 1991, 145).

Another associate of Traven and also a leader of the Bavarian revolution was Erich Mühsam (1878-1934) a fine German-Jewish poet. He was sentenced to five years in prison after the overthrow of the revolution. Mühsam founded the *Tat Gruppe - action group*, a branch of Landauer's *Sozialistischer Bund* and was active in it from 1909-1912 (Michaels 1983, 21). He was also a playwright and member of Erwin Piscator's (1893-1966) *Volksbühne* dramaturgical collective (Willett 1978, 71-72). His play *Reasons of State* was written for the first anniversary of Sacco and Vanzetti's execution. He was also an enthusiastic crusader for the decriminalization of homosexuality (Van den Berg 1996, 18). Traven made no comments on this subject but later on when I examine *The Death Ship* I discuss briefly the suggestion that the two main characters are homosexual lovers and indeed whether Marut/Traven showed any signs of such desire or behavior.

While in jail Mühsam received a postcard from Marut who thought highly of him (*Kidnapped Saint*, 193). In 1927 in his journal *Fanal* Mühsam asked if anyone knew where Ret Marut had gone to (Guthke 1991, 182). In 1934, he was tortured and clubbed to death by the Nazis in Oranienburg prison but not before he had defiantly sung *The Internationale* when ordered to sing the *Horst Vessel* song (Toller 1937, xiv).[7]

Ernst Toller (1893-1939) was an expressionist writer and playwright and the second President of the Provisional Revolutionary Central Council of the Workers', Soldiers' and Farmers' Councils of Bavaria. Before this he had spent some thirteen months in the trenches of the First World War. After the crushing of the Bavarian Soviet he was imprisoned but eventually released into exile. In 1924 he declared that he was a man without a party (Toller 1937, 303). In prison he read at least two of the books that most influenced Traven, Bang's *Denied a Country* and Hamsun's *Hunger* (Toller 1937, 140).

He was born close to the Polish border and his childhood friend was called Stanislaus (the name also of Gales' friend in *The Death Ship* (Toller 1934, 14). He visited Mexico in 1937. He held himself responsible for the failure of the Bavarian Soviet Republic, the collapse of the Weimar Republic and the defeat of the Spanish Loyalists. He was filled with guilt about the suffering he thought he had brought upon innocent people (Gruber 1967, 189). Did he meet again with Traven before his suicide in New York in 1939?

Another prominent Jewish revolutionary was the communist Dr. Eugene Leviné (1883-1919) the head of the Second Bavarian Soviet, When it was defeated he was executed along with most of the senior comrades. Traven also dedicated *Der Ziegelbrenner*'s issue of 20 March 1920 to him as a "revolutionary of unimpeachable integrity and touching selflessness" (Guthke 1991, 145).

The economist Silvio Gesell was also in Bavaria during the Soviet, and as Finance Minister promoted his concept of regressive utopias that would restore natural order and the harmony between man and nature (Mitchell 1965, 312; Seibert 1987, 166-167). This ideal appealed to Traven and we see him referring to it in his fiction especially in *The Treasure of the Sierra Madre* and the "Jungle" novels.

Fraser has written that Traven's philosophy about the interrelationship between things animate and inanimate owes a lot to Martin Buber's I Thou relationship as laid out in *Between Man and Man* (Fraser 1964, 41). Richard Flantz refers to "Traven's profound sense of the 'Thou' as an 'I'" (Flantz 1987, 132n6).[8] Paul Berman has suggested that Traven's position is also close to that of Waclaw Milewski the Polish theorist who argued that there would always be a permanent need for revolution as one tyranny will always follow another (Berman 1978, 95).

In the light of the grisly end of many of his associates Traven's subsequent evasiveness as to whether he was Marut is therefore very understandable. He had helped uncover the secret exploits of the pre-Nazi death squads, *Femgericht* (FEME) which had plotted the murders of Mathias Erzberger and Walter Rathenau (1867-1922), two of the most important statesmen of the Weimar Republic and many other political killings.[9] He knew FEME had a long hand, so preferred a life of obscurity in Mexico – a land where many Germans lived (Kohner 1977, 137-138).

Such had been the shock of his death sentence and the savagery of the German soldiers he did not visit Germany for over forty years until he traveled to Berlin in 1959 as "Hal Croves - Traven's representative" to the premiere of the movie *The Death Ship*. In a conference held in Tucson Arizona in May 1974 Traven's widow remarked that at the end of his life Traven told her he was Marut and authorized her to confirm this fact to anyone interested.

Another influence on his life was Rudolf Rocker. Rocker (1873-1958) was an anarchist and the son of a music printer. Like Wagner he was aware of the difference between a people and a nation. In his major work, *Nationalism and Culture*, he quotes from two of Wagner's most important books, *Art and Revolution*, and *the Art Work of the Future* (Rocker 1937, 396). He writes admiringly about, "the great epoch of the free cities and of federalism" from the tenth to the fifteenth century. "The old city was not only an independent political organism it also constituted a separate economic unit". Such independence was changed through, "the gradual increase of the power of commercial capital" (Rocker 1937, 90-93).

Rocker lived in Berlin in the early 1920s and attended the International Congress of National Syndicalist Organizations held there from 22 December 1922 to 3 January 1923. One of the theories about Traven's antecedents is that he was Bendrich Traven, a Scandinavian who came to Berlin in 1920 and associated with Rocker (Jannach 1961, 28). However, I think we are safe in assuming that if Traven attended the conference he would have taken great pains to hide his identity and disclaim any suggestion that he was Marut.

Rocker had very good connections with Spanish and Latin American comrades and might be the one who cleared the way for Traven's escape to Mexico in 1924 (Guthke 1991, 153-154). Rocker wrote an introduction to the first Spanish translation of *Die Brücke im Dschungel* (Buenos Aires, 1936). Traven is said to have remained in contact with Rocker for years but unfortunately no correspondence between the two has been preserved (Guthke 1991, 373-374). Recknagel says that Traven and Rocker may have met in Brooklyn, in 1945 but once again offers no definite proof (Recknagel, 389).

A painter and Socialist whom Traven knew in his Munich and Cologne days was Anton Räderscheidt (1923-1970). Räderscheidt produced a very striking woodcut of Rosa Luxemburg in a series of six by various artists in Köln commemorating assassinated Socialist leaders (Willett, 1996, 46-47; Richter 1972, 11-12).

According to one source Räderscheidt gave his passport to Marut/Traven in 1923 to allow him to travel outside of Germany (raederscheidt.com, downloaded 3 October 2003). If this is true Marut must have either lost the passport en route to Canada or it was stolen or confiscated by immigration. In any case we know that Marut was refused entry to Canada and sent back to England where he was imprisoned. This episode would be a powerful impetus to the drafting of *The Death Ship* where Gales and all others of the hapless crew are without passports and identity. After Traven's death Guthke found Räderscheidt's identity card among his belongings (Guthke 1991, 43). An ironic twist to Räderscheidt's later life, which was almost as eventful as Traven's is that in 1940 he was living in Paris and interned as an enemy alien in a former brickworks until the German occupation of France.[10] He was deported back to Nazi Germany but survived the war.

I do not know to what degree Traven knew of Joe Hill murdered by the authorities of the State of Utah in 1915. He may have read Paul Brissenden's *The I.W.W.* first published in 1919 which quotes Joe's poems (Jenkins 1987, 212). Joe's last words were: "Goodbye, Bill. I die a true blue rebel. Don't waste time in mourning; organize". Traven's ashes were scattered over Chiapas and Joe Hill's poem resonates here:

> My will is easy to decide
> For there is nothing to divide.
> My kin don't need to fuss and moan
> "Moss does not cling to rolling stone."
>
> My body? Oh! If I could choose,
> I would to ashes it reduce
> And let the merry breezes blow
> My dust to where some flowers grow.
>
> Perhaps some fading flower then
> Would come to life and bloom again.
> This is my last and final will
> Good luck to you all. (Joe Hill)

Non Anarchist Literary and Politcal Influences

As one of the Traven scholars has said so aptly, "one of the refreshing and remarkable things about him is that it is very difficult to name *any* writer to whom he is manifestly indebted" (Fraser 1958, 9). However, I will comment on one or two possible literary forerunners and contemporaries where echoes at least can be heard.

Georg Büchner (1813-1837) the iconoclastic, young nineteenth century dramatist whose work was being reevaluated during Marut's years in the theater relates in *Woyzeck* that paradise for workers meant hard labor, harder even than their life on earth. Traven could well have read Büchner; he certainly writes that the Aztec paradise is the same as the one to which Büchner's workers are condemned. The Aztec are busy all the time, there is no time for sleeping or drinking or good French wine (Stone 1977, 68). Traven also cites the fact that the Aztecs worshipped the evil gods as devotedly as the good ones (*Night Visitor*, 107). Traven considers that paradise is not for proletarians; when they arrive they will find the bosses sitting at the high table just as they did on earth (*Carreta*, 198).

Of other German non-anarchists Traven seems to have admired Gerhart Hauptmann (1862-1946) who was an important dramatist and novelist. Zola and Ibsen influenced Hauptmann's first play *Vor Sonnenaufgang - Before Sunrise* (1889). *Die Weber* (1892) deals with the Silesian weavers' revolt of 1844. Marut's story, *Liebe des Vaterlandes - Love of the Fatherland* (1916) shows his debt to him.

Shiela Navarro sees Traven as sharing characteristics with the German impressionist writer Frank Wedekind (1864-1918). They both rage against the bourgeoisie, intending to provoke and disturb them and have poet-heroes who are rootless (Navarro 1974, 117-118). They share a deeply ironic sense of humor. One of his best lines is from his play *Franziska* (1912) where the Chief of Police is asked why he didn't prevent a suicide: "my dear Sir. I am only the Chief of Police. I can't be expected to know everything" (Wedekind 1998, 66).

Another important and prolific dramatist at the time was Georg Kaiser; no less than seventeen of his plays being performed from 1917-1918 alone. His ability to juggle the passion of a revolutionary with the logic of an intellectual and master of the theater would be admired by Traven. I do not know if he ever saw or commented on Kaiser's trilogy *Gas* (1917-1920), however, the central motif of the clash between the satisfactions of power and the visionary fight for truth and justice would appeal to Traven (Lange 1963, 5).

Richard Mezo sees an analogy between the river in *The Bridge in the Jungle* and the Rhine in Wagner's *Der Ring*. Both allow exploitation of riches, and tragedy attends those who attempt it (Mezo 1993, 77-78). Part of Traven's manifesto *Gegensatz – Contrast* - published in *Der Ziegelbrenner* in 1921 seems to refer to Wagner's *Tristan and Isolde* and *Parsifal*.

> If you can stuff all your earthly possessions into a bag that reaches up to your hips, and if you can carry this bag on your shoulders, then the cannons will rust and the walls of the oppressor's castles will fall down at the sound of a shepherd's pipe. (Cited Guthke 1991, 136)

Incidentally, Traven was musical and played both piano and violin. His library contained "many music books of German folk songs and opera arias" (Guthke 1991, 73, 375). Traven was also sexually active to an advanced age, and I am sure that he would agree with me (and Wagner and Schopenhauer) that the two elements of everyday life which bring one closest to the noumenal (the essence of things as they really are) are sexual love and music (Pateman 2002, 122).

Friedrich von Gagern was a contemporary of Traven who used American Western themes in three of his works published from 1925-1926 (Ashliman 1969, 240-241). However, the similarities between Traven and another earlier and esteemed German writer are more striking. Charles Sealsfield was the pseudonym of Karl Postl (1793-1864). Born in Moravia, he was ordained a priest but became a Freemason; he fled his monastery in 1823 and settled in the USA, thereafter becoming vehemently anti-Catholic and claiming to be a native of the United States (Ashliman, 28). His *Tokeah: or, The White*

Rose (1829) like Traven's *Die Weiße Rose* is set on a Mexican *hacienda* and its entire plot is based on the unjust treatment of the Indian (Ashliman, 151-152).

The Treasure of the Sierra Madre is a book owing something to a fellow revolutionary, Jack (John Griffith) London (1876-1916) who is often discussed in connection with Traven. Writing about the revolutionaries in *The Iron Heel* (1907) London is directly referring to *Parsifal* when he compares them to the knights of the Holy Grail (London 1971, 53). The hero of the book, Ernest Everhard is modeled on Nietzsche's superman. Traven could have read London who was widely available in a German translation.

Terrence Ponick makes a useful comment on another work of London. In *John Barleycorn*, London attacks the American myth of "from rags to riches" with ironic glee; far from marrying the boss's daughter and becoming a senior partner in his firm, he started as a shoveller of coal and never got any further. Gales in *The Death Ship* also muses that he was far from being the President of the California Railroad and Steamship and Fruit Corporation. The men who did must have shined boots of a different sort than him and sold different newspapers from the ones he carried (Ponick 1976, 57-58).

Traven might have read *The Call of the Wild* in English in 1919. I wonder if he was also familiar with one of London's best short stories "The Mexican" published in 1913 (London 1913, 243-290). The Mexican is Felipe Rivera an eighteen year old lightweight prize fighter who boxes in the USA to get money to buy arms to send south of the border to the men preparing to fight Díaz. The gringo supporters in the story are drawn from life; they are the Turners and their friends who devoted much of their time and considerable energies to buying arms for the Liberal Party to use in their insurrections of 1906 and 1908 (Turner 1967, 24, 27). London covered the Mexican Revolution as a correspondent from April to June 1914 until ill health cut short his stay.

In a letter "to the Comrades of the Mexican Revolution" in February 1911 he says in his roustabout rousing style: "we socialists, anarchists, hobos, chicken thieves, outlaws and undesirable citizens of the United States are with you heart and soul in your efforts to overthrow slavery and autocracy in Mexico" (Labor 1994-548). Ethel Duffy Turner offers a necessary corrective to this side of London. She writes that by 1914 London was calling for the U.S. to occupy Mexico by force; "his suicide in 1916 seemed the logical end of his moral collapse" (Turner 1981, 19).

Traven certainly read *The Sea Wolf* in 1929 (Baumann 1976, 169n39). London's Wolf Larsen is a brutally magnificent character (Rideout 1956, 44). Larsen's awfulness would appeal to Traven whose villains always seem to have some maverick quality about them.

Traven told the Gutenberg Book Guild that he and London shared many things. Both were illegitimate, proletarian children, both had been to sea and wrote about the sea. They were self-educated (Raskin, 143). London wrote in 1906 in "What Life Means to Me:"

> I became a tramp, begging my way from door to door, wandering over the United States and sweating bloody sweats in slums and prisons ... I was down in the cellar of society, down in the subterranean depths of misery about which it is neither nice nor proper to speak. I was in the pit, the abyss, the human cesspool, the shambles, and the charnel-house of our civilization. This is the part of the edifice of society that society chooses to ignore. (Labor, 477-478)

However, Traven and London were not the same man – in spite of frequent rumors that London only staged his suicide in order to resurface several years later as Traven.

Traven is very much in the American stubborn, individualist tradition; we have seen that Walt Whitman was one of his favorite authors when he was a young man. Whitman can justly be claimed as an American libertarian; among other pointers he subscribed to Benjamin Tucker's anarchist journal, *Liberty* (DeLeon 1978, 81). He refers in the preface to his most famous work *Leaves of Grass*, to "the swarms of cringers, suckers, doughfaces, lice of politics, planners of sly involutions for their own preferment to city officers or state legislators or the judiciary or congress or the presidency" (Whitman, 1931). Whitman's *Song of the Open Road* and the resounding line "Allons! To that which is endless as it was beginning less" also seems apposite (Whitman 1931, 130).

Traven also may owe something to Henry David Thoreau (1817-1862). There is no hard evidence that Traven had read Thoreau, but many passages in Traven remind one of Thoreau the philosophical anarchist and lover of nature (Baumann 1976, 108). In particular note, Howard's concern in *The Treasure of the Sierra Madre* (128) that the miners show their gratitude to the land they have despoiled as they have been frantically digging for gold. Like Thoreau, Traven sees the state as a Behemoth crippling and deforming mankind (Melling 1975, 144). And he is totally unlike Hernando Cortéz the *conquistador* who said very straightforwardly that he "came to get gold, not to till the soil like a peasant" (Prescott cited Coblentz 1965, 112).

Thoreau's short essay *Walking* (1862) may also have been read by Traven. Most of the action in Traven's novels takes place out of doors, and all of his major characters walk long distances. Thoreau's aphorism that "every walk is a sort of crusade" seems very apt (Thoreau 2001, 225).

It has also been well said that Traven's heroes are the very embodiment of Emersonian self-reliance (Ponick, 16). Emerson along with Hawthorne and Thoreau formed the Boston Club of Transcendentalists who established The Brook Farm Institute for Agriculture and Education (1840-1847), a Socialist utopian commune run on Fouriest principles. This sort of initiative would appeal to Traven and reminds us of the Utopian colony of Solipaz which ends the jungle novels' epic cycle of war and revolution.

Some of Traven's love of nature is derived from his reading of Shelley; this is seen in a long Shelleyan poem *Khundar* published in *Der Ziegelbrenner*, 30 April 1920 (Stone 1977, 40-42). There is also an interesting echo of Wagner's *Siegfried* as well as Stirner in the poem. Stirner wrote, "I sing like the bird sings" whilst Marut says, "ask the blackbird why it does not care if you want to hear it" (Essbach 1987, 102-103). Traven was also in tune with Shelley's distrust of government, his libertarian ideas, hatred of injustice and anti-Christianity (Baumann 1976, 24, 100).

Ambrose Gwinet Bierce (1842-1914) was a brilliant sardonic short story writer and aphorist. He disappeared during the fighting in the Mexican Civil War. Some people advanced the theory that he was born again as Traven but this cannot be true as Traven was still publishing in 1960 and died in 1969; he was an old man but not 127 years old.

Bierce wrote to a relative, "if you should hear of my being stood up against a Mexican stone wall and shot in rags, please know that I think it is a pretty good way to depart this life. It beats old age, disease or falling down the cellar stairs" (cited McLynn 2001, 231). This would strike a chord with Traven, and I am also reminded of Bierce's ironic comment about President McKinley going to war on Mexico for peace, humanity and honor, not for conquest, exploitation or extension of territory (which of course occurred); "observe, now, how providence overrules the intention of the truly good for their advantage" (cited Robinson 1977, 178).

One of Traven's most distinguished precursors and writers on Mexico was the reporter John Reed (1887-1920); but did Traven read *Insurgent Mexico* published in 1914? Reed certainly understood the people and their "inarticulate desires for land and liberty" (Gunn 1974A, 63).

John Roderigo Dos Passos (1896-1970) visited Mexico for a few months over the years 1926-1932. The first book of his trilogy *USA* (1938) *The 42nd Parallel* has a number of references to the Mexican

Revolution (Gunn 1974A, 90-92). Neither he nor Traven recognized each other in print or mentioned the other in conversation.

Of other possible literary predecessors: Theodore Dreiser (1871-1945) was the ninth child of poor German speaking parents. His first two novels *Sister Carrie* (1900) and *Jennie Gerhardt* (1911) were widely attacked for their subject matter and realistic style. He visited the Soviet Union and had hopes at one time for socialism. John Huston very perceptively said that Traven's unique dialogue was a combination of Conrad and Dreiser (cited Kaminsky 1978, 49). H. R. Hays has also remarked on Traven's Dreiser-like treatment of Collins (the villain of *The White Rose*), his mistress and his underlings (Hays 1946, 44).

Richard Henry Dana's (1815-1882) classic *Two Years before the Mast* – which has never been out of print since 1840 must surely have been read by Traven. Dana signed on as a seaman – one of the forecastle hands - and sailed along the coast of California, then a part of Mexico (Gunn 1974A, 19-20). However, Dana's ship the *Pilgrim* "savored not in any way of a hell-ship" (Labor, 504). Dana expresses his amazement at the drunkenness and gaiety of a Mexican funeral wake and how the body of a child is on display throughout the night – just as in Traven's *The Bridge in the Jungle* (Robinson, 98-99).

From 1917 to 1932 there was a strong revival of interest in Herman Melville (1819-1891) both in the USA and England. Traven could well have read Melville while he was in England from 1923-1924 as reprints of *White-Jacket* were available in London at this time (Cowell 1987, 316-317).

Stephen Crane's (1871-1900) *Maggie: a Girl of the Streets* (1893) is a pioneer work in the American naturalism school and described the sordid and ultimately hopeless life of a girl in the Bowery. In 1895 he went to Mexico as a newspaper correspondent and seems remarkably objective. He wrote that, "the most worthless literature of the world has been that which has been written by the men of one nation concerning the men of another" (cited Alarcón 1997, 57-58). As of yet I can find no reference to Traven reading him or commenting on his work.

Of Sinclair Lewis (1885-1951) Traven admires his hidden but corrosive ironies (Baumann 1976, 169n38). I haven't seen any references to any contact he may have had, or contact with John Steinbeck but Steinbeck's uncompromising *In Dubious Battle* (1936) dealing with the bloody confrontation between striking itinerant apple pickers, led by the Communist Party, and vicious owners, law officers and townspeople may have been known by Traven (Perez 1972, 65). We will see later that Traven is much more light handed in his handling of similar dramatic episodes. In *The Pearl* (1945) Steinbeck tells a parable of the northwestern coast of Mexico but his extremely romanticized portrayal of life is far removed from that of Traven.

In 1930 Traven declared that he had long been familiar with the work of Upton Sinclair (1878-1978); indeed *The Jungle* (1906) set in Chicago's meat packing plants, and dedicated to "The Workingmen of America" and dealing with the filth, disease, degradation and hopelessness of meat packers lives, may have inspired Traven to expose the conditions on the Death Ships (Baumann 1976, 45, 91-92). Raskin found a copy of *Oil* inscribed to Traven by Sinclair in Traven's study (Raskin 1980, 42).

In *The Death Ship* there are allusions to Yank, the illiterate sailor in Eugene Gladstone O'Neill's (1888-1953) play *The Hairy Ape* (Baumann 1976, 92-94). Robert Olafson points out that Gales' speech patterns and the filthy interior of the ship may be patterned on this play (Olafson 1976, 167-168). And after all Marut had been an actor for many years.

Helmut Reinecke alludes to some common ground between Traven and Carl May (1842-1912) who was the author of numerous popular adventure novels (cited Keune 1987, 84).[11] May's most successful book is *Winnetou* which has sold over 2.5 million copies in Germany alone; Winnetou is the son of a chief of the Mescalescou Apaches (Green 1980, 398n13). The celebrated photographer and long time resident of Chiapas, Gertrude ("Trudi") Duby Blom read these stories as a child in Switzerland (Blom 1984, 7). It seems certain that Traven would have had, through reading May, a similar introduction to Indian life.

Notes

1. It was to be published only thirteen times.
2. He associated with the young Hegelians known as *Die Freien* - the free ones - men such as Arnold Ruge (1802-1880), Karl Marx (1818-1883), Friedrich Engels (1820-1895), Ludwig Feuerbach (1804-1872), Georg Herwegh (1817-1835), and Moses Hess (1812-1875).
3. In April 1976 Rolf Recknagel found a copy of Nietzsche's *Also Sprach Zarathustra* in Traven's library.
4. John Deathridge entertainingly pursues the "post-modernist" Wagner in his homage to the "Dean of Wagner Studies", Carl Dahlhaus (Deathridge 1992A).
5. Wagner was the obsession of Nietzsche's life; an obsession which undoubtedly contributed to his madness and tragically early death.
6. Only one book of Nietzsche's, *The Anti Christian* fails either to mention directly or allude to Wagner, and much of the later writing consists of parodies of, and attacks on Wagner. As is well known, Nietzsche after a short but

passionate friendship, turned on Wagner, and at the end of his productive life claimed that Wagner and he were, "antipodes" (Nietzsche 1971, 662).

7. Mühsam's wife Zenl went to the Soviet Union where she was arrested during the Great Purge. Happily she survived and in 1956 was allowed to leave for the relative freedom of East Germany (Rühle 1969, 149).

8. Buber (1878-1965) was a cogent critic of Stirner but realized that Stirner was a necessary forerunner of Søren Kierkegaard (1813-1855) (Buber 1965, 44-45).

9. The acronym is derived from *Femgericht* an order which was established in medieval Germany to deliver vigilante folk justice. It was used by virtually all *Freikorps* organizations in post World War I Germany (Waite 1952, 212-213).

10. Wyatt says that Götz Ohly, a pharmacist and reader of *Der Ziegelbrenner* gave Marut his passport which was lost by him somewhere between Germany and England.

11. Incidentally Adolf Hitler's (1889-1945) favorite reading was May's westerns (Tambling 1987, 196).

Chapter 3

Traven's Life, Work and Times

1712	Cancúc uprising in Chiapas
1821	Chiapas joins the Mexican Empire
1858-1872	Presidency of Benito Juárez
1868	"The war of the castes" San Cristóbal de la Casas
1876-1911	Presidency of Porfirio Díaz
1878	Anti-socialist laws passed by the German *Reichstag*
1880	2 July: Charles Trefny born in St. Louis
1882	23 February: Otto Feige born out of wedlock in Schwiebus (Zwiebodzin) then in East Prussia Parents: Adolf Rudolf Feige, potter, and Hormina Wienecke, a mill-hand
1882	25 February: Ret Marut born in San Francisco Parents: William and Helene Marut (née Ottarent) Father's occupation "impresario" Nationality: English, later changed to American

1890	4 March: Traven Torsvan Croves born in Chicago Parents: Burton Torsvan, probably Scandinavian, and Dorothy Croves, (Irish/Scottish)
1896	Feige confirmed
1896-1902	Otto Feige apprenticed with Firma Meier as a locksmith
1901	Ricardo and Jesús Flores Magón jailed in Mexico
1902-1904	Feige: Army service with 7th Jäger Battalion
1904	Feige: reads about anarchism and disappears from home never to return
1904-1907	Feige at Sea?
1905	Ret Marut: talks to Westphalian miners
1906	Cananea copper strike in Mexico broken with assistance of Arizona Rangers San Francisco Earthquake
1907	Ret Marut: as actor in Essen
1908	Marut: meets the actress Elfriede Zielke (born 1886) Marut acting in Suhlendorf
1909	Police issue registration card in Ohrdorf to Marut Marut: juvenile lead in theater at Crimmitschau
1910	The slogan *Tierra y Libertad* first used in journal *Regeneración* Marut and Zielke in Berlin
1910-1911	Marut in *Neue Behne* ensemble touring Prussia, Pomerania, Posen, Silesia, Danzig
1911	January: fall of Mexicali to Magonista rebels April: fall of Ciudad Juárez to Mexican rebels May: Porfirio Díaz resigns as President of Mexico

	Election of Francisco I. Madero as President
1911-1912	Marut at Danzig Municipal Theater
1912	20 March: Ret Marut's daughter Irene Zielke born Marut: first published story, *Der Idiot* Marut: works for the theater journal, *Masken* September: *Casa del Obrero Mundial* founded November: Emiliano Zapata issues Plan of Ayala in Morelos
1912-1915	Marut in Düsseldorf
1913	Traven/Torsvan: enters Mexico at the port of Mazatalán February: murder of Madero in Mexico General Victoriano Huerta assumes Presidency Pancho Villa has series of great victories
1914	First known portrait of Marut by F. W. Seiwert Marut breaks with Elfriede Zielke USA invades Mexico landing at Veracruz Villa and Zapata occupy Mexico City
1915	Ret Marut: appears in Munich and never works in the theater again Marut: meets Irene Mermet (born 27 July 1893) Marut applies to San Francisco for birth certificate Rebellion by the Bachajón in Chiapas April-June: Villa defeated by Alfaro Obregón Venustiano Carranza recognized as President of Mexico by the United States
1916	Richard Maurhut: publishes *An das Fraülein von S...* in Munich
1917	6 April: U.S. belatedly enters World War I April: Marut refused U.S. passport (applied March) 1 September: first edition of *Der Ziegelbrenner* 7 November: Russian October Bolshevik Revolution
1918	7 November: Republic in Bavaria under Kurt Eisner

Wilhelmshaven Naval Revolt
August: Ricardo Flores Magón sentenced to 20 years imprisonment for obstructing the war effort
9 November: Kaiser deposed
11 November: Armistice Day
December: *Der Ziegelbrenner* evenings with readings by Marut

1918-1919   Palmer Raids in the USA and deportation of Anarchists

1919   Murder of Rosa Luxemburg and Karl Liebknecht after the failure of Spartacist Revolt in Berlin
21 February: Eisner killed by Lieutenant Graf (Count) Anton Arco-Valley
21 March: Hungarian Soviet, Béla Kun premier
7 April: *Räterepublik* - Republic of Councils in Bavaria
8 April: Marut becomes press censor
Marut and Mermet living at 84 Clemenstrasse Munich
I May: Marut arrested by White Guards; escapes
Flees to Vienna
June: meets with Mermet in Berlin
Murder of Gustave Landauer
Zapata lured into ambush and killed

1920   January: *Der Ziegelbrenner*, published from Vienna
Later in year published from Cologne
24 February: Nazi Party founded in Munich
16 November: end of Russian Civil War
May: assassination of Carranza; Obregón becomes president

1921   Marut in Berlin
February 28: Kronstadt uprising in Russia
December: last issue of *Der Ziegelbrenner*

1922   Marut in Switzerland, Czechoslovakia, Belgium and Holland. Sends postcard to Mühsam from Rotterdam
Murder of Walter Rathenau German Foreign Minister
28 October: Mussolini March on Rome

Ricardo Flores Magón murdered in his prison cell
Start of the Mexican mural movement

1923	Marut leaves Germany for Canada (June) deported to England (August) July: Pancho Villa assassinated 8-9 November: failed Nazi putsch in Munich First letter from "B. Traven" arrives in Germany Irene Mermet arrives in USA
1923-1924	30 November-15 February: Marut in Brixton prison England Rebellion of Adolfo de la Huerta in Mexico
1924	Marut claims to be Feige March: Feige applies for U.S. citizenship Feige writes to parents 21 January: death of Lenin Plutarco Elías Calles becomes President of Mexico on ambitious reform platform June/July: Marut arrives in Tampico (Tamaulipas state) Mexico 26 July: Marut writes in his diary that the Bavarian anarchist is no more
1924-1930	Traven/Torsvan lives in Columbus near Tampico
1925	June: *Vorwärts* begins serialization of *Die Baumwollpflücker* Irene Mermet in Mexico September: ms. of *Das Tottenschiff* and letters from Traven to Ernst Preczang at *Büchergilde Gutenberg* Kafka's *Der Process* published
1925-1929	*Cristero* uprisings in Mexico
1926	*Der Wobbly* published by *Bucheister Verlag* Traven/Torsvan: takes photography lessons with Edward Weston in Mexico City April: *Das Tottenschiff* published in Germany April: Murder of Primo Tapia in Mexico July: *Im tropischen Busch* short story published

May-August: Traven/Torsvan on Palacios scientific expedition to Chiapas and Vera Cruz as Swedish photographer
Meets Frans Blom and Wolfgang Cordan
Torsvan admits to Cordan he is B Traven
President Calles issues anti-Catholic decrees
Trotsky expelled from Politburo
Publication of Kafka's *Der Schloss*
U.S. troops intervene in Nicaragua – until 1933

1927   *Der Schatz der Sierra Madre* published in Germany
Traven/Torsvan: at summer school of National University of Mexico
22 August: Execution of Sacco and Vanzetti

1928   *Land des Frühlings* translated from English by Curt Reibetanz published in Germany
Der Busch published in Germany
Torsvan: in Chiapas and Guatemala involving a 2,000 mile coast to coast horseback journey
Torsvan: takes up with Maria de La Luz Martinez in Mexico City
May: Chinese Red Army founded in Hunan
1 October: start of Soviet Five-Year Plan

1929   Publication of *Die Brücke im Dschungel* and *Die Weisse Rose* in Germany, translated from English by Rudolf Dörwald
Torsvan: in Merida (Yucatán)
Traven in United States
Black Friday: 29 October New York Stock Exchange collapse
Establishment of *Partido Nacional Revoluciónario* (PNR) in Mexico
Trotsky expelled from the USSR
Hemingway's *A Farewell to Arms*
Nobel Prize for Literature to Thomas Mann

1930   As "Engineer" B. T. Torsvan on expedition to Chiapas
Living in Acapulco at Cashew Park

Starts to travel to San Antonio training for a pilot's license
Dos Passos' *42nd Parallel*

1931 Publication of *Der Karren* and *Regierung* in Germany
El Barco de los Muertos published in Madrid (Zeus)
Traven: gives his address as Tamaulipas State, Mexico
9 December: Spain becomes a Republic

1932 28 January: Japanese occupy Shanghai
Conference in Amsterdam of intellectuals against war

1933 Publication of *Der Marsch ins Reich der Caoba* in Zurich, Vienna and Prague
12 January: Grosz emigrates to the U.S.
30 January: Nazis seize power in Germany
27 February: Reichstag Fire. Banning of KPD
28 February: Brecht goes to Prague; arrest of Mühsam
20 March: opening of Dachau concentration camp
23 March: Kurt Weill arrives in Paris
2 May: Büchergilde offices seized and the press taken over by the Fascist German Workers Front
10 May: Traven's novels - *Der Karren, Die Weisse Rose* and *Regierung* and other black-listed books burned in Germany
Bernard Smith starts to edit Traven's English versions of *The Death Ship, The Treasure of the Sierra Madre*, and *The Bridge in the Jungle*

1934 *The Death Ship* published in English in London (Chatto & Windus) in translation from German by Eric Sutton
The Death Ship in Traven's English published in New York (Alfred A. Knopf)
The Treasure of the Sierra Madre translated from German by Basil Creighton published in England (Chatto & Windus)
Murder of Erich Mühsam in Germany

	General Lázaro Cárdenas del Rio elected President of Mexico - 1940
1935	Traven corresponds with Herbert Klein *The Treasure of the Sierra Madre* from Traven's English version published in New York (Alfred A. Knopf) *The Carreta* translated from German by Basil Creighton published in London (Chatto & Windus)
1936	Publication of *Die Troza, Sonnen-Schöpfung* and *Die Rebellion der Gehenkten* in Zurich Traven and Rosa Elena Luján meet at a party for the violinist Jascha Heifetz in Mexico City *Government* translated from German by Basil Creighton published in London (Chatto & Windus)
1936-1939	Spanish Civil War
1937	*Das Tottenschiff* translated by Wilhelm Ritter from Traven's English version published by *Büchergilde Gutenberg* in Zurich Arrival of Trotsky in Mexico Nationalization of Mexican railways
1938	11 March: Germany annexes Austria 18 March: Cárdenas expropriates foreign-owned oil companies *The Bridge in the Jungle* from Traven's English published in New York (Alfred A. Knopf)
1939	28 March: Franco's troops enter Madrid 8 August: Esperanza López Mateos writes to Knopf in relation to film rights on Traven's novels Suicide of Ernst Toller in New York 22 August: Nazi-Soviet Pact 1 September: German troops enter Poland Start of World War II *Ein General kommt aus dem Dschungel* translated into Swedish by Axel Hölmstrom published as *Djungelgeneralen* (Stockholm)

1940	*The Death Ship* from Traven's English published in London (Jonathan Cape) *Ein General kommt aus dem Dschungel* published in German in Amsterdam *The Bridge in the Jungle* from Traven's English published in England (Jonathan Cape)
1941	*Puente en la Selva* published; translated from English by Esperanza López Mateos Traven starts to use Hal Croves as an alias 21 August: death of Trotsky following attack 7 December: Pearl Harbor attack
1942	2 June Mexico declares war on Germany 17 June: Traven/Torsvan gets Mexican identity card Esperanza López Mateos becomes B. Traven's legal representative
1943	Casa M. L. Martinez offers for sale *The Story of an American Sailor Aboard a Death Ship* (probably the 1934 Knopf edition) Meets members of U.S. Author's Guild in Mexico City
1944	Esperanza López Mateos starts to translate all the rest of Traven's novels 6 June: D Day landings in France
1945	Traven: visits New York and San Antonio, Texas Traven possibly meets Rocker in Brooklyn *La Tercera Guerra Mundial* published Mexico D. F. (Estudios Sociales) 8 May: VE Day 6 August: A bomb dropped on Hiroshima
1946	John Huston corresponds with Traven. Meets Hal Croves *Una Canasta de Cuentos Mexicanos* translated from German by Esperanza López Mateos (Editorial Alas)[1]

1947	Hal Croves on the location of John Huston's *The Treasure of the Sierra Madre* Josef Weider of Zurich becomes Traven's agent in Europe. Weider meets Esperanza López Mateos
1948	Luís Spota's investigation into Traven's identity Traven in Mexico City and San Antonio June: Berlin blockade
1949	*La Carreta* translated from English by Esperanza López Mateos (Compañia General de Ediciones)
1950	*Macario* published in German; translated from English by Hans Kauders (*Büchergilde Gutenberg*).[2] *Land des Frühlings* published in Zurich *El Tesoro de la Sierra Madre* and *La Rebelión de los Colgados* translated from English by Esperanza López Mateos (Compañia General de Ediciones) 25 June: start of Korean War
1951	First issue of *B.T. Mitteilungen* 9 May: *Dennoch eine Mutter* *La Rosa Blanca* and *Gobierno* translated from English by Esperanza López Mateos (Compañia General de Ediciones) Suicide of Esperanza López Mateos 3 September: Traven becomes Mexican citizen as Traven Torsvan
1952	*The Rebellion of the Hanged* translated from German by Charles Duff published in London (Robert Hale) and translated back from Esperanza López Mateos' Spanish version of 1950 into English in New York (Hill and Wang) Rosa Elena Luján gradually takes over functions of Esperanza López Mateos
1953	Essay on the unpublished manuscript of *Kunst der Indianer* (1931) appears in *BT-Mitteilungen* *The Night Visitor* appears in English as *Visitor from Nowhere* *Macario* appears in English as *The Third Guest*

	5 March: death of Stalin
	19 June: execution of the Rosenbergs
1954	*General from the Jungle* translated by Desmond Vesey published in London (Robert Hale)
	Croves on location of *The Rebellion of the Hanged*
	Reunion of Traven and Rosa Elena Luján on the set in Chiapas
	Frans Blom and Gertrud Düby identify Croves as Torsvan while on the film set – as does Humphrey Bogart when shown photographs
1955	August: premiere in Zurich of *Totenschiff: Play in four acts* by H. Croves and Rosa Elana Luján
1956	Death of Irene Mermet in New York.[3]
	Premiere in Mexico City of film *Canasta de Cuentos Mexicanos*
	The Cotton Pickers translated by Eleanor Brockett published in England (Robert Hale)
1957	Torsvan/Croves marries Rosa Elena Luján in San Antonio, Texas
	Death of Diego Rivera
1958	Election of President Adolfo López Mateos - 1964
	Film of *Macario*
	Death of Rudolf Rocker
1959	January: Cuban Revolution
	October: Torsvan/Croves visits Germany for premiere of *TheDeath Ship*; visits London
1960	Publication in Germany of *Aslan Norval* (Desch) copyright Rosa Elana Luján and J. Weider
	Last issue of *B.T. Mitteilungen* (no 36)
	March to Caobaland published in England (R. Hale)
1961	Traven's copyright changed to Rosa Elana Luján and/or Hal Croves
	Stories by the Man Nobody Knows: Nine Tales published in the USA (Regency Books)

	17 April: CIA mount abortive Bay of Pigs invasion of Cuba Start of the Berlin Wall
1962	Filming of *The White Rose*
1963	*Stern* reporter Gerd Heidemann interviews Rosa Elena Luján 22 November: assassination of President Kennedy
1964	Traven moves into Calle Mississippi 61, Mexico City *Sun Creation* published in English fantasy and science fiction magazine
1965	Traven writes script for documentary on David Alfaro Siqueiros *The White Rose* published in London (Robert Hale) in Traven's English
1966	*The Night Visitor and Other Stories* New York (Hill and Wang) October: Judy Stone investigates Traven Federico Canessi works on bust of Traven *El General, Tierra y Libertad*, translated by Rosa Elena Luján published in Mexico (Compania. General de Ediciones) Rosa Elena Luján de Torsvan writes *Der Sarg auf dem Bus - The Coffin on Top of the Bus.* It is often erroneously attributed to Traven.[4]
1967	*The Night Visitor and Other Stories* published in London (Cassell) *El Visitante Nocturno y otras Cuentos*, translated by Rosa Elena Luján published in Mexico (Editorial Diana)
1968	*Creation of the Sun and Moon* published in New York (Hill and Wang) with illustrations by Alberto Beltrán *Salario Amargo* (The Cotton Pickers), translated by Rosa Elena Luján published in Mexico (Editorial

Diana)
4 April: assassination of Martin Luther King, Jr.
Olympic Games held in Mexico City.
2 October: Massacre of students in the Plaza of
Tlatelolco, Mexico City
Traven paid visit by DDR delegation

1969   26 March: dies of prostate cancer in Mexico City as
Traven Torsvan Croves aged 78 and born in Chicago
in 1890 - son of Burton Torsvan and Dorothy Croves
Ashes scattered over Chiapas
The Cotton Pickers published in the USA (Hill and
Wang, translated from German but no translator is
named - probably Traven)
Rosa Elena Luján reveals Traven was Ret Marut

1970   *The Carreta* published in New York (Hill and
Wang); no translator indicated; presumably Basil
Creighton

1971   *Government* published in New York (Hill and Wang,
translated from German but no translator indicated;
presumably Basil Creighton)
The March to the Montería published in New York
(Hill and Wang, no translator named; it is presumably
Traven's English version)
Mexican President Luis Echeverría – until 1976

1972   *General from the Jungle*, translated by Desmond
I. Vesey published in New York (Hill and Wang).

1973   *Marcha al Imperio de la Caoba*, translated by
Rosa Elena Luján published in Mexico (Editorial
Diana)

1975   *The Kidnapped Saint and other Stories*, edited by
Rosa Elena Luján, Mina C. Klein and H. Arthur
Klein, published in USA (Lawrence Hill)

1979   *The White Rose* translated by Donald J. Davidson
published in USA (Lawrence Hill)

1981	Ret Marut's *To the Honorable Miss S. and other Stories*, translated by Peter Silcock published in USA (Lawrence Hill)
1994	January 1, Zapatista Army of National Liberation begins the revolution in Chiapas *Trozas* translated by Hugh Young, published in English in USA (Ivan R. Dee)

Adapted from and indebted to: Treverton, 1999, Recknagel, 1983; Wyatt, 1980; Johnson, 1968, and other sources.

Notes

1. Edward Treverton writes that both Esperanza López and Rosa Elena Luján "probably knew insufficient German to base their Spanish translations on the German texts" (Treverton, 4). I am more persuaded by Guthke's remarks that Esperanza learned German in the late 1940s (Guthke 1991, 322).
2. Ponick says that the name sounds suspiciously like Hal Croves (Ponick 1976, 211).
3. She had been married to a lawyer and seems to have had no contact with Traven since 1925.
4. It was published in Zurich with the subtitle: "A Short Story from South America". Zogbaum incorrectly attributes it to Traven (Zogbaum 1992, 236).

Chapter 4

Traven's American Alter Ego

The Man without a Country is Free. (*Der Ziegelbrenner* 15 January 1919, 93)

Traven first appeared in print as "Traven" in the social democratic Berlin paper *Vorwärts*, in 1925 with a series of stories based on his work and adventures in Mexico.[1] He toiled for a time in the Tampico oilfields; the source also for many of the events depicted in his full length book *Die Weisse Rose* (1929): *La Rosa Blanca* (1932): *The White Rose* (1965). Among other jobs he also herded cattle and picked cotton. Several stories appeared in journals such as: *Simplicissimus*, *Jugend* and *Das Buch für Alle* (Treverton, 113).

These pieces were very well received and attracted the attention of the *Büchergilder Gutenberg*, the book guild formed in Germany in 1924 to enable workers to buy good books at low cost.[2] The directors wrote to Traven in Mexico asking to see some more of his work. He sent them *The Death Ship* first in English and then, at the suggestion of the guild's editor Ernst Preczang, in German (Treverton, 5).

When published it became an immediate and enduring success. His subsequent relationship with the guild was a very intimate one. When it moved to Switzerland after the Nazis came to power he donated many artifacts for the guild to use as prizes and inducement to readers to recruit more members (Spoer, 1936). He had a clear realistic vision of what the guild should try and attain. He wrote that it alone had within it the power to create economically and ideally for the poet a following which is the basis of his activity (Traven 1934, 147).[3]

American publishers however, regularly rejected the work he submitted to them. In a letter to an admirer Arthur H. Klein in 1935

Traven said that he sent his first story in English off to an American magazine as early as 1915 (cited Baumann 1987, 39). It was rejected like many others. The renowned American publisher Alfred Knopf had been in the business for over twenty years, but not until a visit to Berlin in 1932 was he made aware of the existence of Traven who by then had sold millions of books in Europe (Knopf, 1935). Not until the early 1950s did American and British magazines accept his stories; this was long after his success with one or two of his novels. Moreover, several novels did not appear in the USA until after his death. *The White Rose* was not published in the USA until 1979.[4] A searing attack on U.S. exploitation of Latin America understandably was not to all tastes.

Traven's royalties were also reduced because of the proliferation of pirated Spanish editions printed usually in Mexico City and Buenos Aries (Johnson 1947, 13). Nevertheless, Traven managed to survive upon earnings from European publishers, substantially reduced as they were post-1933 after the Nazis seized his royalties and burnt his books. His royalties from the USA were derisory; in 1946-1947 he received $28. Apart from leftists, Traven remained largely unread in the USA for many years. In the first five years of publication sales of *The Death Ship* totaled 3,288 copies and *The Treasure of the Sierra Madre* even less at 2,692 (Hagemann 1959, 43, 45). The low-key nature of Knopf's enterprise is indicated by the fact that in 1958 it was impossible for Alfred Knopf or Herbert Weinstock to say who had translated the German manuscripts of *Das Tottenschiff*, (*The Death Ship*), *Der Schatz der Sierra Madre* (*The Treasure of The Sierra Madre*) and *Die Brücke im Dschungel*, (*The Bridge in the Jungle*) into English (Hagemann Correspondence, Folio 11).

He published seven books between 1926 and 1930, but rather than spend his earnings in the established literary capitals of the world as did his contemporaries Ernest Hemmingway and Scott Fitzgerald he preferred to use his time exploring in south-east Mexico. After rediscovering long forgotten ruins and the tomb of Cuauhtémoc, the last Aztec chief, he completed his only travel book, *Land Des Frühlings - Land of Springtime* (1928) full of descriptions of the Indian nations, native lives and customs. He revised it a couple of times but it has never been translated into English; a Spanish version *Tierra de la Primavera* came out in Mexico City only in 1996.

His desire to live a modest retiring life but at the same time continue his social and political commitments was shown by his donation of the film rights of his most famous book, *The Treasure of the Sierra Madre* (amounting to some $5,000 U.S.) to poets and writers who were more in need of the money than he was.

A fitting comment on Traven's life and work was made in 1977. Of the writings "they are as curious, as ambiguous and as provocative as the author's life". And, "not much that is better has been printed - in German or English since Traven's death" (Skow 1977, 94).

I will deal with each of the novels and significant short stories in the order that Traven suggested one should read them.

The Death Ship

> There are so many ships on sea
> Some do come and some do flee
> Yet none can be so dreadful low
> That none is found so further so.
> (Cited Braybrooke 1963, 140)

I am using a 1959 reprint of Traven's English version of 1940, published in London.

The Death Ship is subtitled: *The Story of an American Sailor* and in my view and Neville Braybrooke's this book is the song of the real and genuine hero of the sea (Braybrooke 1965, 212). Traven is regarded by many people as one of the greatest "American" writers, a writer of the same stature that Herman Melville (1819-1891) showed in *Moby Dick*.[5] When you read Traven's description (116-119) of Gales' feelings on first seeing the *Yorikke* you may agree with this accolade.[6] Traven invites a comparison with Melville or Joseph Conrad (1857-1924) whom he obliquely refers to "that greatest sea-story writer of all times" (148).[7] As John Fraser points out so well *The Death Ship* shares a distinction with Conrad's *Heart of Darkness* for supremely depicting; "an extreme situation that can produce the kind of radical testing-out of human strengths and weaknesses" (Fraser 1964, 40).[8] Although he liked *Lord Jim*, Traven thinks he does better than Conrad as Conrad writes about the bridge and not the crew (Stone 1977, 63).

The first review in English was by James Hanley (himself a former sailor) and he was extremely enthusiastic. It called it "the first *real* book about the lives of the men for'ard of the bridge". He concluded that "no better description of a ship's stokehold and the strange beings in it has ever come my way" (Hanley 1934, 131). Wynard Browne was equally positive. "Traven has experience and sensibility but thankfully eschews the rhapsodic" which in Browne's view scuppers many a sea faring yarn. He said that it was "perhaps the best existing account of the work of the trimmers and stokers under the worst conditions". He thought that Traven's criticism of big capitalists and big states "is the more telling because throughout most of the book the reader can forget its implications" (Browne 1934, 463). Henry Major Tomlinson was overwhelmed. In a full column review he said: "it is a translation not only from the German, but from life, and so is profoundly disturbing" (Tomlinson 1934, 75).

On our side of the Atlantic one of the first reviews had the masthead "A Powerful Book Unfettered, Wild". Lincoln Colcord asked: "has a new genius come out of the stokehold of some ocean tramp" (Colcord 1934, 5). Another of the first substantive reviews - by William Doerflinger for *The Saturday Review of Literature* - was very up beat; "its rough virile style becomes a perfect torrent of slashing description and vivid nightmare" (Doerflinger 1934, 677). Some other early reviews were shorter and less encouraging. A female reviewer showed her incomprehension: "half-way through the first book I had ceased to believe a word that sailor [Gales] said." She complains of a man, "who tells of his difficulties in a pretentious patter that is worn meaningless with effort" (Pier 1934, 149).

However, *The New Yorker's* anonymous reviewer said *The Death Ship* had considerable power and was refreshingly without "the sentimentality of Jack London or Conrad" (*The New Yorker* 28 April 1934, 102). Another influential feuilleton, *The Saturday Review of Literature* in the second time it was reviewed in their pages in a week, called it "a truly remarkable book" "a Moby Dick of the stokehold" (Quercus 1934, 671). Another 1930s review says "its language is so spirited, so opulent, and even in its ghastly fashion so gay; it is the most distressing world I have ever witnessed" (Van Doren 1934, 569).

Traven claims to have first written the manuscript of this book in English and rewrote it substantially at some unspecified time later in German (Spoer 1936, 8). Some of the original manuscript was written in Brixton prison where Traven was incarcerated from 1923-1924 for some months with an unlimited supply of paper and pencils (Guthke 1993, 125). Frank Nordhausen examined these handwritten fragments along with the first German edition. He says that we can see how Traven corrected the formal and textual unevenness of the first English draft so that the concept of the Death Ship becomes clearer. He argues (conclusively to my taste) that it proves the continuity of the Marut – Traven identities (Nordhausen, 1992).

It was first published in Germany as *Das Tottenschiff* in 1926; it became an instant success with a quarter of a million copies being sold over seven years until storm troopers under the orders of Hitler's second in command, Hermann Goering took over Traven's publisher (*Büchergilde Gutenberg* - the Gutenberg Book Guild) printing works. The Nazis subsequently burnt all of the copies of Traven's work they could find in Germany and in other countries of Europe they overran. It is difficult to overestimate the appeal that Traven had; right up to the Second World War he "dominated the reading of the German Left"

(Willett 1996, 193).

Traven translated *Das Tottenschiff* back into English in 1934, rewriting it considerably in the process and adding about a quarter to the length. *The Death Ship* and *Das Tottenschiff* therefore are different works of art just as Nabokov's original Russian stories are different from his subsequent "translations" into the English prose masterpieces such as *Ada*. Traven's translation was published by Alfred Knopf in New York in 1934, and by Jonathan Cape in England in 1940 and the edition I use and normally comment upon is a reprint of this one.[9]

The critic, Arthur Calder-Marshall was very much more impressed with Traven's translation that with another made from the German for Chatto and Windus (also in 1934) by (Eric) Jeremy Sutton (Calder-Marshall 1940, 523). This at times makes a travesty of Traven, reading as if Gales is an Ivy League graduate and not a sailor. This is a grave mistake as although Traven does not describe Gales' appearance it is clear that he is a worker. The most hostile review I have seen of the book concerned this translation by Sutton and started with the resounding if astounding words, "I have never read a duller book" (Bechofer Roberts 1934, 249). Admittedly the review looks as if it was written in half an hour of not too concentrated effort and largely consists of a long extract. *Punch* was equally dismissive of Sutton's effort: "the book is really more propaganda of the UPTON SINCLAIR type than genuine fiction, and, like most of its kind, it suffers a good deal artistically from overstatement; and though it has a certain rough strength of its own, it is not an entirely convincing piece of work" (*Punch* 31 January 1934, 140).

Unfortunately, many of the reviewers do not specify whether they have been reading the Sutton translation, or the Traven version (edited by Bernard Smith). Confusingly both were published in the same year. The general run of reviews for Traven/Smith is much more positive than for Traven translated by Sutton. Whenever I can establish the edition being reviewed I will do so.

A similar problem arises with the other books. The versions published in England and the USA often differed significantly from each other; such as: using a different translator, whether the text had or had not been revised by Traven, and so forth. In my bibliography and in chapter three: *Traven's Life, Work and Times*, I try to give a concise and hopefully accurate summary of the most important editions available in English.

Among the few other hostile or lukewarm reviews is an anonymous piece belaboring the point that Traven "shouldn't have mixed fiction with a diatribe however useful on labor conditions" (*New York Times Book Review* 29 April 1934, 21).[10] In England an ultra nationalist reviewer was incomprehensibly incensed at, "the author who quite evidently loathes England, and is not above a little anti-British propaganda masquerading as art". He also saw it as a straightforward sea yarn incorporating a bitter indictment against the state (Maclaren 1934, 383).

The book subsequently has had a long and complicated publishing history comprising complex translations, unauthorized pirate versions, re-writing and re-translations. Wilhelm Ritter in his part of the publishing cycle translated Traven's English version back into German and this was brought out by *Büchergilde Gutenberg* in Zurich in 1937. It was also translated from Traven's English into Spanish by his friend and agent Esperanza López Mateos as *El Barco de la Muerte* in 1950 (Hagemann 1959, 43, 44). A pirated version in Spanish *El Barco de los Muertos* came out in Buenos Aires in 1936 and in Mexico in 1945. In his introduction to this free-booting version the putative translator Oscar Cerruto claims (plausibly) that nobody had answered any of the letters he had addressed to Traven. He declared generously that Traven was a lucid writer who laid bare the evils of the civilizations he writes about and he (Cerruto) felt compelled to make it available to the Spanish speaking world (Cerruto 1945, 7-8).

In a statement that Traven put out when the novel was first published he says that it is autobiographical. In 1966 Traven told Judy Stone that Stanislaus was a real person – from the same part of Germany that after 1918 became part of Poland (Garland, 131-132). Traven's widow also said after Traven's death that he identified with Gales, who was his favorite character. This is easy to believe even if it is not necessarily true; Traven as Marut had an intimate knowledge of post World War I conditions in Europe. Traven as Torsvan was an experienced seaman and wrote the notes for the book in ports scattered throughout the world, and in his breaks from watches. Torsvan was a fireman on board the ship which took him first to Mexico in 1924.

Much of the book's strange air is achieved through a convincing portrayal of the reality of workers' lives seen through the alert, supple and agile mind of a young anarchist; Gales, a man not constrained by any ideology, "Communists in Russia are no less despotic than the Fascists in Italy or the textile–mill magnates in America" (109-110).

Traven's clear sighted and prophetic assessment of Soviet Communism jarred with many of the left and liberal reviewers of the time. Herbert Klein in the flagship of American Communist intellectuals, *The New Masses* while adoring the story referred to Traven's "wild wobbly prejudices" (Klein, 1934). Writing after the war D. Lynn highlighted the crux of Traven's view, "he sees 'the State' with its creatures, religion, big business, war, as Behemoth crippling and deforming men out of all human semblance" (Lynn 1950, 91).

On the face of it *The Death Ship* is a simple and straightforward tale but a more detailed look shows that it is really written in a very sophisticated style. John Mair writing in 1940 said; "from whatever angle it is regarded it shows outstanding merits, not the least of which, perhaps, is the skill with which Mr. Traven veils his own fundamental intentions" (Mair 1940, 340). Granville Hicks comments that although the structure of *The Death Ship* is very like that of thousands of other simple adventure stories its texture is revolutionary (Hicks 1935, 318).

One feature of Traven's writing which we will find later in most of his novels lies in the inclusion of long interpolated stories that give him an opportunity to bring in universal issues and theories. They serve to still the action of the narrative and build suspense further (Ponick, 35). In the opinion of most of his readers Traven succeeds brilliantly.

Olafson remarks that the book "is ladened with a heavy manifest of literary allusions" (Olafson 1976, 163). There is a great deal of humor and very subtle irony – irony that has escaped some of the less alert critics.[11] It is full of paradox. Just compare: "if you do not wish to be lied to, do not ask questions!" (253), with: "the word 'why' with a question mark behind it is the cause, I am certain of all culture, civilization, progress and science" (83).

Traven continually shifts the plane of meaning from anger to satire to despair. Some critics have termed Traven's writing "halting" but most of his commentators fervently disagree. Some others have complained of his gallows humor. As Hamlet has it, "has this fellow no feeling of his business that he sings at grave making".[12] Lynn called its style; "a tough argot reminiscent of Brecht and Toller in its irony and accent" (Lynn, 89-94).

We know that Traven was most at home when writing and speaking in German and that even at the end of his long life and after spending forty years in Mexico, he still spoke English as well as Spanish with a German (or Norwegian) accent. It is partly this that gives *The Death Ship* much of its force and impact. In English, *The Death Ship* reads as though it were written by an immigrant or second generation self-educated American worker, and to my mind it has the same power and eloquence as the writings of the anarchists Sacco and Vanzetti, unjustly electrocuted in America in 1927, in the midst of anti radical and anti immigrant hysteria.

> If it had not been for this thing I might have lived out my life talking at street corners to scorning men. I might have died unmarked, unknown a failure. Now we are not a failure. This is our career and our triumph. Never in our full life could we hope to do such work for tolerance for justice, for man's understanding of man as now we do by accident. Our

words – our lives – our pains – nothing! The taking of our lives – lives of a good shoe-maker and a poor fish-peddler – all! That last moment belongs to us – that agony is our triumph. (From a statement by Vanzetti after receiving sentence of death) [13]

The book can be read on many levels of meaning. Quite clearly it is an allegory; death after all is the destination to which, like it or not, we are all sailing. Tomlinson draws on the analogy that the *S.S. Yorikke* is the Ship of State (Tomlinson, 215). The sea is what Auden calls "a place of purgatorial suffering" (cited Melling, 147). Traven's view of the ship of death as a microcosm of society could be descended from Sebastian Brandt's *Ship of Fools*, which Traven may have known either through the popular German text or via Melville's *The Confidence-Man* (Chankin 1975, 125n20).[14] Katherine Anne Porter's foreword to her *Ship of Fools* (first published in 1945) is appropriate in this context and worth citing:

> When I began thinking about my novel, I took for my own this simple almost universal image of the ship of this world on its voyage to eternity. I am a passenger on that ship.

Traven had a copy of William Clark Russell's novel also called *The Death Ship* (1901) (Guthke 1991, 375). Geoffrey Fenton a master mariner is picked up at sea by the "Flying Dutchman", Captain Cornelius Vanderdecken and sails on his death ship. An even earlier treatment of this myth which dates back to Ahasuerus, the wandering Jew is Captain Frederick Marryat's *The Phantom Ship* (1839).[15] And of course the influence of Richard Wagner's first mature opera *Die Fliegende Holländer – The Flying Dutchman* cannot be discounted. Traven was musical and it is difficult to see how such a man who lived in Germany for so many years, and who associated with keen Wagnerians such as Gustave Landauer could have resisted the magic of the score and story.

As a sea faring man Traven may have read one of America's most famous short stories, Edward Everett Hale's, "The Man without a Country" (first published in *The Atlantic Monthly* December 1863). A young Lieutenant, Philip Nolan is tried for treason and says "Damn the United States! I wish I may never hear of the United States again!" And his judge grants him his wish. He is imprisoned on ships for the next fifty-six years until he dies, and no one is allowed to mention his country's name again. He bitterly repents his rash words and dies with a fervent prayer on his lips for the United States. As he says to a young midshipman: "stand by her boy, as you would stand by your mother" (Hale 2002, 20). Traven was no flag waver but certainly sympathized with seamen wherever they sailed and under whatever flag.

There is fantasy but not self-indulgence in Traven's adventure story of a sailor. It is anything but an escapist yarn and the story in my view is much superior to the output of a much higher rated author, Hemingway. It reads as an indictment of capitalism and state bureaucracy, and in particular of that document – the passport – so beloved of every government under the sun. Traven saw the world as full of dead men, of ghosts; millions of people adrift without a country or a passport (Traven, 1926). It is very relevant today with ever more starving, ill and desperate people searching for sanctuary which is refused them with such heartless cruelty. In chapter two I mentioned a recent disclosure that Traven traveled for at least one journey on a borrowed passport.

It is a work which employs a variety of techniques for describing experience; this is used to such an extent that you may at first be in some doubt as to the way you are meant to read certain passages. For instance, the treatment of the French prison workshop warder (87-89) is mainly ironical but after all "screws" the world over act this way. There is never enough real work for the prisoners to do – indeed usually there is no real work at all – but the inmates must be seen to be occupied, no matter how pointless the task. When Gales is told by the Dutch police that his ship "the *George Washington* has never yet come to Rotterdam so he is lying" he is not bound by the laws of logic, but by surreal humor which reminds me of the Marx Brothers, when he responds, "that's not my fault officer; I am not responsible for the ship" (50).

The book is also strongly rooted in fact. There is a particular word for the all too frequent crime of scuttling a ship in order to obtain the insurance money – "barratry". There is an earlier reference to this crime in Melville's amusing and ingeniously written *The Confidence Man* (1857) set on a Mississippi steam boat. One of the dupes of "The Confidence Man" mentions heavily insuring a ship and deliberately sending her down, and quotes "a wet sheet and a flowing sea!" (Melville 1964, 126).

There are many intriguing elements in the book. One of them is a powerful psychological presentation of a man who loses his possessions, money, passport and name in quick succession. And he is then forgotten by the world, left to travel on the death ship. But Gerry doesn't give in to brooding self-pity; he finds within himself the strength to survive the most fearsomely hard conditions without becoming degraded. Gales is a universal figure "we cannot give you anything which you do not find within yourself!" (373); and of course he is not alone; Stanislaus is another man without a country although in his case he had no choice in the matter. Indeed *The Death Ship* could fairly be called the story of two sailors one American and one German/Polish. At risk to their own lives these two men save Daniel. They have not been defeated by the death ship. "All the filth is only outside. Don't let it go to your soul and spirit and your heart" (177).

The Death Ship can also be seen as a symbolic presentation of human existence in a very black universe, a universe similar to that of Céline's first book *Voyage au bord de la nuit - Journey to the end of the Night* (1932) Louis-Ferdinand Céline (Louis-Ferdinand Auguste Destouches) (1894-1961) volunteered and fought in the cavalry, in World War I, and sustained serious injuries. His works have a nightmarish fascination. As he said - the truth of this world is death. *Voyage au bout de la nuit* was acclaimed on the right (Léon Daudet) and left (Leon Trotsky) alike.[16]

Céline's prose at times is so insane and violent that it can be mistaken for a satire, a *reductio ad absurdum* of racism (Sinclair 1968, 11). Céline unlike most writers was intimately aware of the lives of the proletariat having been both a ship's doctor and practicing among the poor of Meudon (Rühle 1969, 357-358). He was an anarchist, pacifist and (for which he is best known) an extreme anti-Semite. Our life said Céline is a journey from life to death. Céline differs from Traven in that he takes a fundamentally pessimistic view of this journey while Traven holds out some hope for us on the way.[17]

There are also similarities with Kafka's work most notably *The Castle*. Gales' tussles with bureaucracy are very reminiscent of Kafka's "K" and remind me how resigned most people are to the bureaucrats who make or break our lives. "How humble these people are – they come to us with requests! Instead of storming into the office and smashing it to bits, they come with requests" (Kafka's *Diaries*). Other possible sources in Kafka are *The Penal Colony*, *The Trial*, and the short story "The Stoker" which was first published in a German magazine in 1913 and also forms the first chapter of *Amerika* (Olafson 1976, 165).[18] Like Gales, the protagonist of "The Stoker" becomes a coal-drag by accident. *The Trial* first appeared in 1925 so it is conceivable that Traven could have read it whilst working on *The Death Ship*.

Gales and Traven are ultimately detached from the suffering they feel and describe. Traven is committed but not bitter; he is a writer of great poise. He describes hardship convincingly but not to the extent that he is overwhelmed by it and consequently incoherent with anger and unable to express it. He is sanguine, not racked by inner conflict, and so able to take an ironic view of life. Consider the telling phrase; they had the "sour faces of string savers" (9). His description of the *Empress of Madagascar* "elegant dame, silk outside, crabs underneath"

(336) could be an indictment of European civilization (Fraser 1973, 72). And the bizarre sequence which follows from Gales being stuffed full of food by the good village people "if I had not escaped, there might have come a day when I would have started to kill them, one by one" (106). He muses that; "if you are happy and contented, you want to be still happier?" (129). This, all too human, trait could be the cause of much of our suffering.

In these passages Traven reminds me of other writers of the "hard-boiled" school such as Dashiell Hammett - incidentally a man who to his everlasting credit refused to testify against his friends during the McCarthy anti-liberal witch hunts in Washington and when accused of contempt of court replied in measured tones, "there are no words to express the contempt I feel for this court":

> I had never shot a woman before. I felt queer about it. "You ought to have known I'd do it!" My voice sounded harsh and savage and like a stranger's in my ears. "Didn't I steal a crutch from a cripple?" (*The Gutting of Couffignal* in Hillerman 2000)

John Reilly makes a similar point; the narrator of *The Death Ship* is a brother of Sam Spade and "like Sam he speaks as people really do when they are free of illusion" (Reilly 1977, 115). Traven writes in a short story written about the same time that Hammett's tale was first published (1925) that he who carries a gun always has the right to give orders and the one who has no gun always has the damn duty to obey (*The Night Visitor*, 122). I discuss Traven's relations with some of the blacklisted writers during their time in Mexico in chapter six.

The Death Ship is still famous as a genuine "proletarian protest" novel and many of his other books depict an individual worker standing up to capitalist and communist bosses alike. A rather stodgy, short and anonymous review says "he demonstrates a revolutionary spirit and sense of human comradeship reminiscent of many American novels of the 1930s" (*Choice* September 1973, 968).

However, Traven stresses very carefully that although he writes with passion and sympathy about workers he doesn't write only for proletarians.[19] He is an internationalist, but he is also perfectly aware of how difficult it sometimes is for us to remain so: "each protects his own kind" (41). The well fed sailor's attitude to the bums is like that of most of us (112). At times, Traven too takes a very dim view of his fellow man "the thought that I would have to meet somewhere all the rabble that I have met quite unnecessarily here on earth would alone induce me not to die" (Stone 1967, 43). Gales also tellingly remarks that workers might have a bigger say in world affairs but only as soon as they can shake off the middle class ideas they have (112). Joseph Davis made a very shrewd point when he says that "if the common man were as skeptical as Gerard, demagoguery would be impossible" (Davis 1974, 141).

An anarchist reviewer made a crucial point. Fred Woodworth says admiringly that Traven "represents Anarchism in a powerful way, but without stridently proclaiming it. "He is a propagandist who creates works of art, not ephemeral leaflets" (Woodworth 1974, 6).

Traven (like Marut in *Der Ziegelbrenner*) was not entirely immune from the vicious virus of anti-Semitism (66). Not surprisingly he criticized Jewish bankers and industrialists along with their German counterparts. But in a dispute with the notorious anti-Semite Dietrich Eckhart (1868-1923) he said defensively that as far as he knew not a drop of Jewish blood ran through his family (Guthke 1991, 73).[20] He had "many Jewish friends" but complained that "I haven't found any decent people among them" (Stone 1967, 40). He is also no ardent feminist. In the short story "Submission" an independent woman learns obedience as Traven believes that in bed things only work if the man orders and the woman submit herself "willingly and expectantly" (*The Night Visitor*, 221). An alternative title is "The Tigress – *Die Tigerin*". It was made into a short film and screened in Mexico in 1956.

And – as we will see later when we discuss the *Cotton Pickers* - he as Gales is not always sympathetic to black Africans or African-Americans (353). But all of this shows that Traven writes from the experiences of his life; he has a real and not feigned sympathy with the lowest and most despised section of the working-classes; he is with them in spite of their faults and his faults. This is shown most movingly in the description of Kurt cutting off the steam from the water-pipe and being scalded to death in the process (295).

Not one of the consular officials, customs men or policemen who appear in this book is a very unpleasant character. Traven can show these people as human beings because he is not cooped up in any ideology; he gets beneath surface impressions. His treatment of the skipper of the *Yorikke* is particularly subtle. Gales knows full well that the master has connived with the first mate's hoodwinking of him onto the ship. He describes the dreadful food, and the infernal conditions in the hold, circumstances of which the skipper must be perfectly aware. But Gales still admires him because he does his job superbly well, "I had more admiration for that skipper than ever before" (311). The crew wouldn't dream of losing their self-respect by squealing to police, customs officers or arms chasers. A strong thread running throughout the book is that "a working-man that is not respected has only himself to blame" (332).

Traven writes with great gusto and at times reminds me of a fellow anarchist Jaroslav Hăsek's *The Good Soldier Svejk and his Fortunes in the World War*. Traven's message is this:

> I can laugh at a thousand things and situations, even at the brutalities of fascism, which as I see them are but a ridiculous cowardice without limits but I can never laugh at the love shown by men for those of their fellow men in pain and sorrow (*Bridge in the Jungle*, 211).

Although Traven may seem to stand apart from the world, he is totally involved in it; as he told one of the editors of *The Death Ship*, "the sailor peeps out from every page" (Miller 1987, 76). He retained a lifetime fascination and affection for the sea; he answered to the name "Skipper", referred to his den as the bridge, and called his wife and step daughters "First, Second and Third Mate".

And a real measure of the book's greatness is that Traven can write such an ending – one of the most moving in fiction. It has justly been compared to the passing over of Mr. Standfast in Bunyan's *The Pilgrims' Progress* or the death of Mrs. Gradgrind in Charles Dicken's short and jewel-like *Hard Times* (Fraser 1973, 92). As Braybrooke says Edgar's lines (Act IV, Sc. I, l.27-28) from *King Lear* are relevant here: "And worse I may be yet. The worst is not so long as we can say 'This is the worst'" (Shakespeare 1940, 78). As an actor for so many years Traven was very familiar with the writings of Shakespeare.

It is also uncannily prescient. I was reading Primo Levi (an author I am close to on two accounts, one being that we are both Jewish, the other we both lived for years in that magical but forbidding city Torino) and was struck how like life on the death ship foreshadowed the hideous reality of the death camps.

The book seemed destined to be made into a film. But, unless you lived in Germany you were unlikely to be able to see the only film made so far of *The Death Ship* with Horst Bucholz, who played Gales, Mario Adorf as Stanislaus, and Elke Sommer (1959); for complicated legal reasons for many years it couldn't be shown outside of that country. However, by 2002 it had obtained vintage status and was shown in Washington D.C., and in March 2003 it was screened in Harvard. I give a fuller filmography in chapter six.

Most critics claim that Gales (as befits Traven's *alter ego*) survives the shipwreck and appears again in *The Cotton-Pickers* and *Die Brücke im Dschungel* (1929) - *The Bridge in the Jungle* (1938) set deep in the Mexican bush, and as the narrator of several of the short stories. The Gales' novels and stories are Traven's only first-person narratives. In the conclusion to the story *The Night Visitor* (1928) Gales disappears into the bush never to be seen again.

But is he the same man in all these works? Does he survive the shipwreck? Logically as the narrator he should, but then Traven's writing often defies logic. Traven never links the novels and stories together or refers back, and as Baumann points out Gales cannot physically be in Europe and Mexico at the same time as the novels' chronology would seem to demand (Baumann 1976, 31). "Gales" is not necessarily identical with Traven, just as Traven is not all Gales. Jenkins makes a grave mistake when on the basis of Gale's ironic remarks, he conflates Traven with Gales and draws a conclusion that Traven is ambiguous about politics and even sympathetic to communism when the reverse is true (Jenkins 1987, 206).

A possible precursor of Gales/Traven is mentioned by Jim Seymour. In 1920, he recalls a hobo companion in Mexico, a Scandinavian seaman who is forever deserting ship and who "knew every grogshop and other places of abiding interest in every port under the sun" (Seymour, 1920). It is certainly possible that Traven could have seen this article.

The core of Traven's philosophy of life is encapsulated in two lines of Gales in *The Night Visitor*; "enjoy it as long as it lasts and get the most out of it-for death is within you from the moment you were born" (16). Gales disappears from Traven's fiction but he may still be out there in the bush. And as one of the most memorable characters in fiction he will probably live for as long as people read.[21]

The Cotton-Pickers

> In landlessness alone resides the highest truth. (Melville)

I am using a 1969 reprint of Traven's English version published in New York.

Traven sent the manuscript of this novel to Germany by September 1924; the parts written in English were translated into German and serialized in twenty-two installments in the daily newspaper *Vorwärts* in 1925.[22] Recknagel discovered 105 sheets (46,000 words) of a handwritten copy of an "original manuscript" among Traven's effects when he inspected the house in Mexico City after Traven's death (Recknagel 1983, 330-331).

Its writing was praised for being "exceptionally plastic and flowing" (Scherret 1930-1931, 389). At first it was in two distinct parts "The Cotton Picker" and "The Wobbly" the latter being an account of Gales after he leaves the farm and returns to Tampico (Spoer, 15). It was first published as a whole in German as *Der Wobbly* in 1926 and later retitled as *Die Baumwollpflücker* (1928). It came out in English only in England in 1956 translated by Eleanor Brockett. It did not appear in an American edition until 1969. It was then reviewed by

Stephen Geller and he points to a "problem of dramatic rhythm in the book". "Many times what was important to the hero has ceased to be important to the reader." However, he sees the book as a necessary beginning for Traven before he found his sure hand in the other books and stories set in Mexico (Geller 1969, 40).

Tampico where most of the action takes place was the center of Mexico's booming oil industry and the I.W.W.'s most important area of activity outside the USA. For many years the wobblies had been strong in the Marine Firemen, Oilers and Water Tenders Union and claimed effective control of America's Atlantic and Gulf coast (Jenkins 1987, 205). The Western Federation of Miners (WFM) under its leader Big Bill Haywood also took a revolutionary syndicalist position and had a major impact on Mexico, both through the cross-border flow of Mexicans who had worked in the USA, and the visits and support of American labor organizers (Gilly 1983, 57). The I.W.W. left a militant legacy in Mexico and in many other South American countries (Renshaw 1967, 289-290).

The wobblies set up their headquarters on a farm just outside González; Traven lived there in 1924 (Zogbaum, 2). Incidentally, the American writer Joseph Hergesheimer came to Tampico in 1925, and in 1926 published an indifferent novel *Tampico* which has little of the impact of Traven (Gunn 1974A, 90). In contrast, Olafson praises Traven's deft un-didactic writing about the wobblies. He also says that Traven avoids the flaws of Dos Passos' wobbly character Mac in *The 42nd Parallel* who acts stereotypically (Olafson 1972, 57).

Kingsley Widmer suggests that Traven owes a debt to the American hobo who unlike his European counterpart was "assertive, achieving considerable pride, bravado and, at times social militancy." He wonders whether Traven may have come across the writings of another hobo writer, Jim Tully such as *Beggars of Life* (1924) (Widmer 1968, 7). Tully says: "at times, I cursed the wanderlust that held me in its grip. While cursing it, I loved it. For it gave me freedom undreamed of in factories, where I would have been forced to labor" (Tully 1924, 235). Traven would have sympathized with these feelings.

There is a very long tradition going back at least to the late Middle Ages of wandering holy men, many of them rogues. The Free Spirit German millenarian anarchists of the fourteenth century preached untrammeled freedom and that man should live without looking behind or before (Cohn 1970, 177). Chaucer's "Pardoner", one of the many tens of thousands of transient beggars and conmen of the times, is a forerunner of the picaresque peddler, traveling salesman and riverboat gambler of American fiction (Davis 1974, 6).[23] Traven drew upon "The Pardoner's Tale" for his plot for *The Treasure of the Sierra Madre*.

The cotton pickers sit down strike described in the book is probably the first to be depicted in American fiction (Olafson 1973, 2). Traven is quite obviously on the side of the workers in this book but he doesn't depict them as angels; he is no dogmatist. Migrant workers could also be racists. Kenneth Allsop refers to a strike by Mexican citrus workers in Southern California in 1941. Migrant workers from Oklahoma "Okies" enrolled as strike breakers and attempted to drive all remaining Mexicans from the fields (Allsop 1967, 383). As in *The Death Ship* Traven is tolerant toward his adversaries. He depicts the gringo ranchers as likeable human beings just as he describes the newspaper publisher in *The Death Ship* in the most amiable and droll way.

Gales is a Wobbly and therefore like Traven no Bolshevik. He became a rebel and a revolutionary because the sight of injustice and cruelty revolted him (68). He doesn't parade his allegiance but his shrewd employers suspect he is a red. As Mr. Pratt says good-humoredly he is a Wobbly and a troublemaker (200). And Mr. Shine is in doubt about this when Gales joins the strike humming along as he does so to the song of the cotton pickers with its menacing last line of each verse which tells the boss that they will destroy the crop if he doesn't meet their demands (38-39).[24]

It was not published in an English version until 1956 in England and 1969 in the USA. Some short reviews appeared in the USA. An anonymous reviewer in *Choice* called it "a successful tale of adventure written in the Hemingway plain style" (*Choice* 1970, 1579). Mark Neyman complained that "the dialogue is often crude" (Neyman 1969, 2003). This aspect of the novel may not seem so surprising when we consider that the characters are all working men who might be expected to have a narrower vocabulary than the average college educated man. At least *Book List* called it an "eloquent statement on the poverty and helplessness of the poor" (*Book List* 15 July 1969, 1261). An anonymous short review in *Publishers' Weekly* observed that, "their experiences en route and at the farm are carved out of terrible poverty and pain, yet there is cheer, humor, incredible hard-core human dignity" (*Publishers' Weekly* 1969, 64).

It fared a little better at the hands of reviewers in England, and Dillibe Onyeama (whom I presume is West African in origin) said it was, "a powerful indictment of social injustice, and in spite of the author's dry sense of humor, is essentially a tragic story of human endurance in the face of terrible indignities" (Onyeama 1980, 28-29). I expected a lot from a review by Alan Hollinghurst, a man I know to be one of the keenest quotation sleuths in England and one of the best read. Unaccountably, he writes that "Traven's anarchist position ... may seem a little incomprehensible in this sketchy novel" (Hollinghurst

1979, 948). I think I have shown that Traven's anarchist credentials are overtly and skillfully displayed in this book.

The Treasure of the Sierra Madre

> The vagabond who's rapping at your door
> Is standing in the clothes that you once wore. (Blind Boy Grunt)

Astonishingly this gem of a book was rejected by one publisher. However, it was then quickly snapped up by *Büchergilde Gutenberg*. It was published by them in German as *Der Schatz der Sierra Madre* (1927). It came out in English, translated by Basil Creighton in 1934. The copy I work from is a paperback version of this English edition (1962): however, for some reason Creighton doesn't get the credit.

On its publication fortunately it was reviewed by one of England's most brilliant men of letters – V. S. Pritchett who said it was the best book of the four he had to read that fortnight; one of the others being Ignazio Silone's *Fontamara* – a searing tale of Italian Fascism that has also stood the test of time. Moreover, Traven's book was the best he had read in a year, "humane and powerful, quivering with life" (Pritchett 1934, 639). A thoughtful review by Clyde Hunter says that although it lacks organic unity nevertheless, "it is a whopping good story with a salty picaresque tang, a wealth of social and psychological perspective and an ironic sense of humor" (Hunter 1935, 342).

Very interestingly the German edition has a note that it is translated by Curt Reibetanz from the English – presumably Traven's. The original English and/or German manuscripts no longer exist nor have the proofs been found (Kutt 1979, 315). The 1930 German edition was reviewed favorably for the "fine analysis of the gradual change in the character of the young fortune seekers" (Malthaner 1933, 76). The translation into German of the 1935 Knopf New York edition (Traven edited by Smith) was praised as "admirable, especially effective in hard boiled dialogue" ("M. H." – Halperin 1936, 101).

It was translated into Spanish by Esperanza López Mateos from Traven's English as *El Tesero de la Sierra Madre* and published in Mexico in 1950 (Hagemann 1959, 45, 47).[25]

More than any other, this book has its roots in Traven's experiences (Berman 1978, 84). An early reviewer made the very perceptive comments that "in all his books he is almost entirely free from the greatest of all vices of the contemporary writer which is to work from the idea to the experience". Daniel Guillory reviewing a reprint in 1980 says that "Traven tells his tale in language as real and hard edged as the rocks mined by the three men" (Guillory 1980, 22). *The New York Times* used the opportunity of another reprint of this enduringly popular tale to recall Fred Marsh's comments in 1935 "it is not a fancy or a sentimental story. In fact it is as hard and tough as nails" (*New York Times Book Review* 8 July 1984, 30).

The virtues of Traven's writing; "do not suffer in translation" (Troy 1935, 79). They do not suffer in condensation either. Donald Yates reviewing a Spanish version *El Tesoro de la Sierra Madre* (1963) condensed and simplified to eighty-seven pages of text from an original 366 says nevertheless, that the action moves a leisurely pace and not in fits and starts (Yates 1964, 442). George Edberg reviewing the same edition says that second semester college students of Spanish will be immediately attracted by the story. He mentions that the preface claims that the text is Traven's original prose and wonders whether this is true and if the easy conversational Spanish is the work of the translator (Edberg 1964, 393).

Dobbs, Curtin and Howard are the same sort of men whom we met in *The Death Ship* and the *Cotton-pickers* - hobos, bums and drifters. Robert MacDougall, reviewing the first American edition, called the book, "a burning narrative of human derelicts" (MacDougall 1935, 14). However, Traven shows his sympathy with the dispossessed. He is convinced that it is the system that has made Dobbs "a vicious and yellow underdog in the first place" (Marsh 9 June 1935, 6). Dobbs is the villain of the piece but Howard and Traven say that deep down he might be a decent man; possibly his war experiences have brutalized him like so many others.

Granville Hicks thinks that the appeal of the book also comes from Traven "speaking always and in every slightest phrase as a class conscious worker" (Hicks 1935, 310). Another 1930s reviewer speculates that the writer has not only "dug for gold in Mexico himself, but has also dug into the workings of rough men's minds and enriched his story thereby" (S.W. 1934, 275).

Traven says that the moment you possess anything you belong to the minority and become the slave of your possessions (65). In *Der Ziegelbrenner* he urged people to discard their possessions and not buy shoes or stockings (Raskin 1980, 171). However, Traven like Howard respects the property of men who have obtained it by the toil of their own hands and sweat of their brow (166).

Smith (Traven's invaluable editor) writes that the story is a retelling of Chaucer's *The Pardoner's Tale* (Smith 1970, 2). In fact Chaucer's version is a comparatively late version of an ancient and widely spread folk tale of the adventures of two or three treasure seekers who murder one of their number (Kirby 1951, 269). "The Pardoner's Tale" is one of the most discussed parts of *The Canterbury Tales* and Marilyn Sutton's Bibliography of it has well over a thousand entries (Sutton, 2000). One interesting echo in Traven is suggested by the Pardoner's determination not to try and "live by making baskets" (Morrison 1977, 321). Unlike the Indian in Traven's short story *Assembly Line* that I discuss later in this chapter.

In Chaucer's tale, three young roisterers set out to seek Death but find instead a treasure. One of them goes into town to buy provisions and also purchases poison. While he is gone the other two agree to kill him on his return. He returns, is murdered, and the two others drink the poison (Morrison, 327).

The Treasure of the Sierra Madre has been misinterpreted widely merely as an adventure yarn; a reviewer in *The Christian Science Monitor* said, "the action is so thrilling, the setting so vivid, that it remains a thrilling story" (cited Farmer 1968, 20). Chamberlain calls it "a superior thriller" (Chamberlain 1935, XII). However, the same reviewer redeems himself later in the review when he says, "by the use of the most time-worn thriller material Traven miraculously conveys to us the overtones of 400 years of Mexican folk-wisdom" (Chamberlain, XII). In another review Chamberlain comments on Traven's view of the malevolent effect that Spanish imperialism and Catholic dogmatism have had on the Indians (Chamberlain 1935A 19). Gregory in a review published two days before Chamberlain's commented (independently I assume) to the same effect (Gregory 1935, 5).

William Plomer (himself a distinguished poet and novelist) said that it was "one of those rare books that may be recommended almost without reservation to almost any kind of reader" (Plomer 1934, 454). He continues that one of the novel's strengths is that the miners "speak a more universal and at times a much more elaborate language" than American workers in many of the rather dreary American proletarian novels of the twenties and thirties. An American reviewer persisted in dubbing Traven "an expert teller of grown up adventure tales" but he did praise it for being "without a touch of conventional sentimentality" (Fadiman 1935, 67). A fellow writer, Percival Christopher Wren (1885-1941), author of that diverting and hugely popular tale *Beau Geste* (1924), said:

> I read it at a sitting because I could not put it down – by reason of the fact that it is one of those rare books written by an adventurer who can write – a writer who can adventure. It has the ring of truth, and bears the seal of authenticity as well as the priceless appeal of simplicity. (Cited Powell nd, 5)

James Hilton (1900-1954), the esteemed author of *Goodbye Mr. Chips* (1934) and *Lost Horizon* (1933) praised it in the following terms:

It is indeed, one of the very best adventure stories I have ever read. The entire narrative is tense, unpretentiously told and astonishingly vivid. B. Traven has a profound knowledge of humanity as well as a profound pity for it. (*Daily Telegraph*, 11 September 1934)[26]

It is certainly a brilliant exploration of masculine character as well as a grand yarn. Rather patronizingly and pointedly Fred Marsh says that "male readers of all persuasions should enjoy it" (Marsh 1935, 6). John Beevers pursues this theme: "he uses a plain masculine prose, well braced with nouns and verbs." But he is aware of the great subtlety of Traven. "It is impossible to read it without some associative tremor, some obscure feeling that there is a great deal going on below the straightforward narrative of violence, greed and murder" (Beevers 1934, 1144). Indeed there is.

The tale is profound; one reviewer said that its subtle but ironic treatment of morality reminded him of the coachman in Shaw's *Pygmalion* who said that he was not rich enough yet to perform a moral act (Scherret, 1930-1931, 389). Stuart McDougall very perceptively points out that in the film made from the book John Huston groups the three main characters as a unit. Only when this unity unravels does order break down. This is crucially important when Howard remains in the Indian village and thus allows Dobbs and Curtin to be alone together (McDougall 1985, 118-119).

I am tempted to employ Freudian symbols here. Dobbs clearly represents the Id, the unconscious, irrational amoral basic drives demanding instant gratification. Curtin personifies the ego that emerges from the Id in childhood. It is largely the conscious and mediates between the Id and the external world and is intent of self-preservation. We are left with Howard, the superego, the home of repression, conscience and guilt. It is the main instrument in civilizing the wild child and turning it into a social and moral being. The film, if not the book, ends with Curtin, the ego, leaving to do good works.

When we finish reading the novel we are left with several tantalizing loose ends – not least based on the grounds that because it is very different in style than his other novels – whether he even wrote it (Stone 1977, 85). Also what happens to the important if secondary character Lacaud – did he know or sense there was still a lot of gold to dig and would he be allowed to get it (152).[27] William Johnson makes an apt comment "fame is a cruel master, but it also blows away on the wind" (Johnson 1967, 38).

A sound comparison has been drawn by Peter Christensen between *The Treasure of the Sierra Madre* and Conrad's *Nostromo* (1904). In both novels there are three main characters involved in the search for treasure, a search that ends in tragedy (Christensen 1987, 330). Both authors also use legends and flashbacks to dramatize their tale (Chankin 1988, 233-234). *Nostromo* is set in an imaginary Central American Republic and is based upon a yarn that Conrad heard while he was at sea twenty-five years previously (Walker 1974, 11).

It is almost impossible to discuss the book without taking into account the gigantic shadow cast by John Huston's film of it – almost universally agreed to be one of the finest films to be made by Hollywood and on many people's list of the top ten. This is in spite of the fact that there is no romantic element in the film and it has a distinctly unhappy ending with the mega star dead in a ditch. Indeed one reviewer who has obviously read nothing else of Traven compares the book on the whole unfavorably with the film. He grudgingly admits that "the Mexican peasants are much better than in Huston" but concludes "on the basis of this novel alone it is not clear why anyone would want to go farther than across town to track down B. Traven" (Sale 1967-1968, 672).

The film certainly stimulated a great interest in the book as shown by the fact that between 1948 and 1965 it was reprinted or issued in a new English edition no less than thirty-five times (Treverton, 40-49). On the occasion of one of these reissues John Anthony West called Traven, "one of the few writers of the century actually worth reading". He comments that "all the virility, tenseness and tension that Hemingway worked so hard for – and which, in his case, so rarely amounted to more than hirsute affectation – seem to be Traven's by birthright" (West, March 1967, 28).

John Engell makes one of the most perceptive comments in the course of a short piece where he shows how the script and the film differ from the book. He speculates whether Traven/Croves fundamentally objected to Huston's deletions and additions and whether his resentment – hidden during the shooting of the film surfaced later and caused his indignant and waspish letters to *Time* and *Life* (Engell 1989, 252). In Chapter six I discuss this film and other dramatizations of Traven's work at greater length.

An important collection in the library of The University of Texas is devoted entirely to editions of this work. By 1968 it contained fifty items, eleven of which are probably pirated versions for which Traven would not have received royalties, or payments for translation rights (Farmer, 3). Treverton's bibliography published in 1999 listed 172 separate printings (Treverton, 37-49).

K. Payne perceptively notes that this book marks a turning point in Traven's creative thrust. Together with its predecessors, *The Death Ship* and *The Cotton Pickers* it is predominantly concerned with the lumpen proletariat. All of Traven's following books center on Indian

Mexicans (Payne 1988, 46). Of course in this one the Huichole Indians of the Sierra Madre also play a significant part.[28] The land plays the major role "vast, cold isolated stretches of mountain, desert and sky" (Garland, 135). Antonin Artaud (1886-1948) visited the same area and commented on its overwhelming aura of mystery and death (admittedly he was a manic-depressive and founder of the "theater of cruelty").

It recently occurred to me that one contributing factor toward Traven's identification with native Mexicans and their fight for land and liberty is related to his awakening awareness of the reactionary role sometimes played by *Casa del Obrero Mundial*, the anarcho-syndicalist trade union movement in the Revolution. Its Red Battalions enlisted with Carranza and Obregón against the armies of Villa and Zapata. After Obregón became President in 1920 the unions were integrated into the new state structure and emasculated as a revolutionary force.

The episode of the winning lottery ticket which is such a crucial part of the plot of *The Treasure of the Sierra Madre* may have influenced Graham Greene when he came to write his short story "The Lottery Ticket". His hapless character learns in "a grim little tropical state" (Tabsaco/Chiapas) that he has won the lottery (Greene 1947, 126). As a good "Liberal" who is comfortably well off he gives his winnings to the state believing it will found a hospital or a school. Instead the governor diverts the money to pay the wages of the police who use it to get drunk and summon up enough courage to kill the opposition candidate for the Presidency. As in T*he Treasure of the Sierra Madre* wealth has brought death.

The Night Visitor (1953) - *Der Nachtbesuch im Busch* (1928)

The copy I work from is *The Night Visitor and Other Stories* published in London in 1967 where it is the lead story.

This is one of Traven's most celebrated tales and includes an important part where Gales breaks into an ancient tomb and is thereafter haunted by an Aztec prince. Traven's widow says that this is his most autobiographical work (Raskin 1980, 67-68). The relentless night visitor is an archetypical figure in the dream-world of Mexico and has troubled many a foreign traveler (Walker 1978, 15). John Warner cogently remarks that this story is "a confrontation with the darker side of life equal in its tragic reverberations, to much in Conrad" (Warner 1970, 377). The English poet and critic John Wain says it is notable for the author's "complete imaginative identification with ancient Mexican beliefs about the soul." Wain concludes with the resounding remarks, "he is the only living writer who is capable of rivaling the Conrad of

Nostromo and *The Shadow Line*" (Wain 1966, 24). Like Conrad, Traven was an émigré, they both chose to live in a foreign country and write about it. They were both able to survey their adopted country from a broader perspective than the native born writers and make the best of a complex rich pattern of culture (Eagleton 1970, 14).

It was first published in the collection of stories *Der Busch* brought out by *Büchergilde Gutenberg* in 1928 (Recknagel, 406). It was published in English for the first time under the title "Visitor from Nowhere" as the featured story in *Cosmos Science Fiction and Fantasy* pulp magazine in 1953.[29] It is assumed that the translation is the work of Traven, but this is not stated either here or in the English collections of short stories.

It came out in *The Night Visitor and other Stories* in New York in 1966, and in London published by Sphere in 1967. Jack Durant signaled out this story as the best of the collection when he reviewed the book in 1967. He says that "only when his characters lay arbitrary claim to mortal or social superiority do they become unattractive and unsympathetic" (Durant 1967, 93). An anonymous reviewer in *The Times Literary Supplement* said that all the stories were good (*The Times Literary Supplement* 1967, 553). Another prestigious literary and political weekly said: "these stories are timeless in their quality, the work of an undoubted master, who uses a tongue not native to him with amazing economy and force" (Buchan 1967, 24). Desmond MacNamarra wrote that even his most trivial short stories are still good reading, and "he is far better than Jack London" (MacNamarra 1967, 880).

Of the collection as a whole Mary Sullivan writing in the British *Listener* wrote, "the stories...are told with an utter lack of artifice and a direct logic; they are about what is" (Sullivan 1967, 25). When the book was reprinted in 1983 Michael Barber included it in among his choice of paperbacks and advised the reader to, "ignore the often-clumsy dialogue and let yourself be carried away by the momentum of his narrative drive" (Barber 1983, 36). The reviewer in the frequently humorous magazine *Punch* highlighted: "the extraordinary magic of Mexico is best evoked in the stories which deal ostensibly only with the present" (Bonney 1983, 72).

In the United States, Frederick Kidder in the *Library Journal* said that it was a "delightful collection, gentle humor, warm sympathy and deep understanding" (Kidder 1966, 2367). An anonymous reviewer said of Traven, "he reveals in these skillful diverse pieces a deep and warm understanding of his adopted country, Mexico" (*Choice* 1966, 413).

The only sour note in a generally appreciative audience appears to be from a one time lecturer at Harvard who said that, "Traven is neither a profound nor a subtle thinker". The stories (even *Macario*) "are light literature – often witty and deft, but nevertheless, light literature" (Keeney 1967, 1058).

Die Körbchen = Der Großindustrielle - Assembly Line

This story was first published in German in *Der Busch* in 1930. In English it appeared in the book *The Night Visitor and other Stories* in 1967 and I work from this. A short film made from it was shown in Mexico City in 1956. It had been translated earlier in 1946 into Spanish, by Esperanza López Mateos – and called *la Canasta*. It also appeared in English as "A legend of Huehuetonoc" in 1952 in a short-lived Californian journal (Traven 1952, 56). Olafson comments of Traven's deftness in the satirical treatment of the American tourist Winthrop (Olafson 1973, 3). The copyright is held by Contemporary Publications Inc. It remains one of his most popular stories.

When the Priest is not at Home

As far as I know this story unlike many of his others did not appear in German in any of his early collections such as: *Der Busch.* (A German translation is: *Wenn der Priester nicht zu Hause ist*). John Simon included it in a collection of contemporary stories designed to appeal to the young reader and published in 1969. Cipriano, an Indian Sacristan takes the opportunity when the priest is away to repaint a status of Judas.[30] During the process he inadvertently burns a wooden figure of the Virgin. He manages to survive any possible disgrace because of the good fortune of a storm hitting the Church. The charred figure of the Virgin is discovered, and the Priest and his flock mistakenly believe that she had taken the full strength of the lightning and saved the church. A miracle is pronounced and pilgrims start to come to the church.

In a commentary of what, on the face of it, is a mordant tale of religious gullibility Simon makes a spirited case that the moral is that Cipriano has discovered his creative side and also has reason to be grateful to the Virgin who has saved his skin (Simon 1969, 18). I am dubious as to this reasoning but certainly Simon has opened up a new readership for Traven.

The other stories in the collection in order of appearance are as follows. The original German title is also given and the date it was published. "Effective Medicine", (*Wirksame Medizin* 1928); "The Cattle Drive": this is an excerpt from *Die Baumwollpflücker* and was first published as *Das Viehtreiben* (1929); "Midnight Call", (*Der Ruf um Mitternacht = Der Banditendoktor* 1930); "A New God was Born", (*Ein neuer Gott wurde geboren* (1925); "Friendship", (*Freundschaft* 1995); "Conversion of Some Indians", (*Bekehrung einiger Indianer* 1966); "Burro Trading", (*Der Esselskauf* 1927); "Tin Can" (*Blechkanne* 1967); "Frustration", (*Enttäuschung* 1967).

Another of these stories *Submission* (*Unterwerfung* 1930) is about the traumatic therapy given by a husband to a feisty wife has given much offence to feminists. At the time of its publication in German it was described in rather unfortunate terms as: "a jolly counterpart to Shakespeare's *The Taming of the Shrew*" (Spoer, 1936, 21). As Traven always says he wrote from experience it is interesting to speculate on who was the model for the wife in this story. I deal with "Macario" (1950) the last story in the next chapter as it was written originally in English, and is probably the most highly regarded of all Traven's considerable output of short fiction.

Some of these stories had been published in English earlier in the collection; *Stories by the Man Nobody Knows* (1961). They are "Burro Trading", "Tin Can", "Midnight Call", "Frustration", "When the Priest is not at Home", "Assembly Line", "Submission", and "Effective Medicine" and "Macario" - but titled "The Third Guest". The volume is long out of print and because of its fragile condition hard to find in second hand bookshops.

I deal with a third collection of stories by Traven/Marut called *The Kidnapped Saint and Other Stories* (1975) and a collection of mainly early stories by Ret Marut/Richard Maurhut titled *To the Honourable Miss S. and Other Stories* (1981) in the next chapter.

The Bridge in the Jungle

My copy is the edition published in London in 1969; it is a reprint of Traven's English language version of the 1930s.

This widely acclaimed novel was originally written as a short story *Die Brücke im Dschungel* and serialized in *Vorwärts* in 1927. It was expanded and published as a book in German in 1929; in Traven's/Smith's English version, in America in 1938 and in Great Britain in 1940 – also from Traven's English. It was published in Mexico in 1941 translated by Esperanza López Mateos as *Puente en la Selva*. Another edition was published in 1950 (Hagemann 1959, 50, 51).

When it was first published in America Alfred Kazin praised Traven's work as "a minor joy of contemporary literature" and said that Traven was "a glowing example of the soul-stricken urban man"

(Kazin 1938, 6). Ralph Thompson in *The New York Times* wrote "it is at least in part autobiographical, the extraordinary descriptive passages could hardly have been written otherwise" (Thompson, 1938). On its publication in England, J. D. Beresford enthused, "it is a remarkable book and reads throughout as if it is an inspired account of an actual happening. Mr. Traven writes so well that one forgets to notice it" (Beresford 1940, 215).

It is certainly a powerful and moving tale of the death by drowning, the recovery of the body and the funeral of a small Indian boy. Grace Flandrau (bearer of one the most distinguished names among Mexican writers) says it is "a strange and, I think a remarkable book" (Flandrau 1938, 6). It is also one of his most sensitive books. A female reviewer said; "it is rendered with a degree of insight which does credit both to the author's knowledge of female nature and his understanding of the savage temperament" (Neville 1938, 134). William Soskin writing in *The New York Herald Tribune Books* said that "with thoroughness and quick understanding" he has written what amounts to a "sound anthropological study" (Soskin 1938, 5).

One of the features of the book that has attracted much comment is the dressing up of the boy's body and leaving it the midst of the wake until it begins to putrefy. This is based on the long established tradition in poor Mexican families of suspending dead babies for the edification of the neighbors for twenty-four hours or more so they can decorate them with silk wings, paper crowns, ribbons and flowers; this follows the Aztec practice. These *angelitos* were sometimes hired out to *pulque* merchants to attract trade (Herrera 1983, 469-470n221).

Of the other American commentators Granville Hicks writing in the strident flagship of the left *The New Masses* praises him for "a deep and genuine love of the exploited masses of the world" but deplored his "eccentric" political views (Hicks 1938, vi). A short, glib notice in *Time* says confidently that the author is undoubtedly an American. The book though "is written in a dry travel-talk style, as awkward as a letter home" (*Time*, 18 July 1938, 51).

It was chosen as one of the top novels of 1940 by the most prestigious British literary weekly, *The Times Literary Supplement*. The first review praises it for being "quietly hard-bitten in tone" (*The Times Literary Supplement* 2 March 1940, 109). John Mair reviewing it in the left wing *New Statesman* along with *The Death Ship* said it was an equally interesting novel. He wonders if "the secret of his popularity ... is that he provides the final kind of escapism" (Mair, 340).

Another notice in the *TLS* is far less enthusiastic and whines about his "diatribe against more civilized societies" (*The Times Literary Supplement* 16 March 1940, vii).[31] In 1969, the venerable *TLS* was even more dismissive. "An unfortunate B-feature opening;" "he makes his points with relentless heavy-handedness" and the dismissive, "it would have made a powerful short story" ("Stumbling" 5 June 1969, 601). The same type of comments about its rightful place as a short story had been made in the1930s by Granville Hicks and an anonymous reviewer in *The New Yorker* (Hicks 1938, 23; *New Yorker* 23 July 1938, 59).

However, when the book was republished in the USA in 1967 it received at least one thoughtful reassessment. The book showed "the contrast between a simple, elemental and honest community relationship and the fraudulent, overbearing, flamboyant organization of industrial society" (Sheppard 1967, 31). And on the occasion of a reprint in England a review in the right-wing *Spectator* was most appreciative. Maurice Capitanchik said it was "a powerful and convincing plea for conciliation and tolerance" and that Traven, "chose, like Joyce 'silence, exile and cunning' for his protection. He deserves his republication" (Capitanchik 1969, 856-857). An exception to a generally positive reception was the unknown reviewer of *Publishers' Weekly* who was of the opinion, "the book is primarily a platform for the expression of anti-capitalist sentiments directed against the 1930s brand of imperialism" (*Publishers' Weekly* 1967, 59).

Traven suffuses the book with subtle ironic asides but never loses his love and admiration for the poorest of the poor. He says that he can laugh at most things even at fascism but he can never laugh at the love shown by men for their fellows in pain and sorrow (211). Here there is a powerful allegory of death as the "great music-master" who is charge of the events, just as in his last major story, *Macario*, the bone man is in charge of Macario's life (Mezo 70; 149). Ponick sees Traven here as harking back to his image of "The Great Skipper" in *The Death Ship* (Ponick 1976, 130).

It is a masterpiece even though Flandrau complains about "the irrelevant political harangue" of the last few pages (Flandrau, 6).[32] Otis Ferguson stands out for arrogant incomprehension with the careless remark, "B. Traven hasn't read enough to know the difference between tragedy and truism" (Ferguson 1938, 341). John Marks hits the right touch with his concluding remarks that "probably against his will" the reader "is made to mourn" (Marks 1940, 424). Thompson summed up his impression by saying it epitomized "the tragedy of all Mexico's years from stout Cortez to Standard Oil" (Thompson, 1938A). And many Mexicans obviously support that opinion, it had gone through fourteen printings by 1996 (Treverton, 57).

Notes

1. Kurt Eisner (1867-1919) the first Premier of the Bavarian Republic had been editor of this paper.
2. Membership of the guild grew to 80,000 by the end of 1932; it also published several of Jack London's novels as well as works by Upton Sinclair, Arnold Zweig, Otto Bauer, Fyodor Mikhailovich Dostoevski, and Vicente Blasco Ibáñez. I am reminded of "The Left Book Club" that operated in England from the 1930s onward; my father and uncles were enthusiastic members, and my first introduction to socialist letters was by this means.
3. I am struck by the use of "poet"; Traven saw himself as primarily a poet – just as did Richard Wagner.
4. Approximately the first thirty-five pages were published in 1975 in the collection of stories called *The Kidnapped Saint*. Only five of the novels had been published in the USA as of 1967.
5. After Huston had finished with *The Treasure of the Sierra Madre* he naturally wanted to proceed with *Moby Dick* but was initially thwarted in this project just he was with plans for Dreiser's *Jennie Gerhardt* and Steven Crane's *The Red Badge of Courage* – also logical follow-ups to Traven (Agee, 427).
6. In his acting days Marut/Traven appeared as the second gravedigger in *Hamlet*. It is possible that the ship's name in the book, *Yorikke* is derived from Yorick. You may recall that Hamlet sails for England on a death ship and is rescued by pirates (Mezo 1993, 18).
7. For an autobiographical account of the hard life on sailing boats just before the start of the Second World War there is no better read than Eric Newby's *The Last Grain Race* (Newby, 2001).
8. There is an interesting echo of Melville in that Gales is sometimes called PipPip. Braybrooke refers to Pippib: I assume that he was reading a version different from mine (Braybrooke 1965, 212). In *Moby Dick* the black cabin boy is called Pip; Gales spends most of his time dragging coal and consequently is black from head to toe (Olafson 1976, 167).
9. Bernard Smith, Alfred Knopf's brilliant editor in New York turned Traven's text into "acceptable" English - a process which involved treating about twenty-five percent of the text (Guthke 1991, 308-309). Smith had worked on the communist journal *New Masses*, and was one of the foremost literary figures and intellectual thinkers of the period. Smith also helped to fine tune the writings of Chandler, Hammett and Langston Hughes for publication. He then moved into the film business producing many films for Samuel Goldwyn, Paramount and MGM. Among his most successful were: *Elmer Gantry*, *Cheyenne Autumn* and *How the West Was Won*. He died in 1999 aged 92.
10. A review in *The Nautical Magazine* perceptively said of *The Death Ship* "we recommend this book to every officer in the Merchant Navies of the world." I am reminded of the no doubt apocryphal tale of the hapless reviewer on *The Gamekeeper's Gazette* who was sent a copy of Lawrence's *Lady*

Chatterley's Lover. He remarked that there was nothing new to be learnt about the raising and care of pheasants from the sordid pages he was forced to turn.

11. Traven is so subtly ironic that Fraser misreads him and sees him as accepting or tolerating something when clearly he is poking fun (Fraser 1973, 87-88).

12. Gales was also once a grave-digger's assistant (127).

13. Traven says in a short story *Mother Beleke* (1919) "can there be a death more enviable than one that is joyful. Why then do you mourn?" In most of Wagner's operas, the final stage is as littered with as many corpses as is *Hamlet*. It is an unpleasant truism that we all must die. I have often thought that the reason why so many of us scream so loudly the moment we are born is that we realize that we must die. Wagner's characters die with some of the most sublime music ever written; as Elizabeth Magee says of Siegfried's end, "it is an excellent way to die, the mood jubilant, the shadows of misunderstanding finally dispelled" (Magee 1990, 105). In every tradition there is the myth of the honorable death. James Fennimore Cooper (1789-1851) says of the death of Uncas, the Native American Indian:

> Why do my brothers mourn! Why do my daughters weep that a young man has gone to the happy hunting grounds; that a chief has filled his time with honor? He was good: he was dutiful; he was brave. Who can deny it? The Manito has need of such a warrior and he has called him away. (Cooper 1962, 414)

It is probable that Cooper's depiction of the American Indians, Uncas and Chingachgook in *The Last of the Mohicans* influenced Traven (Spoer, 15; Baumann 1976, 168n18). However, in one of his essays in *Die Büchergilde* Traven explicitly rejects Cooper as his model (cited Steele 1987, 309n5).

14. *Das Narrenschiff* was first published in 1494. This allegorical poem has been hugely popular mainly in the German speaking world, but also published in many other languages. It is a broad criticism of the faults of Brandt's contemporary world and its greed for wealth and luxury (Van Cleeve 1993, 85-93). It also contains the first known reference to the noble Indian savage in German literature (Ashliman 1969, 114).

15. The Wanderer had struck Jesus as he was being dragged to his place of crucifixion saying "go faster Jesus, why doest thou linger?" To which Jesus replied, "I indeed am going, but thou shalt tarry till I come".

16. In his second novel, *Mort à credit - Death on the Installment Plan* (1936) Céline "was still enough of an anarchist ... to mock against Nazi racist theories" (Sinclair 1968, 10). He was invited to the Soviet Union in 1936 and when he came back he wrote a bitter attack on Stalin. In the late 1930s, revealed himself as a fierce Nazi sympathizer. He was punished in 1945 for collaborating with the German occupation force in Paris, but was exonerated later by the French government, even though he never apologized for his conduct. His worst attacks on Jews, Freemasons, Communists and democrats occur in pamphlets such as *Bagatelles pour un massacre - The School of Corpses* (1937).This strange book largely consists of five ballets. Céline was obsessed with ballet –

his wife was a dancer. It shows his usual obsession with physical, mental, cultural and racial purity. Like Wagner he blames the Jews for his lack of success in getting his work performed in Paris (McCarren 1998, 172-220).

17. It has been suggested that Céline's *Voyage Au Bord de la Nuit* is indebted to *The Death Ship* (Fraser 1964, 37). Also note the same author's reference to Hamsun's *Hunger*. Traven admired Hamsun and spoke about him (Guthke 1991, 377).

18. This fragmentary novel is largely set in the American West and concerns the Oklahoma Theater Organization. Unlike Kafka's other works he envisaged an optimistic ending (Ashliman, 250-253).

19. Some critics get into a terrible muddle when they try to write about the proletariat. Charles Miller carelessly refers to them as "the drone class" (Miller, 1968, 114). I can say in parenthesis that born as I was in an inner-city slum, the son of a highly skilled printer temporarily out of work because of his union activism, I have never underestimated my class, or its ability to succeed given the opportunity.

20. Moreover, when he was involved in a furious dispute with the newly appointed Nazi director of his publishing firm he labeled the new management's practices as "Jewish" and un-German (Guthke, 305).

21. The book continues to make ripples throughout the world. I watched the movie *Fight Club* a couple of years back, and a shiver went down my spine as the camera slowly tracked to a table and rested for a moment on a copy of *The Death Ship* on a table.

22. In a letter of 1929 Traven claimed that his native language was English (Baumann 1976, 88-89).

23. A pardoner had a collection of ancient holy relics, such as a lock of the Virgin's hair, a bone of a saint or a piece of the true cross (all of course fake). If a gullible soul would but buy a relic or pay gold to kneel down in front of one his sins would be absolved

24. Traven wrote the song. The I.W.W was an effective if often invisible movement.

25. In the *Treasure of the Sierra Madre* collection at the library of the University of Texas at Austin there are over fifty editions of the book.

26. It was perhaps appropriate that Hilton became a Hollywood scriptwriter and died in California.

27. He appears as "Cody" in Huston's entertaining – if rather overfull of complacent morality - screen play (Naremore 1979, 20).

28. President (from 1913-1914) Victoriano Huerta was a *huichole* Indian; because of this he suffered racial slurs from much of the population (Rutherford 1971, 172n79).

29. *Cosmos Science Fiction and Fantasy* 1 2 (November 1953): 1-43.

30. A Judas candlestick was once to be found in many churches. It is a tall thick piece of wood – often reaching almost to the ceiling of the church - inserted in to the center branch of a seven branched candlestick. It held the wax Paschal candle. It appears in many Mexican paintings and works of art by masters such as Rivera and Kahlo.

31. In the unlikely event of the reviewer being alive he must still regret these remarks. Just a few months later a supposedly more civilized nation Germany launched a series of air attacks on English civilians (including the five year old author of this book).

32. She makes an interesting observation that the idiot brother was probably responsible for pushing the child off the bridge (Flandrau, 6).

Chapter 5

Tierra y Libertad

There are not criminals, but only men. (Michoacán legal code)

Land des Frühlings (1928) - *Land of Springtime*

I am using the 1936 German edition which has twelve new photographs but is otherwise the same.

In *Der Ziegelbrenner* (23/25, 20 March 1920) Traven had raised the possibility of fleeing European civilization and hiding out in primitive surroundings (Goss 1987, 97n41). Ernst Preczang on behalf of the *Büchergilde Gutenberg* suggested that he write a travel book about Mexico. *Land of Springtime* resulted from his journeys in the remote areas of Chiapas starting in May 1926. It is a big book of 429 pages and some 140 photographs taken by Traven spread over 64 more pages. It is specifically addressed to the German working-class reader. Incidentally, many of the big coffee planters in Chiapas were German (Knight 1986, 56).[1] Baumann praises it highly saying that it is "surely the most important book Traven wrote" (Baumann 1977, 75). In it Traven writes that communism is as bad as capitalism in spite of the latter's multiple sins (Baumann 1971 15n9). However, he asserts his anarchism in saying that man's struggle has been and always will be a struggle "against uniformity, against a binding, coercive organization" (Baumann 1971, 35n2).

It was published in Berlin in 1928; in a translation from English by Curt Reibetanz (Hagemann 1959, 49).[2] It was reissued in Zurich in 1936. and again but in a shorter version in 1950. It has never been translated back into English; one compelling reason is that it probably tells us more about Marut-Traven than Chiapas (F. Baumann 1987,

246). Traven quickly became unhappy with the book and stipulated that no translation should be approved in his lifetime. He had realized quickly that he had drawn hasty, untenable conclusions from too brief an observation of a tiny part of Mexico, and in the process, had vastly overstated the progressive nature of President Plutarco Elías Calles' regime (Zogbaum, 36). There were numerous assassinations during Calles' reign "one of the blackest pages in Mexican history" (Friedrich 1970, 111). It was finally released in Spanish (reduced in size to 370 pages) as *Tierra de la Primavera* in 1996 (Treverton, 52).

It is a very eclectic book and shows Traven to be as enthusiastic a naturalist, and a man as close to nature as Thoreau. Baumann comments on the similarity of Thoreau's description of the battle between the red and black ants in *Walden* and Traven's interest in spiders, bees and wasps (Baumann 1971, 125). James Herndon writes that Traven's view of Indians corresponds entirely with Claude Levi Strauss' notion of "hot" and "cold" cultures (Herndon 1971, 53). Cold cultures are those that resist any modification to their structure "that would enable history to burst into their midst". The driving force of hot societies is the change and energy that derives from clashes between power and opposition, exploiters and exploited (Lévi Strauss 1976, 28-29).

Traven contrasts the white man's ambition, greed and lust for power with the Indian communal sense or feeling (Baumann 1971, 70-71). Robert Berkhofer shows how this represented one fundamental conception of Indian culture – the "Noble Savage". It was opposed by the opposite and more dominant paradigm of the "bad" Indian – nakedness and lechery, passion and vanity; constant warfare and brutish revenge, cannibalism, human sacrifice and witchcraft (Berkhofer 1979, 28).

One of the most interesting short accounts of the book came out appropriately enough as a result of a conference on the 500th anniversary of Columbus' voyage to America in 1492. Peter Monteath shows how Traven is an exception to most European and American writers and statesmen before him who failed to see or admit that the people who were colonized by settlers were equal to and different from them. Traven in this book and the following Jungle Cycle affirms the validity, vitality and forecasts the viability of the Native American (Monteath 1994, 87-88).

His trip to Chiapas was sponsored by the President of Mexico but was dogged by bad luck from the start. He had a brief meeting with the only other foreigner on the expedition, Frank Tannenbaum (1893-1969) but a smallpox epidemic caused the promising expedition to dissolve barely as it began. Interestingly it seems that Tannenbaum was a member of the I.W.W. (Britton 1987, 37). Traven then arranged to travel through the Lacandón Forest with Frans Blom (1893-1963) the Tulane University archaeologist but broke his leg while crossing a bridge (Zogbaum, 63-66). Understandably his mobility and usefulness were much diminished.

Blom's co-worker Oliver La Farge was a novelist as well as an archaeologist. His *Laughing Boy* (1929) about the love between a young Navajo man and woman thwarted by the conflict between native and white American cultures won a Pulitzer Prize (Berkhofer, 107). It seems likely that Traven would have read it and mused on La Farge's introductory note that "the picture is frankly one-sided. It is also entirely possible" (La Farge 1929, viii).

Chiapas has always been a frontier region remote from central power. The ancient cities of Palenque and Bonampak were located at the northern edge of Mayan civilization (Benjamin 1981, 8). Even when Traven traveled there Chiapas was the most underdeveloped region of Mexico. Some thirty years later Eric Wolf wrote that a diligent ethnologist could still find "patriarchal kinships units sharing a common name, a common saint, and a measure of social solidarity among the Tzeltal-Tzotzil-speakers of Chiapas" (Wolf 1959, 220).[3]

Traven in the nineteen twenties missed the significance of the ubiquitous slavery – peonage - of the region; it was still being practiced in 1952 (Zogbaum, 112). And he seems to have been unaware at the time of the significance of the important role played by Indian *caciques* (bosses) in contracting Indians to work in the forests, mines and plantations (Zogbaum, 147).

Jan Rus and Robert Wasserstrom give a good succinct account of the civil-religious hierarchies or cargo system that emerged among the Chamula and other peoples of Chiapas in the nineteenth and early twentieth century. The Chamula were reluctant to work on ladino plantations knowing that they would build up impossible communal debts and obligations. Under Díaz they were forced to do so with the state providing armed guards to take the *peones* to their servitude.

The Chamula were largely left alone during the revolution even though Chiapas was the only region in Mexico where a counterrevolutionary movement was in power for most of the time. But by 1926 things were just as bad as before (Rus and Wasserstrom 1980, 472). A very informative and moving fictional account of Chamula culture is given by Ricardo Pozas. Called *Juan Pérez Jolote* (1948) and *Juan the Chamula* in translation it is ingeniously told by a first-person narrator, and almost every page corroborates Traven's depiction of this indigenous group of Tzotzil-speaking Indians (Pozas, 1962).[4] Its feel is that of a good historical novel (Brushwood 1966, 25-26).[5] Traven's novel *The Rebellion of the Hanged* takes place near the Chamula town of Palenque (Rosa Elena Luján 1981, xi).

According to Heidi Zogbaum, the Chamula accustomed to the cool highlands were not contracted to work in the steamy jungle. Therefore, she says that Traven was historically inaccurate in depicting Celso as a Chamula (Zogbaum, 124-125). This is a somewhat tangential and carping qualification – after all Celso is a superb characterization.

The classic anthropological account of the life and views of a Tzotzil Indian is given by Calixta Guiteras-Holmes who spent some weeks from 1953-1956 having exhaustive interviews (mainly in Spanish) with Manuel Arias Sohóm. One of the very few Tzotzil who were literate in Spanish, he had been President of the small town of San Pedro Chenalhó. Born in 1900 he fought General Pineda and the rich landowners in the Revolution (Guiteras-Holmes 1961, 322-323). Guiteras-Holmes was a student of the distinguished anthropologists Sol Tax and Robert Redfield who peddled the line that ethnically different groups of Indians shared "the cultural trait of indifference" toward other ethnies.[6] Sol Tax also argued that acculturation was synonymous with culture loss, the displacement of indigenous culture with that of the West (Wasserstrom 1983, 1-2). We will see that Traven's sweeping epic of the Revolution differs from this conventional depiction; he shows Indians from different groups bonding together in order to overthrow dictatorship.

The Indians depend on each other; they share property in common do not need government imposed on them, and do not want to be anybody's master. "The Indian blends in the landscape until he is an indistinguishable part of the white wall against which he leans at twilight, of the dark earth on which he stretches out to rest at midday" (Paz 1985, 43). Their sense of honor and truth has been described ironically as "their fatal flaw" (Olafson 1987, 143).

These trips formed the basis of Traven's life-long involvement with the poorest region of Mexico. In his later jungle novels he gives a devastating account of the hopeless indebtedness of the *peones*. He says clearly that he is opposed to whatever form the state takes and that man should struggle against any binding coercive organization (Baumann 1976, 162n2). His love for Chiapas continued to the end; his last wake was a Tzeltal ceremony in the poorest hut on the outskirts of the village of Ocosingo after which his ashes were scattered over its jungles (Womack 1999, 106). After his death Ocosingo was renamed Ocosingo de Traven.

He was followed to Mexico by several other distinguished foreign visitors. The authors Evelyn Waugh and Graham Greene came within a few months of each other in early 1938 and were equally depressed by the country. Greene spent most of his two month trip in Chiapas (Gunn 1974A, 186). As Walker remarks Traven, unlike other visitors such as Waugh, Greene or Aldous Huxley, seized upon examples of an alien mysterious reality, accepted them eagerly and used them in his fiction, rather than feel threatened by their inaccessibility (Walker 1978, 11).

Greene's *The Power and the Glory* (1940). is set on the border between Tabasco and Chiapas. In his travel book *Another Mexico* (1939) he shows his deep disgust at Mexico, "how one begins to hate these people... the intense slowness of that monolithic black-clothed old woman" (Greene 1964, 246). And, unfortunately there is much more of the same.[7]

Waugh's even more bilious travel book *Robbery Under Law: the Mexican Object-Lesson* (1939) written after all of eight weeks spent in the country, is just as hostile to Mexico, the government and in particular the Indians as his fellow Roman Catholic, Greene. By "robbery under law" Waugh means President Cárdenas' nationalization of the oil industry and the agrarian reform policies (Walker 1978, 216).

Aldous Huxley spent some time in Mexico in 1933. A crucial part of his novel *Eyeless in Gaza* (1936) is set in Mexico, while the concluding section of a travel book, *Beyond the Mexique Bay: A Traveler's Journal* (1934) deals with Mexico; it is highly regarded (if not by Mexicans). His experience can be summed up by his comments, "human life seemed, somehow, too hopelessly irrelevant to be possible" (Huxley 1949, 288).

All of these British writers had read D. H. Lawrence before they set sail for Mexico (Walker 1974, 28). This deeply troubled genius affects and infests their work. Carleton Beals got Lawrence right, "At bottom he was terribly afraid of the country, always saw some secret menace in it" (cited Walker 1974, 57).[8]

Since then, Chiapas has attracted the attention of many other writers, social scientists and historians. In the thirty years prior to 1987 more than thirty books on the Chamula and Zinacantan were produced (F. Baumann 1987, 245).

The neighboring region of Yucatán which also includes the Mexican states of Campeche, and Quintana Roo was visited by Traven in 1929. Its Mayan civilization dates back to about 1500 B.C.E. Spaniards launched an expedition against the Maya from 1531-1535 and, when they had defeated them, systematically set about destroying their culture and religion. The Mayans were enslaved to work on plantations. The region was in rebellion against the Mexican state from 1821; in 1916 and again in 1924, Mayan and *mestizo* leaders declared Yucatán independent from Mexico. After a short lived period of freedom Mayans again were reduced to the status of *peones* on large estates. Spurred on by Mayan rebellions in neighboring Guatemala from 1975 and Chiapas from 1993 nationalist groups began to organize for autonomy, land and cultural rights.

Indianische Kunst von B. Traven

In 1929 an article in *Typographische Mitteilungen* announced that *Indianische Kunst von B. Traven* would be published in 1930. As a teaser a chapter entitled *"Das Spielzeug"* was printed. In it Traven discusses Mexican toys and praises the handwork of the Indian craftsmen. He also roundly criticizes the inferior machine made toys stamped out of tin metal sheets that were replacing them (Jannach 1965, 405-406). For unexplained reasons the book never came out. Hubert Jannach claims carelessly, and certainly inaccurately, that the end of Traven's active literary career was heralded by the non-appearance of this book.

Die Weisse Rose (1929): *The White Rose* (1979)

I am using the 1979 English translation from the German by Donald Davidson. He seems to have done a very satisfactory job; the only alarming feature being that he has deleted several short passages he regards as "implausible" and "corrected" Traven's slang (vi).[9] He was using Traven's own "corrected copy" of the revised German edition of 1962 (Treverton, 59).

The first German edition of *Die Weisse Rose* was translated from Traven's English by Rudolf Dörward (Hagemann 1959, 51). The first Spanish edition *La Rosa Blanca* was translated from English by Esperanza López Mateos and published in 1951 (Hagemann 1959, 52). An English version (at the hands of Traven) came out in London in 1965, but we had to wait a further fourteen years before it was published in a satisfactory edition. When it emerged at least one reviewer appreciated it immensely. Dayle Manges writing in *The Library Journal* said, "this is one of Traven's best novels and it deserves to be in most fiction collections" (Manges 1979, 2666). Left wing readers saw the worth of Traven's depiction of American capitalism. In *Changing Times* an anonymous reviewer wrote in 1979, "the theme of this story may be as timely as when it was written in the late 1920s) (*Changing Times* 1979, 31).

An unsigned American review in 1980 reminded us that it "has long been regarded in Germany, Mexico and much of the Spanish speaking world as one of the author's most interesting and important novels". The reviewer also names Don Jacinto, the owner of the White Rose *hacienda* and Mr. Collins as two of Traven's most fascinating characters (*Small Press Review* 1980, 8). However, in the USA this is still generally the least regarded of Traven's novels. In 1929, the editorial board of *Büchergilde Gutenberg* rejected the first two chapters as they felt they were unrelated to the rest of the book. Two chapters entitled "The Beginning of a Novel" were found in Traven's estate; they may be the missing chapters (Treverton, 60). They are to be found in German in Guthke (1987A).

Baumann argues (unconvincingly) that it is the work of two writers; a native German speaker who correctly uses German idioms and expressions when ideas are being expressed, and a non-German speaker who is guilty of much incorrect German in the narrative and dialogue of *Die Weisse Rose* and the other Traven books published during the 1920s and 1930s (Baumann 1987, 38-39). It was lambasted by contemporary German communist critics for its "exoticism and lack of proletarian optimism" (Seibert 1987, 158-159).

Mr. Collins the owner of Condor Oil Company is based on Edward L. Doheny the founder of Huasteca Petroleum Company and seemingly a particularly vicious capitalist (Zogbaum, 32). Doheny owned five oil companies producing thirty-six percent of Mexico's oil production in 1926 (Britton, 58). As the American Embassy in Mexico City stood upon land donated by Doheny we can assume that he was relatively safe from harassment by the authorities (Gruening 1928, 604). Ambassador Henry Lane Wilson's (1856-1932) careful and crafty retelling of his inglorious residency as envoy during the Revolution includes a glowing endorsement of "the benevolent and generous administration" of Doheny and "the fair and just" treatment accorded to the native laborers and their families" (Wilson 1927, 238).

The role of Ambassador Wilson in fomenting dissension and the fall of President Madero is instructive. "An inveterate alcoholic, apostle of dollar diplomacy, and conspirator in Mexico's internal affairs, Wilson is sometimes considered the worst ambassador the United States has ever sent abroad" (West 2003, 251n196).

In 1938 the oil industry was expropriated and this action of President Cardenas was carried out not for economic but for political and moral reasons. In Mexico it was seen as an extremely worthwhile move (Tannenbaum 1966, 197-198). Not surprisingly, the United States government immediately imposed economic sanctions on Mexico; however, they were not especially harsh, nor did they last for a long time. This "leniency" was because wise heads in Roosevelt's administration prevailed with their argument that effective sanctions would destroy the Mexican economy and foment a real Communist revolution. Moreover, some seventy percent of the important Silver mining operation in Mexico was in the hands of North Americans and harsh reaction by the U.S. could trigger off its nationalization (Lipson 1985, 78).

John. D. Rockefeller (1839-1937) who appears in this book as a real life character also had important interests in Mexico. The manager of the Green Consolidated Copper Company of America – President William C. Green (at Cananea, the site of a famous strike in 1906) was in daily contact with John D. Ryan one of Rockefeller's most trusted aides (Hart 1978, 90-91). Baumann claims that Doheny's fraught conversation with Rockefeller is based on a similar scene in Frank Norris' *The Octopus* (Baumann 1987, 41).[10]

The banker John Pierpont Morgan (1837-1913) also appears as the "other king who really rules America". Traven could well have portrayed other American capitalists. For instance, the unscrupulous media baron William Randolph Hearst, publisher of the *San Francisco Examiner* had been given hundreds of thousands of acres of land at ten cents an acre by Díaz and could be relied upon to support the Mexican government through thick and thin (Turner 1967, 31).

The Cananea strike forms the basis of Traven's description of Doheny's crushing of the workers as well as his fellow capitalists. The strike was suppressed by American Rangers ordered into the plant by Galbraith, the Consul General of the United States; they shot twenty three workers and wounded twenty-two more. The Mexican government imprisoned fifty strikers but took no action against the military (Rochfort 1993, 220n4). Green appears in Siqueiros' mural *From the Dictatorship of Porfirio Díaz to the Revolution* (Chapultepec Castle, 1957-1965). Lázaro Gutiérrez de Lara who later went with the socialist journalist Kenneth Turner to the hellish plantations of henequen in Yucatán and the tobacco field of Valle Nacional was agitating at the plant (Turner 1967, 14-15).

It is interesting to compare this book with Upton Sinclair's *Oil!* (1927). This bestselling panorama of the oil bonanza and consequent scandals and ruin draws upon many live real people. Pete O'Reilly is based on Edward Doheny and his role in the Elk Hill naval oil reserve scandal and subsequent lavish endowment of the private University of Southern California (USC). Unlike Traven, Sinclair had a very sanguine view of the Bolshevik dictatorship in Russia but they join together in their vision of a transformation of the societies about which they write. We know that Traven had a copy of *Oil* in his library but we do not know to what extent he was familiar with the book, or even whether he liked it.

As in *The Land of Springtime* Traven shows the vital importance of the age old Indian economic system of the commune that was destroyed by the white invaders (Baumann 1966, 162). The laws of the *hacienda* are the laws of the blood, founded in the *peon*'s instinct for justice and not dead laws (Mezo, 93). Traven is however no sentimentalist and observes that the *peones* of the hacienda were probably better off for being forced off their land to find more pay and a fuller life in the oil fields. But I am not sure how much of Traven's deep irony is at work here (194-196). Traven is well aware of how unbeatable an incentive money is; "show a worker a twenty dollar bill and he becomes a capitalist" (208).

He relates how a large rapacious company is usually better organized and more rationally and cleverly run than a state (3-4). Such a corporation has immense power and can overthrow governments and ruin peoples with no fear of repercussion (56-57). Traven also shows the hypocrisy of those capitalists who, just like governments, will go to war justifying it on the moral grounds of serving the unavoidable common good (158). He bemused some middle class reviewers with his rhetoric; *The Bookman's* anonymous reader lost for words could only say "Herr Traven has distinct narrative powers" (*The Bookman* 1931, 162).

I have seen one review of a German edition (I am not sure if this is of the 1929 edition or that of 1931 - which doesn't say who translated it?). It is "grotesque, impossible, pedantic, peevish, abusive, unfair – but it is both gripping and impressive" ("R. T. H." = Roy Temple House 1932, 238). In 1940 a translation from the German into Spanish by Pedro Geoffroy and Lisa Kostakowsky came out in Mexico. This was not a success, and one review said that the book "falls a good deal below the standard of his earlier novels" ("M. H."= Maurice Halperin 1941, 336-337).

The book certainly had an effect in Germany. One of the most surprising offshoots was *The White Rose Group*. This was a band of anti-Nazi resistance fighters founded by Sophie and Hans Scholl in Munich in 1944; they took their name from Traven's novel.[11] In recent years activists against the U.S. government and military occupation of Iraq took the same name – I presume because they argue that the occupation is to ensure U.S. supplies of oil at a low price for the foreseeable future.

In 1951 Traven announced that he had written a new chapter for the novel; it was printed in *BT-Mitteilungen* No. 2 February 1951. This introduced a new allegorical character who calls Collins to account for his fraudulent practices (cited Seibert 1987, 177n32).

It remains after *Aslan Norval* Traven's least regarded novel. American scholars, reviewers and critics take exception to what they see as stereotypes of businessmen and U.S. companies. My guess is that Traven was giving his famous ironic humor full play in his depictions of Collins, his company and his minions. Terrence Ponick compares *The White Rose* to Frank Norris' *The Pit* and declares both to be cliché-ridden and hampered by weak characterization (Ponick, 63). In my view Ponick does less than justice to Traven.

Tierra y Libertad

> Mexico is a country where only the dead are heroes. (Fuentes cited by Langford 1971, 130)

Traven's greatest achievement is probably the six "jungle" novels written between 1930 and 1939 which together amount to some 1,500 pages. Garland has compared the saga known in German as "*Caoba-Zyklus*" to the famous Mexican murals of the 1920s and 1930s with "their large-scale, multi-focused view of history, their stirring revolutionary message" (Garland, 147).

The Mexican Revolution was one of the most significant events of the twentieth century for a number of reasons. Firstly it was a genuine movement that broke the power of the ruling class – the church, army and landlords. Secondly it was a civil war with workers sometimes pitted against Indian peasants and sometimes against each other. Thirdly, as it occurred before the Russian Revolution of 1917 the Mexicans did not have the model of a Marxist Revolution nor yet (thankfully) a Communist Party vanguard to copy. Fourthly, the Revolution was a nationalist revolution directed as much against American imperialism as against Porfirio Díaz. Lastly the Revolution was associated with an explosive cultural renaissance in art, literature, films and philosophy (Mulvey and Wollen 1982, 11-12).

The term "revolution" is more often than not used very loosely and imprecisely by unaware and uniformed writers. The best typology of the Mexican Revolution I have found is by Hans Werner Tobler who convincingly divides the period into: the revolution proper - the armed phase (1910-1917); the late revolution - the political phase (1917-1940) and the post revolutionary period - the economic phase (after 1940) (Tobler 1980, 304n1).

It has been well said that "the novel of the Mexican Revolution stands as one of the significant literary achievements of our century" (Carter 1954, 155). Traven is acknowledged by some to be "the most complete, profound, broad, tense, and keen novelist of the Revolution" (Luis Alberto Sánchez cited by Langford, 59). However, many literary critics persisted in a refusal to consider him along with other Mexican writers and, until his death he received less scholarly recognition than he was due. Lydia De Leon Hazera makes no reference to Traven in her

La novela de la selva hispanoamericana (1971) even though she discusses the Anglo Argentine, William Henry Hudson's (1841-1922) *Green Mansions* (1904) and the British author and explorer, Henry Major Tomlinson's (1873-1958) *The Sea and the Jungle* (1912). As we have seen in chapter four Tomlinson reviewed *The Death Ship* in 1934 in extremely glowing terms. De Leon Hazera redeemed herself somewhat in 1987 when she compared Mariano Azuela's *Los de abajo - The Underdogs: Pictures of the Revolution* (1915) with Traven's jungle novels (Hazera 1987, 345-355).

The "Caoba Cycle" is one of the great classic tales of Latin America on a par with Ricardo Güiraldes' (1886-1927) sweeping novel of the Argentine *pampa, Don Segundo Sombra* (1926). And like Güiraldes' book Traven's is about a rural Utopia.[12] Traven also deals briefly with the life of a cowboy and horse-breaker in his short story "The Cattle Drive" and shares Güiraldes' keen and well informed observation of horses and cattle.

In one of the most significant articles on slavery in Mexico, Alan Knight makes considerable use of Traven's "fictional but convincing" account of the ordeal of the *peones* (Knight 1986, 51n46). Most of Traven's details seem to present an accurate portrayal of life in the south of the country at the turn of the century. However, it has a universal significance and appeal; Berman has written of Traven's debt to Zola's *Germinal* and the timeless story of how the dumb acquire speech (Berman 1978, 91).[13]

As a result of his travels in the 1920s, Traven developed an intimate and deep knowledge of Chiapas, the mountainous and heavily forested province where the novels are set. The series is an epic, if melancholic tale of the life and precarious liberation of rural Mexican Indians during the revolutions of 1910. Observations on Traven/Torsvan were made at the time of his visits by the archaeologist Wolfgang Cordan. He comments that after Traven had described the atrocious conditions in which *indios* lived he "had to flee to the States". He is alone in making this claim.

This is the first time I have heard this story but then Cordan is not the most reliable source; later on he gets the title of *Die Rebellion der Gehenkten* wrong – he refers to it as *Der Aufruhr der Gehenkten* (Cordan 1964, 16, 21). However, it must be significant that between 1930 and 1954 Traven never returned to the Lacandón Forest, and even in 1954 he traveled as Croves and not Torsvan. Zogbaum also says this is because he had received death threats from planters and estate owners. During this period he spent much time in San Antonio Texas training for his pilot's license (Zogbaum, 98-99). He also visited Los Angeles and became enthralled by the movie industry.

But clearly Cordan met Torsvan in 1926 who admitted in "American English with a slight foreign accent" to writing books under the name B. Traven. Cordan says that in 1926 Torsvan never made it to the *monterías* or to the camps of San Quintín and Agua Azul of ill repute on the Rio Usumacinta (Cordan, 20-21). Traven certainly visited Agua Azul in 1930; it appears in *Die Troza* as Nuevo Filadelfia (Zogbaum, 172).

The revolutions of 1910 onward were provoked by and followed the corrupt and vicious rule of Porfirio Díaz (1830-1915) from 1876, - the *Porfiriato* - a rule ensured by the brutal militias, the *rurales*. The *rurales* have aptly been described as dispensing justice according to Díaz's famous telegram: "catch in the act, kill on the spot" (Brenner 1971, 116). Although Pope Paul III had decreed in 1537 that from a religious point of view Indians were people, even as recently as the 1910 centenary celebration of independence, Indians were not allowed on the streets of the capital so "that they may not offend the eyes of our guests with their ridiculous and immoral aspect" (Brenner 1970, 95).

In one of his stories, *The Diplomat* (first published in German as *Diplomaten* in 1930) set in the *Porfiriato* Traven describes a system of organized venality – what has been called today a "vampire state". The ruling class robbed because of insatiable greed, the non-ruling class robbed of bitter hunger (Pearson 1976, 210n33).

Revisionists have tried to show Díaz as an effective if harsh leader. The truth is that nothing at all beneficial was produced throughout his long reign (Mezo, 103). The catchwords of Díaz were "order and progress" but the reality was large scale exploitation by feudal landowners aligned with foreign capital (Revueltas 1966, 146-147). Most of the land was owned by fewer than a thousand families (Tannenbaum 1966, 201). The revolution reduced or ended their power but created a new dominant class of *nouveaux riches* and merchants.

John Kenneth Turner (1879-1948) adds a codicil that is still relevant today; "the United States will intervene with an army, if necessary, to maintain Díaz or a successor who would continue the special partnership with American capital" (Turner 1910, 5). Turner's book *Barbarous Mexico* (1910) was much praised by Mexican revolutionaries and David Alfaro Siquerios (1896-1974) included him in one of his murals (Gunn 1974A, 55n4).[14] Traven read Turner in 1925 shortly after his arrival in Mexico (Raskin 1980, 166).

Turner along with his wife Ethel Duffy Turner played an important role in aiding the Revolution in Baja California. From the time they arrived in Los Angeles in the fall of 1907 they were important allies and financial backers of Ricardo Flores Magón; they also sheltered other revolutionary leaders on the run (Turner 1981, 14).

The town of San Cristóbal de la Casas (previously called Ciudad Real) the site of at least four significant Indian rebellions, plays an important part in Traven's fiction. In the Cancúc uprising of 1712 the Tzeltal with their living "saint", María Candelaria moved on the city to be defeated by the settlers and the Army coming from Guatemala. In 1868 in "the war of the castes", 5,000 Tzotzil warriors with their saint the Indian girl Augustina Gomes Checheb, reached the outskirts; the Spanish fled in panic but the Indians left the city alone (Cristóbal Molina 1934, 365).

In 1915 the Bachajón began to collect arms for a rebellion but the leaders were caught and hung before they formed a serious threat (La Farge and Blom 1927, 404). And on I January 1994, *Ejército Zapatista de Liberación Nacional* (EZLN) guerrillas ransacked San Cristóbal de la Casas' town hall and burned district attorney, judicial and police records (Collier 1994, 1).

Traven's information about the Bachajón seems to come from non-Indian sources (Zogbaum, 116). Tannenbaum recalls that in 1926 there was no Indian in Chamula with any knowledge of Spanish; Traven seems to have relied on his *mozo* "Felipe" – Vitorino Trinidad, who was not a Chamula (Zogbaum, 71).

The first novel to be published, but second chronologically, *The Carreta* (*Der Karren*) describes the life of almost incredible hardship suffered by some of the lowest workers, and others depict the gradual awakening of political awareness by the Indians, in particular Celso and Andrés. Traven sees an important analogy and bond between the European proletariat and the Indians and mixed race Mexicans who are all proletarians.[15] Traven has shifted his position significantly on mixing of the "races". In *Land Des Frühlings* he said of the merging of Indian and European that uniformity kills, that any form of uniformity be it political economic or racial will bring about a uniformity of thought and intellectual death (Monteath, 81-82).

The series culminates in *The General from the Jungle* (*Ein general kommt aus dem Dschungel*), where the peasants and the mahogany lumber camp workers wage a bloody but successful guerrilla war against better equipped, fed and trained troops. This is only to find in a typically brilliant Traven ending that the dictator Porfirio Díaz has long been overthrown and the revolutionary generals are squabbling over the spoils. John Womack captures this chaotic situation in 1911 when chiefs led by Zapata declared themselves formally in revolt against the federal government of Francisco Madero (1873-1913).

> Tell (Madero) this for me to take off for Havana, because if not he can count the days as they go by, and in a month I'll be in Mexico City with twenty thousand men, and have the pleasure of going up to

Chapultepec castle and dragging him out of there and hanging him from one of the highest trees in the park. (Womack 1969, 127)

As even an especially cynical *gringo* onlooker said of Zapata "I cannot but believe that the basic Indian population of Southern Mexico is the better for his life and works (Dunn 1933, 303). Tens of thousands of public papers were destroyed and the Indians formed their own free communes, setting the seeds for the uprising in Chiapas in the 1990s.

Many casual readers of Traven have dismissed his work as now of merely historical interest, and if they are cheerleaders for various Mexican statesmen over the years have applauded the land reform and modernizing measures of whichever is the ruling party. Zogbaum makes a great deal of the fact that the rebellion described by Zapata in the last two novels of the cycle is not based on an actual event – but after all it is fiction and very gripping.

However, it seems clear that Traven's writing and supporters have also played a significant role in subsequent Mexican land reform. During his term in office as President (1958-1964) Adolfo Lopéz Mateos (1910-1970) – the brother of Traven's close friend and collaborator, Esperanza Lopéz Mateos – nearly forty million acres of land, a quarter of all that redistributed in the country's fifty year old agrarian reform law was given to peasants. Some of this land came from the President himself as a direct result of Traven's influence (Humphrey 1965, 222).

Traven may have been influenced when he came to write his revolutionary jungle saga by the genre known as novels of the revolution; including the work of Mariano Azuela (1873-1952), Gregorio López y Fuentes (1897-1966) and Mauricio Magdaleno (born 1906) all of whom made important contributions (Gunn 1974A, 96).[16] Azuela has made the biggest impact with his cycle, *Cuadros y escenas de la revolución mexicana*. Diego Rivera said of him that Azuela was "the only great writer that the Mexican Revolution has given us" (Luis Leal, cited by Berler 1979, xv).

Azuela's most highly regarded novel, and the only one about revolutionary peasants is *Los de abajo - The Underdogs: Pictures of the Revolution* (1915). In it the guerrilla chief, Demetrio Macías is a composite of the revolutionary leaders that Azuela came to know intimately whilst practicing as a doctor in his native town, Lagos de Moreno (Jalisco state) (Hazera 1987, 347). The most important influences were men such as General Julián Medina and Colonel Manuel Caloca.

Under Madero, Azuela was elected by acclamation in May 1911 as *Jefe Político* for Lagos de Moreno and later Director of Education for the State; but after Madero's fall he served the local revolutionaries as their doctor with the less elevated rank of lieutenant colonel. He finished the book while in exile in El Paso Texas in 1915 where it was serialized in the daily *El Paso del Norte* in twenty-three installments from 27 October to 21 November rather as Traven's work was serialized in the German daily newspaper *Vorwärts*.[17]

The Underdogs has been widely praised and even compared to the *Iliad* (Fuentes 1992, 133). It is an apt comment, and after all, Azuela studied Greek at school. Azuela's first-hand experience of guerrilla warfare and the waste of lives it entails led him to take a very pessimistic view of the Revolution (Rutherford 1972, 36). But as Brushwood says he is "disillusioned, but not cynical" (Brushwood 1966, 180). The best short account of his life and work is given by Jefferson Spell (Spell 1968, 64-100).

Los caciques – the bosses (1917) was written while Azuela was in hiding from the police, and before he became a revolutionary. It deals with the effects of the Revolution on the trading community of a provincial town. It shows a strong anti-clericalism – something that is largely absent from the other one hundred or so novels about the Revolution but something that would certainly have appealed to Traven.

Las moscas – the hangers-on (1918) deals with the bureaucrats and hangers-on that buzzed around the peasants in the wake of the withdrawal of Villa's forces to the north in the summer of 1915.

Domitilo quiere ser diputado – Domitilo aspires to Congress (1918) is a short satirical novel dealing with the ways in which the chief of a small town attaches himself to whichever revolutionary general seems to have the upper hand at the time.

Las triblaciones de una familia decente – The Trials of a Genteel Family (1918) is the last of his five revolutionary novels. It caricatures the reactions of a rich *hacendado* family to its loss of wealth and painful readjustment in Mexico City from 1914-1920. He completed *La Luciérnaga – The Firefly* in 1923 but it was not published until 1932. It is regarded as his second best novel. It shows the deeply upsetting effects of the Revolution on all sections of society as well as the redemptive role of a self-denying wife (Hendricks 1979, xxiv).

He also wrote a novel "about sex and murder during the last days of Porfirismo", *Mala Yerba* (1909). He depicts the degrading relationships of masters and *peones* with his customary detachment (Carter 1954, 148-149).

In *Nueva burgesía – the New Bourgeoisie* (1941) he turns his attention to what he sees as the manifold follies of people who have the opportunity for the first time in their lives to accumulate material goods. It is profoundly reactionary but not unsympathetic.

Gregorio López y Fuentes (1897-1966). According to one critic Traven, unlike some of the writers of the 1930s opposed President Lázaro Cárdenas' (1895-1970) "benevolent paternalism" toward the Indian (Steele, 312-313). Cynthia Steele unfairly lists López y Fuentes' *El indio - The Indian* (1935) for indictment as one of novels that blindly followed the Cárdenas party line.[18]

This became one of Mexico's best known and influential novels. Steele's criticism maybe on the grounds that the people in the book are not referred to by their names; presumably López y Fuentes does this to get us to accept the Indians as a significant coherent social group. He certainly shows both state and church mercilessly exploiting the Indian (Brushwood, 216-217). It has interesting echoes of *The Treasure of the Sierra Madre* and the jungle cycle; white men looking for gold cause their Indian guide to be crippled. He is then denied permission to wed his sweetheart.

In his second novel *Los peregrinos inmóviles - the immovable pilgrims* (1944) López y Fuentes attempts to show how the white man has been seen by the Indian through the broad sweep of Mexican history. In addition to these *indigenista* works he also wrote two novels about the Revolution. *Tierra* (1932) is a documentary style account of the impact of *Zapatismo* on a typical Morelos *hacienda* from 1910-1920. In a very Travenesque touch, Don Bernardo sends a young peon Antonio Hernández away to the army. He returns and leads a small band away from the *hacienda* to join Zapata. Antonio and Zapata are both killed.

¡Mi general! (1934) deals with the last two years of the Revolution and political corruption in post-revolutionary Mexico. It is about a humble man who becomes a general during the Revolution but when it is over, because of his lack of education and influence, he is unable to remain in the circles of power. He returns to his beginnings.

He also wrote a very illuminating story *Campamento - Bivouac* (1931) that graphically reproduces the reality of one night in the long guerrilla struggle (Brushwood, 209).

Mauricio Magdaleno (born 1906) best known for *El resplandor - Sunburst* (1937) was a Marxist who argued vehemently that the Indian's needs could best be met in a reformed economy (Steele, 313). *Sunburst* is about an extremely poor community of Otomí Indians before, during and after the Revolution. A *mestizo* child raised by them betrays their faint hopes (Brushwood, 217). In 1941 he brought out *Tierra y viento - Land and Wind*. He says quite accurately that the Indian is more forgotten and oppressed than before; still "he has only heaven to look forward to" (cited Carter, 153).

La Tierra Grande (1949) is about the dissolution of the old order on the *pulque*-producing *haciendas* of Tlaxcala. He shows the Indians as occupying just as lowly a position in the new order as before (Rutherford 1972, 67). *Cabello de elote* (1949) is a post-revolutionary novel about the expropriation of an Indian *hacienda* set in Michoacán during the Cárdenas regime. This is a similar theme to *The White Rose*, an unauthorized Spanish version of which had appeared in Mexico in 1940.

A film using a screenplay adapted from his book *El Compadre Mendoza* was shown in 1933; it is the second in Fernando de Fuentes' (1894-1958) revolutionary trilogy. It is about the self-interested ambivalence of the middle class during the Revolution.

Ermilo Abreu Gómez's (1894-1971) *indigenista* story *Canek* (1940) is regarded as one of the three most important works of the decade about the Indian issue even though it is barely thirteen pages in length; it may have been read by Traven. He was a Marxist, but according to Steele closest in spirit to Traven than any of the other people writing at the same time (Steele, 313). Canek leads an uprising and philosophizes "it is the white man who made the Indian a stranger in his own home, made him pay with his blood for the air he breathes" (Abreu Gómez 1940, 10).

Martín Luís Guzmán y Franco's (born 1887) historical novel of the Revolution *El águila y la serpiente - The Eagle and the Serpent* (1928) in which the focus is on Pancho Villa may have been read by Traven. The author who was from well-placed society came to know Pancho Villa intimately; he eventually became disillusioned with the whole movement. He is widely regarded as one of the greatest stylists in Spanish writing, and his characterization of Villa is masterly, showing a man who combined naivety, brutality and strength (Brushwood, 201).

The opening of the book which declares that the border town of "Ciudad Real is a sad sight; sad in itself, and still sadder when compared to the bright orderliness of that opposite river-bank, close but foreign" would strike a chord with Traven (Martín Luís Guzmán 1930, 1).

El sombra del caudillo - The Leader's Shadow (1929) is based on the murder of fourteen political prisoners during Calles' dictatorship.

Rafael Felipe Muñoz (born 1894) wrote a number of highly praised short stories - two collections being, *El feroz cabecilla – The Ferocious Chieftain* (1928) and *Si me han de matar mañana* (1933) as well as two novels about the Revolution, and also *Memorias de Pancho Villa* (1923), a novelized narration of the last seven years of Villa's life. *El feroz cabecilla* is an amusing satire of the exaggeration that is usual in military dispatches (Rutherford 1972, 298n120).

¡*Vámonos con Pancho Villa*! -*Let's go with Pancho Villa*! - (1931) traces the active life and death, one by one, of a small group of *Villista* soldiers from 1915-1917 who become *dorados* Villa's golden boy escort. The men are held together by an extraordinary bond of loyalty. His reporting ability enabled him to show that the Revolution was fundamentally about people playing an active part in their lives not an abstract ideology. In 1935, Fernando de Fuentes made this into a famous film of the same name. It was funded by Lázaro Cárdenas' administration. Gabriel Figueroa, who subsequently shot a numbers of films made from Traven's novels and short stories, was one of the cinematographers. It seems highly unlikely that a film buff such as Traven would not have seen the film.

Se llevaron el canon para Bachimba (1941) is about General Pascual Orozco and his *colorador*'s revolt against the government of Madero and their slaughter at the hands of General Huerta and his heavy artillery at the battle of Bachimba. It is seen through the eyes of a thirteen year boy.

The latter stylistic ploy is also used by Nellie Campobello in her celebrated *Cartucho* (1931); in a series of sketches she attempts to capture a child's view of the Revolution in Chihuahua from 1915 onwards.

General Francisco L. Urquizo's *Recuerdo que... Visiones aisladas de la Revolución* (1934) consists largely of his reminiscences. *Tropa vieja* (1943) is an unusual story for the period in that it deals with a common soldier conscripted into the federal forces in the transition from the Díaz period to the Revolution and not officers or revolutionary fighters.

José Rubén Romero (1890-1952) wrote a novel dealing specifically with his own minimal participation in the Revolution. *Mi caballo, mi perro y mi rifle* (1936) ends with the *caciques* back in full control.

Miguel Ruiz's story *El Prisonero Trece* was filmed by de Fuentes in 1933. It is about a corrupt colonel who through avarice causes the execution of his son. The censor changed the ending so that it seems the colonel dreamt the whole thing after a drinking bout.

Ricardo Flores Magón's play: *Tierra y Libertad - Land and Liberty* which received its premiere in Los Angeles in December 1915 was highly effective in the struggle against "despotism and in fomenting the agrarian revolution" (Siqueiros 1975, 187).

Some other Latin American writing is also worth mentioning. The Ecuadorian writer Jorge Icaza published *Huasipungo* in 1934. It is a horrifying tale of exploitation, misery and despair of Indians who formed the majority of that country. It was not translated into English until 1964, and the translator remarked that the author asserted to him that the Indians still lived in the same situation as thirty years before paralleling conditions in Mexico before their revolution (Dulsey 1964, xi, xv).

The Jungle Novels

The distinguished writer and traveler Arthur Calder Marshall was so impressed by Traven's first two jungle novels that he heralded Traven as one of three writers in English who had succeeded in depicting Mexico accurately. He said that Traven's characters "by reason of adversity" retain "the qualities we admire, courage, tenderness, selflessness, endurance" (Calder-Marshall 1940, 528).[19]

Raskin claims to have found a hitherto undiscovered two page introduction by Traven to the jungle novels while he was ferreting about in his study in Mexico City. In it Traven says plausibly that "the only ideology and desire of the Mexican Revolution was to get rid forever of the military dictatorship" (Traven 1976, 113). And he concludes that "rulers and politicians never learn from history and repeat the same mistakes over and over again" (Traven 1976, 114).

Regierung (1931): ***Government*** (1936): ***Gobierno*** (1951) – translated from the English by Esperanza López Mateos.

The version I am using is the 1971 American version which is a revised edition of Basil Creighton's translation published in England in 1935. It does not have the final chapter of the British version. This, the only one dealing with Andrés Ugaldo, has been moved to *Der Karren*. This was done in accordance with revisions made around 1950 by Traven (Treverton, 65).

This is the first of the six books in which prison and punishment plays a large role; as Traven says with his usual anarchist irony, everywhere the building of a prison is the first step in the organization of a civilized state (6). The prevailing ideology of the *ladino* settlers was that the Indians were incapable of learning anything, acquiring knowledge and governing themselves – even though they had been doing it for thousands of years (36). Indeed, they were not even sufficiently civilized to have the proper feelings of a human feeling (*March*, 71).[20] The independent Indian nations attempted to coexist with the *ladino* government and sometimes a chief would prefer the government to take a decision so he didn't offend his own people but on the whole they thought that it would be best if the government forgot them for good (167).

Conditions in the twenty or so large mahogany logging camps in the *montería*, in the jungles where the borders of Chiapas, Tabasco and

Guatemala meet, were so appalling that a third of men died within a year; the rest never got out of debt. The whole business was a case of finding the right formula; when this is achieved any crime can be justified and sanctified in ones own eyes and before the world (139).

There is no sentimentality in his treatment of the Indian; the people cannot afford to be sentimental. And there are no illusions on the nature of all power; his description of a new chief sitting over hot coals in order to be elected is an especially memorable scene (175-177). As he says every tenth "man" is capable of governing. And he shows that without exception independent Indians live in decentralized autonomous units of a republican and democratic nature (Mezo, 99).

There have been fewer reviews of this novel than others in the cycle. The general tone of those from the U.S. is shown by Frank Cinquemani's in *The Library Journal*, "simple and direct, it reveals Traven's characteristic concern for the underdog. But much of the writing is didactic" (Cinquemani 1971, 1639). *Publishers' Weekly* evaded the political implications; the reviewer declaimed, "only when dealing with the small personal tragedies of individuals does the genius of the author shine through" (*Publishers' Weekly* 15 March 1971, 72). John Avant in the course a few lines review in *The Library Journal* said "the story, basically leftist propaganda fiction of the 1930s is very dated" (Avant 1970, 915). An anonymous short notice in *Choice* placed him in the "Germanic category" and commented "like the irony the book's melodrama is frequently heavy handed, yet it is never false and it successfully skirts the maudlin" (*Choice* 1971, 680). On the occasion of a reprint in 1973 *Publishers' Weekly* said generously, "if it lacks something as narrative, it is an engaging, at time appealing, introduction to probably what is to come" (*Publishers' Weekly* 1973, 48).

It was left to an authority on Traven, William Weber Johnson to even the score. In *The New York Times* he said it was, "an informed, sensitive and detailed look at one of the most fascinating and least known primitive areas of the continent" (Johnson 1970, 5).

Der Karren (1931): ***The Carreta*** (1935): ***La Carreta*** (1949) - translated from the English by Esperanza López Mateos.[21]

This was titled *Die Carreta* in some later German editions. I am using the American edition of 1970 which is a slightly revised version of the British translation by Basil Creighton of 1935. The 1953 German edition published in Berlin was a revised version by Traven (Treverton, 67).

When this book starts slavery – peonage – is still almost universal in the south of the country. The first and last duty of the peon is obedience to his *patrón* (44). The *carretero* like the *peón* never gets out of his financial debt until he dies, but even when he dies, his son or nearest relative has to take it on to be added to his own debt. Traven's irony is always present; he says the greatest of all a worker's liberties is the taking on of debt or the refusal to get into debt (91). This characteristic of Traven's was picked up by a reviewer who unlike some was familiar with Traven's other work; he praised "its pleasing irony" and at the same time was aware of that "it is a remarkable achievement" (Burdett 1935, 755-756). Oscar Burdett was reviewing Basil Creighton's translation from the German. Reviewing *The Carreta* the *London Mercury* said that it is "vividly and vigorously handled, though somewhat marred by the fact that the author has allowed his sympathy with the underdog and his anger against the social conditions that produce him to reveal itself in bitterly ironic comment" (*London Mercury* 1935, 194). Again in England it was said: "certain of his charges against Catholicism have the crude naïveté so characteristic of the German" (*Life and Letters* 1935, 99).

The anonymous reviewer in *The New English Weekly* dealing with the novel in the same month of 1935 makes an allusion to Eisenstein's film *Thunder Over Mexico* that had just been released in England, and dubs Traven, "an ironist first and novelist second" (*The New English Weekly* 1935, 198-198). The fine English poet William Plomer had a very different reaction; in his opinion Traven is a moralist like all great novelists but he is also an artist and an image-maker. However, even Plomer misses some of the Traven irony; for example his remark that Mexico has the most generous and humane penal system in the world. Traven shows that a criminal is saved the horrors of prison only by being executed on the spot.

The anarchist shines through this book; he says again that healing change can never come through governments but only through the violent overthrow of government (106). He is as healthily skeptical of the Church as ever. It is nothing but magic and mummery and dressing up (135). The book has something in common with Lawrence's *The Plumed Serpent* (1926) where the church is seen to be primarily a yoke binding the Indian to his white or half-white masters. Both Traven in this book and Lawrence raise the case of Benito Juárez who managed to achieve an education in spite of the Church's efforts to keep Indian children in ignorance and innocence. And of course Juárez became President. In Traven's final years he had plans to write a biography of Juárez, and an outline of the book is in his estate (Guthke 1991, 403).

Lawrence despised and was afraid of the Indian. He was very disturbed by both the old and the new Mexico. He saw José Clemente Orozco's caricature frescoes on the second floor of the Preparatoria School in Mexico City which were started on 7 July 1923 and used his impressions in *The Plumed Serpent* where Kate calls them "vulgar abuse, not art at all" (Charlot 1963, 239).

However, unlike most of his contemporary British writers Lawrence spent quite an extended period in Mexico. In the course of three trips between 1923 and 1925 he traveled and explored for a total of ten months. Some of his most important work was set in Mexico or written there. His short story *The Woman Who Rode Away* (1928) is one of the most significant. It was written shortly after he had completed a trip to western Mexico in 1923, It opens with the woman's unflattering description of her husband "a little, wiry, twisted fellow, twenty years older than herself" (Lawrence 1995, 47).[22]

Another arch reactionary Englishman (if man of parts) Cyril Connolly erroneously says of *The Carreta* that is "written from a vigorously communistic point of view" but "it makes very good reading however" (Connolly 1935, 594). This book has been misread by other journalists and even Ph. D. students. Sheryl Pearson devotes nearly a hundred pages of her thesis to the novels and stories that Traven set in Mexico; she still hasn't understood his politics - for example she writes blithely of "his overtly Marxian formulations" (Pearson 1976, 152).

Sonnen-Schöpfung:Indianische Legende (1936): **The Creation of the Sun and the Moon** (1968).

I am using an English language version published in London in 1971 with some very fine illustrations by Alberto Beltrán.

This seems to have been written first in German but translated into Czech as *O Cloveku Ktery Stvoril Slunce* in 1934 before the first German edition appeared in print (Hagemann 1960, 376). The American First Edition of 1968 is Traven's original English version (Treverton, 137).

The bulk of this Aztec legend is also to be found in *The Carreta* (175-182) when Estrellita tells it to Andrés.[23] Pearson comments on how the image of the lost sun is also present in D. H. Lawrence's novel, *The Plumed Serpent* (*Quetzalcoatl*) (1926) and the short story, *The Woman Who Rode Away* (1924). A plumed serpent also appears in Estrellita's story as a symbol of the world (Pearson 1976, 211n41). In Aztec legends Quetzalcoatl is the god of civilization and learning.

Traven does not draw upon the better known and more unified Aztec legend that they are living on the fifth sun. Parmenter notes that the dust jacket to the first English edition says that Traven "directed" the production of the book the copy right to which lies with Rosa Elena Luján. He senses a "somewhat feminine sounding tone" to the book (Parmenter 1969, 26). Incidentally Parmenter is wrong because the German edition predates by about twenty years Traven's literary and business cooperation with Rosa Elena Luján.

It has been well received. Clara Hulton praised "Mr. Traven's sonorous prose", the attractive format and Alberto Beltrán's illustrations (Hulton 1969, 3824). *The Library Review* described it as "a poetic tale, vividly retold and strikingly illustrated" (*Library Review* 1972, 206).

Der Marsch ins Reich der Caoba (1933): **March to Caobaland** (1960) – London: **March to the Monteria** (1964) - New York

I am using a 1971 Penguin books reprint of Traven's English language version of 1960.

Traven continues his deconstruction of government; no system is capable of satisfying one quarter of the people on whom the system is imposed (103). He is very clear about revolution - one either wins or dies (120). His view of Christ as a revolutionary is especially interesting (Mezo, 71). At the same time he continues his ruthless depiction of the state established Catholic religion as absolutely thoughtless (190). And although Traven had been an actor (or maybe because he had trod the boards for so long) he is very dismissive of the theater (24).

It would be interesting to know if Traven/Marut/Croves/Torsvan was a Freemason. The tenets of Mexican Freemasonry dovetailed with those of the hard-line anti-Catholic early revolutionaries. It is difficult to overestimate the influence of masonry; few educated Mexicans build a career without Masonic affiliation. Presidents: Juárez, Díaz, Carranza, Obregón, Alemán and Cárdenas were all thirty-third degree masons (the highest order) or Grand Masters. Moreover, all of the senior American diplomats and businessmen working in Mexico were invariably masons, and for much of post colonial Mexican history controlled the network of lodges (Brandenburg 1964, 191-204).

Traven is no ideologue and again shows some of the agents and traders as brave and resourceful men (203-204). The Indian puts up with a great deal of suffering because he could not bear to be despised by members of his clan (93). *Publishers' Weekly* felt, "especially noteworthy is the way in which Traven conveys the bewildered inability of the Indians to act decisively or in an organized way against their oppressors" (*Publishers' Weekly* 30 August 1971, 273).

Reviewing this book along with *Government* Herndon said "Traven is a very great writer, and his work must be read." He concludes by musing "one wonders what its effect will be on readers of Fanon and Che when they finally get around to Traven" (Herndon 1971, 52-53). It received few other reviews. Neyman in a brief dismissal complained "Traven's style is often awkward and rough" (Neyman 1971, 2794).

Die Troza (1936): ***Trozas*** (1994) translated from the German by Hugh Young.

I am using this English translation published by Ivan Dee in Chicago in 1994.

The model for the Montellano *monterías* where most of this action takes place was Fernando Mijares Escandón's Casa Romano where conditions were even crueler than depicted in this novel (Zogbaum, 94).[24] Many *monterías* did not survive the Revolution; explorers who visited the region in 1948 reported that whereas before the Revolution there were large houses and groves there was now only stubble (Blom and Duby 1955, 110).

Gertrude Duby Blom (born 1901) was one of the most interesting foreigners to devote much of her life to Mexico. She was a journalist and socialist activist in Switzerland and other parts of Europe until 940 when she was imprisoned by the Nazis before being allowed to leave for Mexico. She became a distinguished photographer and first rate archaeologist making San Cristobál de las Casas her home in 1950.

In 1993 she wrote about the destruction of the Lacandón jungle which accelerated from 1960 assisted by cheap bank loans and encouraged by the government. There are now huge flat plains totally denuded of trees, running large herds of cattle; very few indigenous inhabitants are left (Blom 1993, 146). From the 1950s increasing numbers of mainly young colonists (and refugees from an even more vicious dictatorship in Guatemala) settled in what was known as *El Desierto de la Soledad* - the wilderness of solitude (Womack 1999, 16). By 1970 some sixty percent of the Lacandón was in communal holdings or *ejidos*. By 1993 and the eve of the Zapatista rebellion there were some 1,800 colonies and communities and yet another irreplaceable rain forest had disappeared.

In this book, Traven deals in further detail with the debt system. Ironically he calls it fair; after all every worker could pay it off between 6,000-10,000 years time. The Indians believed that not even death freed them from their fate; they will be hauling logs in heaven evermore for twelve hours every day (257-258).

Traven shows how it is always those who are uncertain of their own dignity who demand definite recognition from the defenseless (4). There is no single action on earth no matter how despicable that is not praised by somebody (132). In this very thoughtful book he shows that an action purportedly carried out for the public welfare (interest) is always inimical to the workers and never for the good of the people (164).

I am reminded of the fate of another lumberjack, Wesley Everest, an I.W.W. member murdered in 1919. He was dragged from jail (wearing his army uniform) in Centralia, Washington State by an American Legion mob, castrated, hung and riddled with bullets. His last words were: "Tell the boys I died for my class." Ralph Chaplin has a fine poem on him:

> Torn and defiant as a wind lashed reed,
> Wounded he faced you as he stood at bay;
> You dared not lynch him in the light of day,
>
> But on your dungeon stones you let him bleed;
> Night came ... and you black vigilantes of Greed.
> Like human wolves, seized hard upon your prey,
>
> Tortured and killed ... and silently slunk away
> Without one qualm of horror at the deed.
> (Ralph Chaplin, *Wesley Everest*)

Traven's widow at some stage translated *Trozas* into Spanish; this was presumably from Traven's English version, but no Spanish edition had been published as of 1999 (Treverton, 13n9).

This was the last of the Jungle Cycle to be published in English. By 1994 Traven's greatness as a writer was being appreciated. The Indian uprising in Chiapas had also focused attention once again on Mexico. In *The Publishers' Weekly* the reader was warned it was, "not for everyone... this nonetheless offers a fascinating look at a terrible place and time" (*Publishers' Weekly* 1994, 42). Ali Houissa thought how relevant the novel was, "this literary classic still resonates for the disenfranchised in Chiapas. Highly recommended" (Houissa 1994, 135).

Die Rebellion der Gehenkten (1936): ***The Rebellion of the Hanged*** (1952) translated from the German by Charles Duff: ***La Rebelión de los Colgados*** (1950) translated from the English by Esperanza López Mateos.

I am using a 1971 Penguin paperback reprint of Charles Duff's translation into English.

This is a book with a wonderful opening reminiscent of Ignazio Silone's (1900-1978) early stories of Italian peasants (Geismar 1952, 15). An anonymous reviewer in *Newsweek* quipped, "this certainly does not read like the work of a restaurant owner" (*Newsweek* 21 April 1953, 124).[25] Milton Byam warned sensitive readers that "the unrestrained cruelty of this uneven tale may be too shocking for some" (Byam 1952, 717).

Maxwell Geismar writes about the dreadful and horrifying middle of the book "a travelogue of counter terror" (Geismar, 16). In *Trozas* Traven had said that war and freedom cannot be had at the same time, and from now on he writes of brutalities conducted by the guerrillas as well as the bosses and their minions. In a pointed reminder of conditions in a land where he had lived and worked for many years he says don't mention the screams from the tortured in the camps near your home or you will join them (77-78). Ignore them, and just as the hundreds of thousands of Germans who lived next door to the Nazi's death camps, one can hope that they might go away.

The hope of all revolutionaries is that tyranny lasts only for a finite time not for ever (140). But the dilemma is that it is always better to agree with the powerful of the earth – that way you stand a chance of surviving (145). The poor have one right the right to obedience (216). If you want a revolution carry it through to the end (185). Thrice damned are those who weaken and don't return blow for blow (191). That Traven is an anarchist is obvious because if a man doesn't fight each day for his freedom he is not free (218). All revolutions that have failed have failed because they didn't burn all the paper; marriage and birth certificates, land deeds, and pay slips (219).

The "wild men" to me seem to share many similarities with Kenya's Mau Mau (237).[26] The revolutionary armies were no saints, even though it is going too far to refer as the right wing always did to Zapata as the "Attila of the South". There is no idealization and sentimentalizing of the peasant revolutionaries in this book; indeed at the end the Professor falls flat on his face in the mud (258). This reminds me of a scene in Azuela's *The Bosses*, when in his mad haste to escape the latest military advance the poet and parasite, "Neftalí Sancho Pereda de la Garza tripped over his broken shoe and left an imprint of his handsome face in the mud" (Azuela 1956, 74-75).

Traven has no illusions that the revolution is bound to succeed; the talking capacities of revolutionaries usually succeed in bringing ruin on them. There is an interesting parallel here with the student rebellion of the late 1960s. I am thinking in particular of the stirring occupation of the art college in Hornsey England in 1968 and its feeble ending, along with the petering out of student revolts all over the world.

Geismar complains about the flat and rhetorical ending – but this criticism probably arises from the fact that he, like most other reviewers, was unaware of the existence of the final novel in the sextet. Some other reviewers also appear to be unaware that this is the penultimate novel of a series of six that all hang together. However, Geismar's citation of Samuel Butler is very apt. When the meek inherit the earth they are no longer meek (Geismar, 16). The Indians are Stirnerite in that they have no plan or blueprint for the society they want; they just intend to destroy the old order (Baumann 1976, 165n46).

This is probably the most difficult book to come to grips with of the six and the one that has received most critical attention. A review in the Catholic literary journal *Commonweal* praises Traven for using words carefully but complains that "he asks us to retreat into literary simple-mindedness" (Krim 1952, 250). Harry Sylvester reviewing the 1952 New York Knopf English language version by Traven (and accepting the book's rather unbelievable claim that it had been translated from the Spanish rather than it was translated from Traven's English into Spanish by Esperanza López Mateos in 1950 and then translated back by Esperanza López Mateos into English in 1952) complains that Traven gradually loses his hold of the story when Cándido arrives in the mahogany camp (Sylvester 1952, 5). Edward Treverton thinks that claiming that the book was originally written in Spanish was a ploy by Traven; but he doesn't elaborate on the reasons why (Treverton, 134).

Incidentally in the real world of 1911 during the counter-revolutionary offensive ten Chamula soldiers had their ears cut off - *desorejamiento* - to serve as an example of what happens when *indios* fight *Ladinos* (Benjamin, 125).[27]

An anonymous reviewer condemned Traven tersely as "a matter of fact rather wooden writer" (*New Yorker* 10 May 1952, 137-138). *Time* said it "winds up as a third–rate *Uncle Tom's Cabin*". However, even he had to admit that Traven writes "a prose of such naturalness that it gives an indelible illusion of truth-to life" (*Time* 21 April 1952, 114). Edgar Acken thought the story was an, "intense monotone of misery, corruption, and oppression, objectively, almost casually written, but hypnotically compelling" (Acken 1952, 8).

Reviewers in England in 1952 were looking at Charles Duff's translation from the German. One of them didn't like the blunt irony, the over explanatory narrative style, or the over didactic conclusion (Charques 1952, 122). Another said that "the individuals do not for the most part stand out very distinctly" but found it "very uncomfortable fiction" (Kennedy 1952, 161). George Painter reviewed the book although he blithely confessed that he had neither read *The Death Ship* nor even seen the movie of *The Treasure of the Sierra Madre*. Patronizingly he said that Traven's "belief that art is short and life is long is shared by his enormous public" (Painter 1952, 161).

But it was Morchard Bishop who gave the most muddled, disconnected, and misinformed impression of the book. He said right enough that it was a "sickening account of the brutalities employed upon the Indian workers". He concludes that "one cannot but feel that the book is propaganda – and when one reads of the author's vast sales in the U.S.S.R one is almost sure of it" (Bishop 1952, 111). It was left to the comic magazine *Punch* to find some levity in a somber tale. Carole Mansur in a very short review summed it up breezily as "plenty of drama and, well, suspense, without too much rhetoric" (Mansur 1984, 74).

A reviewer (now justly forgotten) dismissed Traven as "the insurgent's Alistair MacLean" and his writing as "drab but efficient" (Mano 1972, 2). This was the Hill and Wang edition of 1971 for which no translator is given. This attack brought a spirited defense from a reader who pointed out that Traven's portrayal of Indian suffering still aptly described the conditions in the Brazilian logging camps (Nukanen 1972, 51). Alan Cheuse gave his usually scholarly committed review and comments on how some of the barbaric scenes are reminiscent of those in Jorge Icaza's *Huasipungo*. His conclusion is one with which I totally concur: "Traven is a poet, not an historian, and he tells the story of the revolution not 'just as it happened' but *as it ought to have been*" (Cheuse 1973, 58).

An anonymous reviewer in *Choice* starts out by disparaging the book, and comparing it unfavorably with John Steinbeck's, *In Dubious Battle* (1936). However, it ends with an endorsement, 'the novel becomes an important statement of the invincibility of the human spirit. Traven is a fine writer who, although belatedly, must be rediscovered" (*Choice* 1973, 1586).

I have seen one review of the Spanish translation; in 1964 by Joseph Sommers where he compares it with Rosario Castellanos' *Oficio de Tinieblas* (1962).[28] He also looks at other Mexican books of the Revolution such as Gregorio Lopez y Fuentes' *el Indio* and Ramón Rubin's *El Callado Dolor de los Tzotiles*, and compares *La Rebelión de los Colgados* with the Columbian José Eustacio Rivera's (1888-1928) *La Vorágine – the Vortex* (1924) for its relentless confrontation of man and jungle (Sommers 1964, 48).[29] Unlike Traven, Rivera wrote only the one novel; he also drew well known characters from life undisguised by any pseudonyms.[30] A translation by Earle K Jones appeared in 1935 and was reviewed in *The New Republic* – a journal that we know Traven also saw. In it Frances Valensi depicted the plight of the indentured rubber tappers as being every bit as desperate as the workers in the *montería*: "a whole lifetime of work does not suffice to wipe out their debt which is passed on to their children" (Valensi 1935, 175). This strikes a chord with Traven.

Joseph Sommers singles out Traven's deep radical criticism of the Church and comments that the Mexican Revolution never reached Chiapas and not surprisingly that the condition of the Tzotzil was basically the same in 1964 as it had been at the turn of the century (Sommers 1964, 50).

In a two page review of the French version, *la Révolte des pendus* translated from the German by A. Lehmann (1938) Robert Bourget-Pailleron is very appreciative. He calls it, *"un roman de sombre douleur et de goût corrosif"* and hopes that Traven is exaggerating the horrors of the *forestière mexicane* (Bourget-Pailleron 1938, 223).

It has had a checkered publishing career in Spanish. Two pirated versions came out in Mexico in 1938 and 1940 and one in Montevideo in 1943. Translations were from the German by Pedro Geoffroy Rivas. He justifies his piracy by claiming that Traven did not answer a letter he had written him asking for authorization to translate and publish the book. He felt that the problems Traven had written about were still so relevant that the books should be available to Mexican readers. He offered to pay Traven any royalties due to him (Traven 1938 with an introduction by Rivas, 5-9).

Liberation of some Indians from a number of the camps did occur during the Revolution. In March 1913 General Luis Felipe Domínguez in command of the Usumacinta Brigade entered Chiapas and over the next two years freed the *peónes* of all debts, executed administrators and overseers and reduced the camps "Santa Margarita" and Santa Clara" to ashes. All *monterías* were put out of business for two to three years (Benjamin 1981, 132).

Ein General Kommt aus dem Dschungel (1940): *General from the Jungle* (1954).

I am using the 1972 American edition which is a reprint of Desmond Vesey's translation from the German, published in England in 1954.

According to Edward Treverton, Traven completed the manuscript in 1937 and offered it of course to The *Büchergilde Gutenberg* who in exile in Zurich rejected it on the grounds that it now had to cater for a bourgeois Swiss clientele (Treverton, 8). So it was translated into Swedish and published by an anarchist first in Stockholm in 1939 and then in Amsterdam in 1940.

The major theme running through this last book of the cycle as indeed the whole of the sextet is the simple desire of the Indians to be left alone from anything connected with government or the state (7). But after being in servitude for four hundred years it takes time to learn how to be free (19). Traven has been criticized for starting from the simple premise - the rebels are always right (142). But I cannot fault his logic that to break off a revolution too soon is worse than never starting one (280). "General" is a superb tactician and strategist and he must partly be modeled on Zapata (27). Never leave an enemy in your rear is a cardinal rule of successful battle (136). Traven thought that Emiliano Zapata (1877-1919) was extremely important, and used the war cry of the Zapatistas' "*tierra y libertad*" in his books (Stone 1977, 73). He also admired Pancho Villa (1877-1923).

Judy Stone reviewed the book along with a reissue of *The Death Ship* when it appeared in the USA in 1973 in a translation from the German, and used the appropriate heading "revolution when there's nothing more to lose" (Stone 1973, 4). Alan Cheuse ended an enthusiastic review with "American readers who dismiss the genius of B. Traven do so at their peril" (Cheuse 1973, 25). The *Book List* called it, "a masterful portrayal of guerrilla warfare" (*Book List* 1973, 1050). A glib unsigned note in *The New York Times* dismissed it with the comment, "to some readers the book's violent action speaks of left-wing propaganda" (*New York Times Book Review* 1974, 31-32). Another unknown reviewer complained that "the book degenerates into diatribes against authority and much outrage at social inequalities" (*Choice* 1973, 969). Clearly Traven had once again hit the right targets.

The book is a very realistic and unsentimental account of a guerrilla campaign that cost over one million lives and enormous economic devastation (85). In Traven's book, "General" sacrifices the northern army in order to win a battle. In real life Mexico the liberation came in 1914 with the victory of the Northern revolutionary army; even though many *peones* only exchanged one master for another (Knight 1986, 73).

"Never underestimate the enemy" is another cardinal rule of engagement; always assume that he knows more than you, is stronger and better armed. Traven shows his fine balance with his examples of humor and dignity shown by some of the *finqueros* as they face an inevitable death (121). Heinz Osterle gave a fitting summation of Traven when he called him "a man of humor, humanity, sensitivity and commitment" (Osterle 1990, 313).

Traven's cycle ends in Solipaz – in a utopia but one that must be the starting point of humanity's hopeful voyage to another - and we trust a - lasting Utopia. As Oscar Wilde said, "progress is the realization of Utopias" (Wilde 1970, 246).

Macario

I am using the English version included in the collection *The Night Visitor and Other Stories* published in England in 1967.

Macario means healer and is named after an Egyptian saint who lived as a hermit. It was originally submitted to a publisher in English and titled *The Healer*. This short story was published in Zurich in German and was translated from English by Hans Kauders (1950). The German was extensively revised for re-publication in 1961 (Treverton, 95). It was the lead story retitled "The Third Guest" in *Stories by the Man Nobody Knows* (1961). No editor is named but it is known than Harlan Ellison was responsible for arranging the publication. It had first been published in English as "The Third Guest" in *Fantastic* pulp magazine in 1953.[31] Copyright is held by Ziff-Davis Publishing Company. It later appeared in the collection, *The Night Visitor and Other Stories* in 1967. It has been reprinted many times and appeared in the collection *The Best American Short Stories of 1954* of which a reviewer wrote "it is the best in the book" (Pippett 1954, 5).

It won an O' Henry Prize and the film made from it gathered ten international awards. It is Traven's most popular work in Mexico and in 1996 it was reprinted for the forty-seventh time in his wife's translation and has sold over 150,000 copies (Treverton, 95-97). In 1971 Sheilah R. Wilson brought out an unabridged Spanish edition designed specifically as an interesting text to help readers understanding of Spanish. She notes the directness and sparseness of the story and that Macario only keeps alive in an existence of gnawing poverty that "never quite kills but also never quite permits any visible change or hope" by an abiding fantasy (Wilson 1971, v). A reviewer praised Wilson's edition as "interesting to read and most appropriate as a book for the serious learner (Whitmer 1973, 193).

It is a skillful adaptation of two of the Brothers Grimm's "fairy" tales *Der Herr Gevatter-The Godfather* and *Der Gevatter Tod-Godfather Death* (Baumann 1976, 129). In the first story the Godfather gives a poor man the gift of a vial of water that will revive the dead. In the second the poor man is approached in turn by our Lord and the Devil both of whom he rejects; the Lord because he "gives to the rich and lets the poor starve", and the Devil because he "deceives men and leads them astray". He accepts the third godfather, Death as he "makes all men equal" (Grimm Brothers 1960, 158).

Macario, the Mexican poor man with many children meets Death on All Souls' Day, the Day of the Dead – *El día de los muertos*, a very important day and festival in Mexico.[32] And as in Grimm and in all our lives, death wins in the end.

The Kidnapped Saint and Other Stories

This collection was published in English in New York in 1975 and I am using this edition. The stories are - with the title of the original German and date of first publication in brackets: "The Kidnapped Saint" (*Die Heiligen Antonio Kümmernisse* 1930); "The Cart Wheel", (*Das Wagenrad* – a section taken from *Die Weisse Rose* 1929); "The Story of a Bomb", (*Die Geschichte einer Bombe* 1925); "The Diplomat", (*Diplomaten* 1930); "Reviving the Dead", (*Auferwelkune Eines Toten* 1928); "Accomplices", (*Spießgesellen* 1928); "Indian Dance in the Jungle", (*Indianertanz in der Dschungel* 1926). Also included are: "Frustration" and "Submission"; I discussed the latter in the previous chapter. The book also includes a long essay by Ret Marut, "In the Freest State in the World", (*Im Freiesten Staat der Welt*).

Alan Cheuse gave an enthusiastic and informed review. He applauded Traven's "spare but resonant narration" and was sure that "the collection will give readers ample opportunity to discover his distinctive style at its best" (Cheuse 1975, 34). Emile Capouta in *The Nation* was equally positive: "his small-scale epics are written with a particularity about 'conditions' that enlarges our sense of the human condition" (Capouta 1975, 569). Robert Nolan said that, "no sociologist could examine with greater perception the incessant struggle of these people to maintain their identity and common-sense attitude toward life against the encroachment of modern political and economic corruption" (Nolan 1975, 2266).

An anonymous comment in *The New York Times* gave as always the conservative dissenting view, "true to form they're either fables of avaricious gringos or tributes to the native wisdom of Mexican Indians" (*New York Times Book Review* 1977, 19). And *Choice* trotted out their dyspeptic reviewer, "the stories lack distinction, the novel excerpts are essentially random; and the essay stands alone" (*Choice* 1976, 656).

The Kleins who did most of the donkeywork in translating and editing this collection also considered for inclusion a number of other stories by Traven but eventually rejected them. These included: "Burro Trading" (*Der Esselskauf*) that had already appeared in *Short Stories*

(New York) (August 1958) and the collection *Stories by the Man Nobody Knows* (Traven 1961).

Another rejected piece which does not appear in any Traven collection in English is "An Unexpected Solution" (*Short Stories* 1957) a little ironic jewel of a story with an unexpected spin on the consequences of adultery. It had been filmed in Mexico City in 1956 after appearing in a translation by Esperanza López Mateos from the German *Eine unerwartete Lösing* in the Spanish collection *Una Canasta de Cuentos Mexicanos* (Mexico D.F.: Editorial Alas, 1946).

Other stories rejected by the Kleins were (with date of first publication and original German title): "Dynamite," (*Die Dynamit-Patrone* 1925); "Welfare Hospital," (*Wohlfahrts-Einrichtung* 1928); "Foreign Correspondent," (*Ausländischer Korrespondent* 1956); and "The Guard" (*Der Wachposten* 1928).

Judy Stone has read and enjoyed a translation of another German story, *Eine wahrhaft blutige Geschichte* – "A Truly Bloody Story" published in a collection in German in 1957. However, this is the same as "Foreign Correspondent" mentioned above. Unlike the other stories in the collection it is set in Mexico at a specific time, 1915. It is a humorous story of a cub-reporter who is discouraged from pursuing a journalist career when he files a story about six heads – five army officers and one a "goddamned American newspaper correspondent" - impaled on iron spikes on Pancho Villas' orders (Stone 1977, 69).

To the Honorable Miss S and Other Stories (1981)

I am using the English translation by Peter Silcock (1981). I gave the list of stories in chapter one. It was well received. *Publishers Weekly* said that, "this extraordinary collection projects an outspoken original voice finding its full range." *Kirkus Reports* was similarly impressed with: "fifteen brightly scornful short stories, circa 1915-1919, by a youthful German author who went on to become famous as the mysterious 'B. Traven' ... there is intriguing lively work here." A Traven expert Michael Baumann assessed them as "stories sparsely told anecdotal more often than psychologically probing and inventively **Anti**" (Baumann 1982, 32).

Other stories

Traven published a number of other stories in English starting in the 1950s; they appeared in a variety of mass circulation pulp, science fiction and best selling magazines. Two of them that appeared in the collection *The Night Visitor* (1967) were published earlier as:

"Effective Medicine" in *Manhunt* in August 1954, and "Tin Can" in the same magazine in September 1954 (II, 46-56). Copyright to both of these tales is held by Flying Eagle Publications Inc. I give fuller publication details of many of the other stories in the chapter, "Traven, his life, work and times".

Of other published stories the copyright is held as follows: "Burro Trading" (1957) B. Traven; "Midnight Call", "Frustration", and "When the Priest is not at Home" all published in 1961 are held by R.E. Luján and H. Croves. After Traven's death not surprisingly in the majority of cases his widow took over the copyright. The fact that is some cases B. Traven/Hal Croves did not hold the copyright has led some writers to question whether Traven wrote them. I assume that he did and was merely trying to cover his tracks as usual.

According to Raskin he discovered in Traven's library in 1975, a ragged copy of the *Stories by the Man Nobody Knows*, and claims on the last page of the last story "The Story of Bomb" that Traven had drawn a pen through half a dozen sentences and wrote: "I never wrote these words. They were added by an Editor without my permission" (Raskin 1980, 15). This is clearly not true. The story does not even appear in the collection. Under the title "Love Justice and a Bomb" it was published in *Argosy* in February 1966. Not until 1975 did it appear in the collection *The Kidnapped Saint & Other Stories* as the fourth of nine. Raskin claims to have worked on the galleys of *The Kidnapped Saint & Other Stories in Mexico City* with Traven's widow so perhaps now he is just confused (Raskin 1980, 128). He also claims that the two of them changed Traven's original end of the story "The Diplomat" – where President Díaz steals a wristwatch. And that he spent a week changing words and rewriting passages of the Klein's "awkward and archaic" translations (Raskin 1980, 131-132).

Aslan Norval (German 1960)

I am using the 1978 German version which is about half the length of the first edition.

It is set in the USA of the middle 1950s; it concerns the beautiful, rich, young wife of much older man (incidentally Traven married a much younger woman in 1957). Its main plot concerns the building of a new East-West canal across the United States. In it Traven's heroine talks of her dream of a federated America – harking back to a theme found in *Land des Frühlings* of thirty-four years previously (Baumann 1971, 134n47). A subsidiary plot is a brief unsatisfactory love affair between the heroine and a callow but young ex-Marine.[33]

It was initially regarded by some critics as a fake, and received few favorable reviews; it has not been translated into English or Spanish. Even Traven, speaking as Croves told Judy Stone that he didn't think it was a book that should go by the name BT (Stone 1977, 68-69). According to the bilingual scholar Hubert Jannach it is "shallow and trashy" and Traven's "frequent misconceptions and misinformation concerning the United States are glaring" (Jannach 1961, 59). However, Peter Lübbe convincingly links it with Traven's earlier work. He regards the "Atlantic-Pacific Transit Corporation" as a visionary utopian concept designed to take the great powers attention away from the arms race and instead address themselves to the more important matters of alleviating poverty in the underdeveloped world and reducing unemployment (Lübbe 1987, 154).

The manuscript was written in "awkward German" and Johannes Schönherr rewrote it, "toning down the eroticism" (Goss 1987, 48-49; 54n10). At the time Traven defended the book (Baumann 1971, 154). A rather alarming poster advertising it appears in Beck et al. with the subtitle: "The Story of a Millionaire" (Beck *et al* 1976, 12). The copyright of the book is not held by Traven.

Disputed Works[34]

It has been suggested that Robert Bek-Gran who translated Eugen Georg's *Verschollene Kulturen* from German with the title of *The Adventure of Mankind* was in fact Traven writing for an unknown reason in a different pen name (Georg, 1931). If this is true, then I assume that Bek-Gran's *Vom Wesen der Anarchie* (1920) should also be attributed to Traven.

Recknagel suggested in 1966 that Traven in collaboration with Julius Schöffler (1875-1931) wrote a play *Graumulus* (1906) and a novel *Das Große Their* (1918) under the pseudonym Helmut Gubn-Moy.[35] Schöffler spent two years in Central America, participated in the Bavarian Revolution, was an occasional collaborator with Marut and sheltered him after its defeat (Recknagel 96, 104).

Peter Howard lists some stories that I have never seen, nor has any other researcher mentioned them apart from Guthke and Treverton (Howard, 1986 cited Treverton, 18). They include "To Frame or Not to Frame" in *Selected Writings*, 5 (1946): 101-104; it seems to have been written and published in English in *Erzählungen* (1968). The German title is "Der Silberdollar." (Guthke 1991, 361) "How to Tame Them" published in *Short Stories* New York, in November 1956, 59-82, is presumably "Submission". I cannot find any reference to this issue of the periodical in any other bibliography or on the net. He also cites

"The Quarter" published in *Fling* New York, 1966. I cannot find any reference to this journal nor can I find a German or Spanish original for the story. I talked with Peter Howard in Berkeley in October 2003 and he could shed no further light on the matter.

Howard also offered for sale in 1987 Traven's "A Box on a Bus" translated into English by Singer (no date) translation; this was only four pages in length and was first published in German as *Der Sarg auf dem Bus* (1966). It is usually credited to Rosa Elena Luján and *der sarg* is normally translated as a coffin or a casket.

In Traven's estate there is an unpublished novel in German, Das *Vermächtnis des Inders - The Indian's Legacy*. The name on the title page is Georg Steinheb (otherwise unknown) (Guthke 1991, 65).

Uli Bohnen, the expert on Traven's close friend Franz Seiwert nominates the painter/poet as the author of the manifesto, *Gegensatz*, the legend *Khundar* and the prose poems *Totengesänge des Hyotamore von Kyrene* (cited by Guthke 1991, 158).

Notes

1. Foreign growers and plantation owners included the Bulnes family who emigrated from Spain in the middle of the nineteenth century. Torsvan enjoyed their hospitality in 1926 (Recknagel, 216-217).
2. However, Hagemann in an article published a year later than this contradicts himself when he refers to the book being first published in "its original German" (Hagemann 1960, 374).
3. A related smaller group, the Tojolabal, also lives in the Chiapas highlands; further east live the remnants of the Lacondón.
4. The Chamulas believe that each human being has two souls; one, the *chulel* dwells within an animal ("Jolote" is a variant of *guajolote* which means a Turkey) and the other within the body (Paz 1985, 106n4).
5. Carter Wilson lived in Chamula for a year and in his novel *Crazy February* (1974) uses Poza's account to dramatize and exploit the setting for his novel; Lynn Risser sees a parallel with Traven (Risser 1985, 171-172).
6. Oscar Lewis followed Robert Redfield into the village of Tepoztlán seventeen years after Redfield's first stay in the area. In *Life in a Mexican Village: Tepoztlán Revisited* (1951) he exposes Redfield's inability to realize the absolute importance of poverty and landlessness to peasant lives (Risser, 174).
7. I have read all of Greene with great pleasure over the years, but I will admit that there are passages in many of his books, even the entertainments- that are so horrific and cruel that they remain in one's consciousness (unfortunately) for ever.
8. Let me say that I greatly admire Lawrence's novels, stories and poems. For five crucial years of my boyhood I lived in a mining village close to

Lawrence's birthplace Eastwood and being of a similar working class background have always been attracted to him.
9. In Traven's library at his death there was a *Dictionary of American Slang* along with a *Dictionary of Sea Terms* (Recknagel 1983, 328-329).
10. *The Octopus* is the first book in a trilogy "The epic of the Wheat"; it deals with the production of wheat and the conflict between the growers and The Railroad Trust. *The Pit* deals with a deal in the Chicago wheat pit. The third *The Wolf* is set in a village in Western Europe and is about the role the wheat plays in relieving famine. Jack London reviewed it in glowing terms and stresses how Norris shows the weakness of "the agricultural force as opposed to the capitalistic force, the farmer against the financier, the tiller of the soil against the captain of industry" (Labor 1994, 439).
11. In a German Television poll in 2003 they were voted the third and fourth most popular Germans of all time.
12. It must be mentioned (and of course sincerely regretted) that the Utopia described in *Don Segundo Sombra* is free of Indians because the whites had exterminated them all.
13. Emile Zola (1840-1902) more than any other writer, has given us in *Germinal*'s Souvarine a sympathetic portrait of an anarchist "propagandist by the deed". Zola's own views may lie closer to sentiments expressed by Jordan in another work, *Travail*, "while it is with the formula of Fourier that we must begin, it is by *l'homme libre dans la commune libre* that we must end" (Sanborn 1905, 315-316). Zola also contributed to the anarchist journal, *The Torch: A Revolutionary Journal of Anarchist Communism*, published in England by Helen Rossetti Angeli and Olivia Rossetti Agresti, the children of the Pre-Raphaelite, William M. Rossetti (Woodcock 1963, 423).
14. Zogbaum says incorrectly that the mural "The Fore-runners of the 1910 Revolution" was painted by José Clemente Orozco on the walls of the Palacio Nacional in Mexico City (1883-1949) at the same time as Rivera's masterpieces (Zogbaum, 227n90). Turner and Traven can be seen in Siqueiros' huge mural *From the Dictatorship of Porfirio Díaz to the Revolution* (Hall of the Revolution Chapultepec Castle, Mexico City 1957-1965). Turner is on the left among the ideological precursors of the revolution, along with Marx, Bakunin and Proudhon, while Traven finds a place among the journalists and artists who supported the Revolution (Rochfort, 230n30).
15. Nowhere in his writing does Traven mention the fact that Porfirio Díaz was a *mestizo*. But neither does he say that the uprisings and rebellion he writes about are against the specific dictatorship of Díaz; this is part of what makes Traven's writing timeless, and of continuing relevance to us.
16. In the article Drewey Gunn also includes Andrés Henestrosa which is a rather eccentric choice; he was a distinguished writer and collector as well as, along with his beautiful wife Alfa, an adornment of Mexico City's social life, but by no means a writer of the Revolution of the stature of the other three.
17. It faces Ciudad Juárez across the Rio Grande. The inhabitants of the latter city are proverbially credited with the saying: "poor Mexico, so far from God and so close to the United States".

18. In 1937, the author received the first National Prize for Literature for this book. Its ending is anything but paternalist, the people know full well that the *gente de razon* (the whites and *mestizo*) want to attack them (López y Fuentes 1961, 256)
19. The other two being Charles Flandrau, the author of *Viva Mexico*, and the Marquise Frances (Fanny) Calderón de la Barca, a nineteenth century writer of Scottish extraction.
20. I have shortened the references in parentheses to the novels as follows: *Carreta, Government, March, Trozas, Rebellion, General*. In each case I have used the English language version (those of *Carreta, Government, Trozas,* and *General* were published in the USA, while *March* and *Rebellion* came out in England) cited at the head of each section. If I have looked at other editions or versions in other languages I will specifically mention the fact.
21. It is dated 1931 but was published in the fourth quarter of 1930 (Hagemann 1959, 52).
22. This is how Traven appeared to enemies when some thirty years later he married his younger wife.
23. Of course they are both Tzeltal Indians of the Mayan race (Zogbaum, 221n5).
24. As late as 1960, Romano and Co. still had the largest concession in Lacandón, and Dorantes, Romano and Co. were still the largest owners in Palenque (Wasserstrom 1983, 293n22).
25. At this time Traven owned/ran a Bar/Restaurant called *El Parque Cachú* (Cashew Park) in Acapulco.
26. I feel justified in making this statement because I spent two years in Kenya during the Mau Mau Emergency and its immediate aftermath. As a member of British military intelligence I was privy to much material unavailable to civilian researchers. As I am still bound by the Official Secrets Act I unfortunately cannot divulge any of it.
27. Incidentally my spell check insists on the upper case for *Ladinos* but quite happily accepts lower case for *indios*. The implied hierarchy of racial castes is not my intention.
28. This was translated as *The Book of Lamentations*. I look at Castellanos' debt if any to Traven in my last chapter.
29. Hans Otto Storm (see my Epilogue) thought this was one of the two great highlights of South American fiction; he is fascinated by the "inhuman penetration" with which "he looks into the shortcomings of his own class, the literary intellectuals" (Storm 1948, 219-220). As it deals with the exploitation of workers in the rubber plantations it is very well worth comparing with the jungle cycle.
30. It is an artistic equivalent of the hell that Sir Roger Casement uncovered in his report on the Putumayo atrocities in The Ecuadorian *selva* (James 1935, vii).
31. *Fantastic* 11 (March-April 1953): 4-36, 89.
32. And one day I am unlikely to forget as it is the day following my Mother's birthday.

33. It might encourage my older, male readers to learn that she goes back to her older and more virile husband. Moreover, according to John Bright who spent seven weeks with Traven in Chiapas in 1954 Traven then aged 72 slept with Elizabeth Fulano, a much younger photographer from *Life* who was planning a biography of him (Bright 2002, 216).

34. I must give a word of warning to anyone looking at book review indices. In the *Cumulative Book Review Index 1966-1985* there is an entry under Torsvan, Traven "The Complete Book of Cosmetics" This as you may suspect is an error. The two entries are reviews of a book by Beatrice Torsvan. How Traven would be amused!

35. Michael Baumann (1971) claims that Recknagel says this (in his *B. Traven: Beiträge zur Biographie* 1966, 31). I have been unable to get this edition. However, Recknagel has certainly deleted this section in the second edition that appeared in 1983.

Chapter 6

Traven's Legacy

As Traven was the favorite writer of a surprising number of people - famous and unremarkable alike - I will have to be very selective. Famous personalities have included: Albert Einstein (1879-1955), who named Traven as the author he would most want to read if marooned on a desert island (Guthke 1991, 3); Bruno Kreisky (1911-1990) who was an Austrian Chancellor; Luis Echeverría (born 1922), President of Mexico; H. C. Hansen who not only was the Danish Prime Minister but also translated Traven, and perhaps most surprisingly of all Sir Winston Churchill (1874-1965) was an admirer (Miller 1987, 73). I will start with Germany – probably his birthplace - and work out in ever widening circles to encompass the rest of Europe and the continent of America.

Germany and its neighbors

Hanns Eisler (1898-1962) was a prolific composer, who wrote the music for some thirty-eight plays including ten by Bertholt Brecht (1898-1956), and music director of the Agitprop group *Das Rote Sprachrohr*. He went into exile to the USA in 1933, remained a communist and, in 1947 was called up before the House Un-American Activities Committee (HUAAC). Expelled from the USA, he settled in East Berlin. He set Traven's "The Cotton-Pickers Song" to music. A recording of this song won First Prize at the Leipzig Gramophone Exhibition in 1931. It has been suggested that Traven's song is indebted to Brecht (Hays 1946, 44).

Brecht's confidant Henry Peter Matthis regarded *Die Rebellion der Gehenkten* as great literature (Müssener 1987, 278). Brecht had a "silent admiration" for Traven and found in *Das Tottenschiff* that something of himself was anticipated. Indeed Traven's spare and resonant narration has much in common with Brecht's alienated style and is perfectly appropriate for the cinema. Traven spent much of his later life adapting his books and stories for the screen; he makes a number of references to the movies in *The Treasure of the Sierra Madre*. There is clearly an affinity between Traven's hard-boiled naturalism and Brecht. Moreover, Brecht used numerous collaborators throughout his artistic life, and like Traven had an "undeveloped sense of intellectual property" (Osterle 1990, 312-313).

Traven was close friends with a group of artists in Cologne – the *Kalltallgemeinschaft*, the most prominent these being the painter and graphic artist Franz Wilhelm Seiwert (1894-1933). The latter contributed to *Der Ziegelbrenner* and may have collaborated with Traven on a number of non fiction and fiction pieces (Recknagel, 116-117; Guthke 1991, 157-158). In 1919 he produced a couple of very striking woodcuts of Karl Liebknecht and Gustav Landauer in a series commemorating assassinated Socialist leaders (Willett 1996, 46-47; Richter 1972, 12).

George Grosz (1893-1959) may have contributed an illustration to *Der Ziegelbrenner*. One of his most memorable sayings was: "DADA stands on the side of the revolutionary proletariat, *Gott mit uns*". He was a pioneer of photomontage and a highly expressive cartoonist. In some fifteen images created after 1934 he depicted the sadistic sexual torture and murder of his friend, Erich Mühsam (and Traven's); for example see *A Writer, Is He?* (1936). His, *Memorial to Richard Wagner* (1921) depicts a German Burgher dressed up "in romantic longing for his Teutonic past" (Lewis 1971, 168-169).[1]

Clement Moreau contributed twenty-one linocuts to a German edition of *Die Brücke im Dschungel* (1979) (Treverton, 118).

Traven had virtually nothing to do with the German exile colony in Mexico. After 1933, many were Stalinist communists who were as uncomfortable with Traven's views as he was with theirs (Koepke 1987, 296). He doesn't seem to have been involved in any of their organizations such as the *Liga pro Cultura Alemana*, the *Heinrich-Heine-Klub* or the publishing house, *El Libro Libre*. Earlier émigrés who tended to be nationalist, and supported the Nazis were also avoided by Traven (Guthke 1991, 318).

The much admired German/Jewish writer, Anna Seghers – pseudonym of Netty Reiling (1900-1983) is the most interesting of the exiles, and one can see the similarities with Traven in her choice of subject matter; Traven may have provided her and other exile writers with a model of how to write about the Mexican people and feeling lost in a strange country (Koepke, 304). A basic theme in virtually all of her works is the longing for home - *heimat*; Mexico merely "provides colorful backdrops for characters who search for fulfillment, who long for happiness at the end of some symbolic or real pilgrimage" (Baumgerter, cited Lürbke 2000, 171n48). In an interview published in *New Masses* in February 1943 she said that she found the atmosphere of Mexico stimulating, but doubted if she would ever write about it. "Everything is so youthful and I have not quite absorbed it all" (cited Lürbke, 155).

In 1927-1928 she had published *The Revolt of the Fishermen*. At the time she wrote this novel she would have been familiar with *Das Tottenschiff*, published in 1926 and extensively reviewed in Germany (Fehervary 2001, 216). In 1942, she said of Traven that he is a writer who portrays "in an exemplary fashion by means of the German language events among the Mexican people (Volk)" (cited Koepke, 296).

Another well known German exile writer in Mexico was Gustav Regler (1898-1963). He was in Munich at the time of the 1919 Soviet, fought in Spain, and was an anti Stalinist, all of which would on the face of it align him with Traven. However, neither in his autobiography, *The Owl of Minerva* (1959) translated from *Das Ohr des Malchus*, nor his book on Mexico, *A Land Bewitched* (1955) from the German, *Verwunsches Land Mexico*, does he mention Marut or Traven. In 1942 Mexican Communists attempted to get Regler along with Victor Serge and other anti-Stalinist refugees deported (Hope 1983, 13-14).

Victor Serge (1890-1947) the revolutionary novelist escaped from occupied France in March 1941. There was a distinguished passenger list on the *Capitaine Paul-Lemerle* which set sail from Marseilles, including also André Breton Claude Lévi-Strauss and Anna Seghers (Lévi-Strauss 1974, 24; Fehervary, 165). He was given a visa for Mexico by President Lazaro Cárdenas, to whom tens of thousands of Spanish Republican refugees also owe their lives (Serge 1963, 364). He lived in Mexico for a short period and died there (possibly murdered on Stalin's orders) in November 1947; it is possible that he and Traven know each other; certainly Serge talked with Gustav Regler (Regler1959, 358).

Ludwig Renn (1889-1980) was another well-regarded German novelist; it was the pen name of Arnold Vieth von Golssenau. Although a Saxon aristocrat and a Guards officer in the First World War his war novel *Kreig* is written from the perspective of an NCO. He later joined the KPD and was very active in revolutionary writers associations. He was interned in a variety of fascist institutions from 1932 (Willett, 1996). His *Warfare* (1939) is drawn from his experiences in the First World War and in Spain; he shows himself to be a very shrewd observer of war and the politicians who affect its progress so tragically (Renn 1939, 172).

He lived in Mexico until 1947 and in his autobiography reports that in August 1941 *The Rebellion of the Hanged* was adapted for the stage while he was teaching the university students in Morelia, capital of the state of Michoacán. He admired Traven's reputation in Mexico and said that he was a model to follow (Koepke, 296-297).

Traven did not fit into the stereotype of a socialist proletarian writer cultivated in the German Democratic Republic (DDR) from 1945-1990, but nevertheless many editions of all of his novels and stories appeared there. We also saw in "Traven's life, work and times," that in 1968 he received a delegation from the DDR Olympic Committee.

Whilst on the run in Europe from 1919-1923 Traven spent some time in Bohemia. A number of Czech writers have received great inspiration from his life and works. Norbert Frýd who was the Cezch cultural attaché in Mexico after World War II was the most significant of these (Vápeník 1987, 274). We saw in chapter one that there is a rumor which will not seem to go away that the Bohemian writer Arthur Breisky faked his death in New York in 1910 and carried on living with the identity of Traven. The rumor must be laid peacefully to rest.

In Traven's library there was a copy of Tristan Tzara's *Vingt-cinq poèmes* with a handwritten dedication from the author – possibly meant to be for Traven (Guthke 1991, 374). Tzara (1896-1963) born Sami Rosenstock in Romania was a nihilist dedicating himself to confrontation and contradiction for their own sakes (Seigel 1986, 374).

In 1985 I came across a one-man Dutch rock band called "Ret Marut" I presume in some sort of homage to Traven. He has a sprightly remake of Captain Beefheart's classic "I like the way the doodahs fly" and performs it in Dutch and English.

Scandinavia

Traven's Swedish publisher Axel Holmström (1881-1947) was an anarchist with a militant past (Guthke 1991, 288). Arne Holmström (who I assume is a relative of Axel) translated *Regierung* from the German; in Swedish it is titled *Dikatur – Dictatorship* (Hagemann 1959, 54). Holmström published all of Traven's novels. They received good reviews in the radical press but were ignored by the mainstream until his death in 1969. Few workers bought the books relying instead of the excellent free public libraries in that most civilized of countries.

The Nobel Prize winning novelist Eyvind Johnson (born 1900) was an admirer of Traven (Müssener, 278). Pere Albin Hanson who was Prime Minister of Sweden for many years followed suite; he praised in particular *The Death Ship* (Müssener, 287). Swedish fans mounted an unsuccessful attempt to get the Nobel Prize for Traven.

The German anarcho-syndicalist Augustin Souchy (born 1892) lived in Sweden during World War I and later on was an important link between Traven and the Swedes, recommending Axel Holmström for his publisher (Müssener, 290). He also fought in the Spanish Civil War, and after the fall of the Spanish Republic went into exile in Mexico where he lived from 1942 until 1961. Souchy told George Woodcock that while he was working on the journal *Der Syndikalist* in Berlin in 1923 he received a letter from Traven, whose name until then was unfamiliar to him (Woodcock 1976, 1053).

Traven showed a keen interest in the Icelandic author Kilijan Halldor Laxness (pseudonym of Halldor Gudjónsson) (born 1902) who wrote a letter to an Icelandic paper saying that a judicial error had been made in the case of Sacco and Vanzetti. Laxness was summoned to the feared Federal Building in Los Angeles where he was deprived of his passport and told that he would probably be deported (cited Baumann 1971, 95). Charles Miller says that Laxness was very impressed by Traven's novels. He also writes that Laxness is "level" with Traven – I presume he means that they had similar political views (Miller 1987, 82).

Rudolfo Usigli, the playwright and critic was Mexico's Ambassador to Norway and Lebanon for some thirty years (Raskin 1980, 39). He was Traven's most prominent literary friend (Guthke 1991, 379).

The Danish born Bodil Christensen knew Traven from 1927 - when they enrolled for the same summer school at the University of Mexico - until his death (Raskin 1980, 182).

The Rest of Europe

Leon Trotsky (Leon Davidovich Bronstein) (1879-1940) arrived in Tampico on a tanker in January 1937 on the last stage of an odyssey that started in 1929 when he was expelled from the USSR until his assassination on 20th/21st August 1940 by Ramón Mercader del Rio on Stalin's orders. For the first two years he lived in The Blue House, Frida Kahlo's old home in Mexico City until his sexual liaison with the promiscuous Frida became too messy and painful to continue, and Rivera resigned from Trotsky's organization, the 4th International.

There is no record of a meeting or correspondence with Traven although they had a number of mutual friends and acquaintances.

Otto Rühle (1874-1943) Karl Liebknecht's (1871-1919) old colleague was one of the foremost of Trotsky's supporters (West 2003, 29-30). Rühle had lived in Mexico since 1935. A number of American left oppositionists to Stalinism were also very supportive of Trotsky. One of them was a radical journalist and early feminist (and in her later years a conservative libertarian), Suzanne La Follette (1893-1983) (Dugrand 1992, 24). Incidentally, and not surprisingly, Rolf Recknagel (from Leipzig in the DDR) makes no reference to either of them, and their work with John Dewey (1859-1952) on the "Committee for Inquiry into the Moscow Trials and the Defense of Free Opinion in the Revolution", or indeed Trotsky (Serge 1963, 331). La Follette was extremely active and diligent as the secretary of the commission on which Carlo Tresca (1879-1943), the editor of the anti-fascist and anti-Stalinist paper *Il Martello* who was murdered in New York, Wendelin Thomas and Alfred Rosmer (1877-1964) also served (Van Heijenoort 1978, 108). Jean Van Heijenoort (1912-1986) was Trotsky's secretary. Traven had nothing to do with the Committee.

There is no evidence that Traven ever met Tresca or knew about him but words of Tresca's accord with Traven's views. He said Fascism "cannot be stopped except with out-and-out war. Either they get the drop on you, or you get it on them. And if they get it, you can wait for the Resurrection" (cited Hope, 5).

The Italian photographer and Communist organizer Tina Modotti (1886-1942) was in Traven's circle in the late 1920s. Traven, while living in 1926-1927 in the Edifico Zamora in Mexico City, was interested in Tina's photographs of some of the most prominent murals, and wanted to use them in a film about the murals. She gave him scores of prints but when the film was made decades later none of hers were used (Hooks 2000, 132). The source for this observation is Rosa Elena Luján in an interview held in 1990 with the author.

Two things that would have attracted Traven to her (apart from her beauty) was that she was from a working class family and that she had starred in a number of silent films in Hollywood. She was exiled from Mexico from 1930 until 1939: their paths crossed again shortly before her death in 1942, but – surely in a case of the biter being bit - she chose not to talk to him or make any further contact (Cacucci 1999, 193-194).

In Elena Poniatowska's monumental 663 page *novela*, *Tinísima* (1992), Traven appears only once when he is mentioned as attending an exhibition of Edward Weston's photographs in Mexico City. The cameo appearance is somewhat anachronistic because the date is the

10th February 1922 and he is described as the German writer Hal Croves or Ret Barut (sic) or B. Traven (Poniatowska 1992, 133). Ret Marut did not leave Germany until 1923 and did not arrive in Mexico until 1924. Moreover, Traven did not use the name Croves until the 1940s.

She was strikingly beautiful as may be seen from Weston's arousing nude studies of her, and she had an extraordinary impact on most people who met her.[2] She was the model for Rivera's *Germination* and *The Earth Oppressed* – in the frescoes of the Chapingo Chapel (1975) and had a brief affair with him and many others, women as well as men (Wolfe 1996, 189 - plates 73, 74). Her end was problematic; the official verdict was from a heart attack; suspicious friends said she was poisoned. The results of the autopsy were not published (Wolfe 1996, 195). The last line of Pablo Neruda's *Tina Modotti ha muerto* is a fitting epitaph for her:

> *Porque el fuego no muere* - because fire does not die. (Naggar and Ritchin 1993, 201)

Cedric Belfrage was a British subject and newspaper man in New York in the late forties and early fifties, including a stint as editor of the *National Guardian*, until subpoenaed by the House Un-American Activities Committee (HUAAC). He refused to testify, was arrested and then deported. He settled in Mexico, was a fan of Traven and his favorite novel was *Government* (Raskin 1980, 167). He retained his progressive views and in 1980 translated a standard biography of Augusto Sandino into English.

In England, Raymond Postgate who headed the London branch of Alfred A. Knopf dealt with Traven when the books were first brought out in that country. An unanswered question is whether Sylvia Pankhurst shielded Traven from the police in London in 1923-1924 (Guthke 1991, 163). Traven as Marut would appeal to the veteran socialist/feminist. Traven also made contact in London with another formidable suffragist Nora Smythe (Mezo, 6). A radical American journalist Charles Hallinan who had been the Secretary of the American Union against Militarism also gave him some assistance (Wyatt 284, 297).

Basil Creighton, who is justly famous for translating *Treasure of the Sierra Madre*, *The Carreta* and *Government* from German into English, was an author in his own right; his novel *Edwardian Romance* was well received. He also translated Wolfgang Cordan's account of his digs in Chiapas. He made Vicki Baum well known to English readers as well as introducing a generation of hippies to Hermann Hesse's *Steppenwolf*.

J. G. Ballard the writer of numerous brilliant science fiction novels such as *The Terminal Beach*, called one of his main characters, Traven. I do not know if this is a coincidence.[3]

George Orwell (1903-1950) would on the face of it have a great deal in common with Traven:

> I had reduced everything to the simple theory that the oppressed are always right and the oppressors always wrong: a mistaken theory but the natural result of being one of the oppressors yourself. I felt that I had got to escape not merely from imperialism but from every form of man's dominion over man. I wanted to submerge myself, to get right down among the oppressed, to be one of them and on their side against their tyrants. And, chiefly because I had had to think everything out in solitude, I had carried my hatred of oppression to extraordinary lengths. At that time failure seemed to me to be the only virtue. Every suspicion of self-advancement, even to 'succeed' in life to the extent of making a few hundreds a year, seemed to me spiritually ugly, a species of bullying. (*The Road to Wigan Pier* 1958, 148)

Malcolm Lowry paid two visits to Mexico. The first was in 1936, when he arrived on the Day of the Dead and stayed until 1938. He came again from 1945-1946. During both trips he stayed in Acapulco for several months. Did he encounter the elusive Traven? He fell foul of the law on the first trip and was deported in July 1938. But his "affliction" for Mexico was to continue (Walker 1974, 318). This time the trip ended with both Lowry and his new wife being jailed and deported. At his death he had two unfinished novels both of which are set in Mexico. *Dark as the Grave Wherein My Friend Is Laid* (1968) and *La Mordida* (still unpublished).

The French writer Tony Cartano wrote a very entertaining novel inspired by the Traven mystery and especially Will Wyatt's researches. It was published in French as *Bocanegra* in 1984 and translated into English as *After the Conquest* in 1988. Most of the *dramatis personae* we have met with in my early chapters appear thinly veiled in his pages with the exception of Michael Mateos the adult son of the writer W. H. Raven (Traven) and Doña Marina (the name of course of Cortéz's mistress) the owner of the Universal Hotel in Oaxaca (M. L. Martinez). A major subsidiary character is the UCLA literature professor George Lippman, a cuckolded buffoon who is convinced that Raven is a fraud and the novels are the original work of another man who spends most of the time in jail. Michael Mateos is the narrator of the novel and meets his death inadvertently at the hands of the Polish Police during a Solidarity demonstration he stumbles upon while he is tracking down his father's relatives in Schwiebus.

A friend and yet another lover of Frida Kahlo was André Breton (1896-1966)

Neither God nor master Open the prisons, disband the army. (*La Révolution Surréaliste*, 1926, 1)

This surrealist poet, critic and reader of the anarchist press wrote an *Ode to Fourier*. He joined the Communist party in 1927, but because of Stalinist literary policy left it in 1935 to become a Trotskyite (Egbert, 314). He went to visit Trotsky in Mexico in 1938 and collaborated with him on the manifesto "For an independent revolutionary art". He arranged for Frida Kahlo to have a show in Paris in 1939 and also organized the International Exhibition of Surrealism in Mexico in 1940 where Frida showed her two largest pictures. He was a great admirer of her work and said memorably: "the art of Frida Kahlo is a ribbon around a bomb" (Breton 1982, 36).

The French surrealist poet, Benjamin Péret (1899-1959) also lived with Trotsky in Mexico. In 1952 he still sustained a vivid detestation of Siqueiros for the latter's pivotal role in the assassination of Trotsky and in a Paris weekly magazine called him "an assassin who stains the Mexican Art Exhibition with blood by his very presence" (Siqueiros 1975, 148). He was a otherwise a man of flexible beliefs; he joined the Communist Party in 1927 along with his friend André Breton, but later in the Spanish Civil War, 1937 he fought with an anarchist battalion on the Aragon Front. He was imprisoned in occupied France but secured his release; he went to Mexico in 1941 staying there until 1948. Mexico made a profound impression on him (Mathews 1975, 140). Unfortunately neither Péret nor Breton seems to have met, read or commented on Traven.

United States of America

The renowned California photographer Edward Weston (1887-1958) is said to have trained Traven informally in 1925 (Guthke 1991, 187). However, Weston makes no reference to him in his *Daybooks* (1961). Weston was an American individualist and no socialist (Mulvey and Wollen 1982, 22).

Carleton Beals (1893-1979) was a left wing (and some would say communist fellow-traveling) American journalist and explorer whom Traven could also have met in the fairly small expatriate intellectual circle in Mexico (Zogbaum, 53). However, so successful was Traven in concealing his identity that Gunn thinks that even if Beals had met Traven he would not have connected the man and his writing (Gunn 1974A, 100). This alone would justify the title with which Traven was labeled, "the man nobody knows". Beals was an original member of the "Committee for Inquiry into the Moscow Trials and the Defense of Free Opinion in the Revolution" but resigned before the report – exonerating Trotsky - was issued.

Along with Anita Brenner (born 1905), Beals protested at the vandalism of students who mutilated frescoes by Orozco and Siqueiros at the Preparatory School in Mexico City (Charlot 1963, 287). Brenner translated many of the most significant Mexican novels of the revolution and I have read and used these. She was also a very prolific writer in all manner of journals but looking into her archives I have not come across any substantial references to Traven. This is not surprising as Traven did not socialize a great deal. However, he met his future wife Rosa Elena Luján for the first time at a party for Jascha Heifetz (born 1901), the famous violinist, in 1936, and again, on the film set of *La Rebelión de los Colgados* on location in Chiapas in 1954.

In Katharine Ann Porter's (1890-1980) novel *Ship of Fools* (1962) the ship's destination is Germany in the 1930s striking a number of echoes with Traven (Irsfeld 1969, 35). She makes no reference to Traven/Croves in her letters, essays or diaries but nevertheless, her short story "Hacienda" (1932) drawn from her visit to the set of Sergei Eisenstein's *Qué Viva México*! is well worth reading. She was a prolific writer but only occasionally published. Just one line of hers is an appropriate epitaph to the Revolution in its eloquent commentary on the lot of the Indian in the 1930s; "it was just another day's work, another day's weariness" (Porter 1935, 271).

The American Communist writer Mike Gold (born Iztok Isaac Granich) spent almost two years below the border from 1917. He wrote for an English paper, worked for about eight months in the Tampico oil fields, and for about half a year on a ranch (Aaron 1961, 86). He was involved in the influential communist journal *New Masses*. This is one of the three New York journals in which Traven allowed his publisher to advertise his books. However, there is no evidence that Traven read the journal, or that Gold and Traven ever met or corresponded.

Bertram Wolfe (1896-1977) – whose life stretched from heady days in the Communist Party to the hallowed portals of the lily-white anti communist Hoover Institution - does not seem to have met Traven during his years in Mexico, and if he met him he certainly has made no comment on him. However, the opening lines in his autobiography are pure Traven, "I see no reason why the reader should be interested in my private life" (Wolfe 1981, 13).

Jonah Raskin writes that he met William (Bill) Miller in Mexico in 1975 where he seemed to be very friendly indeed with Rosa Elana Luján. Bill Miller was from New York, had fought in against Franco in

Spain and came to Mexico because there was no job afterwards for a red in Hollywood (Raskin 1980, 28-29). Guthke says that Miller introduced Traven to his future wife in 1953 (Guthke 1991, 361-362). Traven also completed an outline for Bill Miller for a film on Pancho Villa which was never shot (Guthke 1991, 386).

Charles Miller was a prolific writer about Traven. He wrote an interesting, if often inaccurate, introduction to one of the most important collections of Traven's short stories in English, *The Night Visitor and Other Stories* (1966). As Miller wrote the introduction in Mexico under Traven's close supervision the obfuscation is not surprising. A number of other fascinating writers and musicians lived in Mexico and the bordering American states, and may have read Traven or even had a brief contact with him. It is tempting to play the game "what if" but it is rather unrewarding as Traven managed very successfully to hide himself as a recluse behind a number of identities.

Traven shares much in common with Harry (Slim) Partch (1901-1974), composer, hobo and poet who said "I would choose to remain anonymous" (Garland, 126). It is virtually certain that they hid from each other rather successfully. Partch says that *U. S. Highball: a Musical Account of Slim's Transcontinental Hobo Trip* (*1943*) is the most creative piece of work he has ever done. I heard it performed in 1997 by the Kronos Quartet with David Barron as Partch's voice. It is of much later date than *The Cotton Pickers*, but it has the vitality and freedom of Gales. Kronos have also recorded Partch's *Barstow: Eight Hitchhiker's Inscriptions from a Highway Railing at Barstow 1941*, arranged like the above by Ben Johnston. Number 1 ends "It's 4.p.m. and I'm hungry and broke, I wish I was dead. But today I am a man."

The composer Canlon Nancarrow (born 1912) lived in Mexico from 1940 after returning from Spain in 1939 where he had fought with the Washington Battalion of the Lincoln International Brigade. He certainly read Traven and commented to a mutual friend "Bill" (probably Bill Miller) about this. After Traven's death he regretted not having followed up this lead (Garland, 177). His wife Annette was an intimate friend of Frida Kahlo; Frida confided details to her about her intention to divorce Diego Rivera and become more assertive (Herrera 1983, 185, 285). She made a charcoal sketch of Traven which hangs in the library of the Traven archive in Cuernavaca (Guthke 1991, 380). Canlon was a close friend of Julian Zimet whom we will meet in the section on the Hollywood blacklist (McGilligan and Buhle 1997, 745).

Ethel Rose Duffy Turner (1885-1969) and John Kenneth Turner were trusted friends and supporters of the Mexican anarchist, Ricardo Flores Magón until he was murdered by a prison guard in Leavenworth, Kansas in 1922. She died in Cuernavaca after living in Mexico in her later years. She corresponded with Herbert and Minna Klein and Charles Miller about Traven. She was of the few Americans from the 1960s colony to be well acquainted with Traven (Guthke 1991, 379).

The Communist author, Lincoln Steffens (1866-1936) was also a firm defender of the Mexican Revolution; he first visited Veracruz in the aftermath of the American withdrawal (Gunn 1974A, 69). He expressed his admiration for Traven in a letter to Lawrence Clark Powell in the following terms: "I am too tired to write to him, but if you can send him a message, tell him that I 'get' what he's doing and that I am very grateful" (cited Hagemann 1960, 379). He also said that Traven was "a unique genius who had glimpsed and given utterance to the very soul of the real Mexico" (Powell no date, 3).

A number of writers on the Hollywood blacklist sought refuge and work in Mexico during the dark and dull years of the right-wing anti-communist hysteria. Albert Maltz (born 1908) was imprisoned for nine months for contempt of the House Un-American Activities Committee – a group whom President Truman once called "the most un-American thing in America" (Salzman 1978, 103). Al Hirschfield commented that anybody who could read or write was on the blacklist (cited Williams 1994, 294n33).

Maltz was unemployed and unemployable in the USA so went to Mexico where he spent the next eleven years. Treverton refers to an English screen play of *The Bridge in the Jungle* by him. Treverton has clearly seen a copy in the Hagemann collection at UCR but does not give the publisher or the place and date of publication (Treverton, 117).

John Bright (1908-1989) was married at one time to Josefina Fierro Bright who was a leading figure in the Congress of Spanish-Speaking Peoples, the main Popular Front organization defending the rights of Mexican Americans. She was deported to Mexico during the McCarthy era. Bright was a founding member of the Screen Writers Guild and one of the original "secret four" members of the Hollywood section of the Communist Party (McGilligan and Buhle, 129). He was in Mexico for ten years from 1949, and was one of the few people to have met Traven officially. Through the actor Pedro Armendariz (1912-1963) he worked with Traven in Mexico City for two years writing the screen plays for *La Rebelión de los Colgados* and *Una Canasta de Tres Cuentos Mexicanos.* He said of Traven, "he was a man of unquestioned integrity but impossible to work with" (Ceplair 1991, 29). While in Mexico he was credited with the screenplay for *The Brave Bulls* (1951); the film was directed by Robert Rossen and James Wong Howe was the cameraman.

He was deported from Mexico and fitfully resumed his career in Hollywood with the highlight being production associate for *Johnny*

Got His Gun (1971), based on Dalton Trumbo's book. He was yet another person who on the basis of very flimsy evidence was said to be Traven (Guthke 1991, 117).

Dalton "Doc" Trumbo (1905-1976) was also in Mexico after he got out of jail. He said of the sixty people who informed on their friends and colleagues when subpoenaed by HUAAC that they were often, just as much as those blacklisted, victims of an ordeal they should never have been subjected to. They were people who chose to abandon honor and become informers. "They lived with that terrible knowledge of themselves for over decades just as – even more terribly their children have lived in such knowledge of their parents" (Trumbo letter to Albert Maltz cited Cook 1977, 312-313). Like most of the American black list colony in Mexico he doesn't seem to have had any recorded dealings with Croves/Torsvan/Traven.[4]

Phillip Stevenson (1887-1965) was a playwright; he ended up as a screenwriter in Hollywood in 1945 with his wife Janet and their play *Counter-Attack* was turned into a motion picture by Columbia. It was based on a positive Soviet theme and as a result Stevenson was blacklisted. Before this he was also credited as a writer on *The Story of G. I. Joe* (1945). Later on he wrote novels and also contributed to films under various pseudonyms. His link with Traven is that he is credited with writing the script for *La Rosa Blanca* (1963). His correspondence with Herbert Klein from 1961 until 1973, and letters from Traven to Stevenson are in the Klein Collection at Stanford.

James Wong Howe (1899-1976), a legendary cameraman with over a hundred films to his credit; a man who won two Oscars for *The Rose Tattoo* (1958) And *Hud* (1963) and numerous other awards, was a friend of Traven's (Wyatt 51, 121-124). Traven had retained a keen interest in photography ever since his first expedition to Chiapas in the early 1920s. Traven introduced himself to James Wong Howe as he was filming *Brave Bulls* in Mexico in 1951; I presume that John Bright who was the writer for the film had informed Traven about the production. Robert Rossen the director was one of the original Hollywood Nineteen. Rossen had directed *Body and Soul* (1947) which starred John (Julie) Garfield (1913-1952) and had a screenplay by Abraham Polonsky a Communist party member and of course blacklisted.

Wong Howe's career went from strength until temporarily denied access to big budget films because of his close association with the Hollywood blacklist such as Rossen and Garfield who became a reluctant witness before HUAAC (Eyman 1987, 61, 78).[5] Wong Howe's wife, the author and literary agent Soñora Babb Howe was also very fond of Traven (Wyatt, 121). Traven wrote many letters to her.

She had a good friend in Esperanza López Mateos. As she was also in trouble through the blacklist, she decamped to Mexico so that her husband Jimmy could keep on working.

Julian Zimet, the screen writer who fled to Mexico in 1951 to avoid the blacklist and adopted the non de plume Julian Halevy, invited the "Beach Boys" production unit of whom Wong Howe was the cameraman to Acapulco in 1958 (McGilligan and Buhle, 746). They could well have met Traven again as it was in the period of his screen writing ambitions, and *Macario* was being prepared for shooting.

Harlan Ellison (born 1934 - the year *The Death Ship* was published in New York) edited nine of Traven's stories for an anthology published in 1961 by his own company Regency Publications, *Stories by the Man Nobody Knows: Nine Tales by B. Traven*, in the process rewriting three of them considerably – with the authorization of Hal Croves (Wyatt, 126). As was previously the case with Bernard Smith, Traven clearly could still be cooperative with a sensitive writer.

Of a newer generation, Jonah Raskin, who has also written a suggestive, if not to say salacious, account of his conversations and relations with Traven's widow over a ten month period in the 1970s, introduces Traven as a character in his sub-Kerouac novel *Underground: In Pursuit of B. Traven and Kenny Love* (1978). Kenny Love is based on Abby Hoffman the hippy fugitive from justice.

Several of Jack Kerouac's novels involve scenes in Mexico and rhapsodizing about Native Americans. In *Lonesome Traveler* and in *On the Road* he says that "the earth is an Indian thing" (Kerouac 1960, 22; 1959, 281). He doesn't mention Traven.

Carlos Castaneda created a considerable stir in the 1970s with his anthropological studies/novels about the Yaqui "sorcerer" Don Juan Matus. This series of novels attracted a world-wide cult following. Don Juan shares the schizophrenic qualities of Traven (Castaneda, 1968, 1971; Berkhofer 1979, 111). On the one hand, he is a stern and fractious taskmaster; on the other hand, he gives the impression of being an earthy, humorous and altogether a delightful old man (Robinson 1977, 293). Another link with Traven is Castaneda's assertion that the purpose of life is to see the miraculous quality of ordinary reality; this is very much what Emerson, Thoreau and Whitman also emphasized time over time (Robinson, 296).

Rudolfo A. Anaya has an entertaining short story "B. Traven is alive and well in Cuernavaca" in his collection: *The Silence of the Llano* (1982). It is suffused with Traven as he comments that "time and space are one" in Mexico, and that the writer had "learned that to keep his magic intact he had to keep away from the public" (Anaya 1982, 130; 140).

Many of the scholars who have contributed most to Traven studies were either born in the USA or are domiciled there. John Fraser, a professor of English literature is one of the most gifted. He was married to an even more famous artist Carol Hoorn Fraser.

The well-known sculptor and brilliant draftsman, as well as a colorful character and lone wolf, Horace Clifford Westermann (1922-1981) painted *The Death Ship* in apparent tribute to Traven's novel and the German film made from it. However, he is best known for his illustrated "Death Ship Letters" of which he penned hundreds of drawings. He volunteered for the Marine Corps in 1942 and served as a gunner on the *U. S .S. Enterprise*. He saw numerous kamikaze attacks including that on the *U. S. S. Franklin*. Such was the devastation this caused that three months later the ship was still too hot to board (Westermann 1988, 184).

He also produced many sculptures of death ships drawing inspiration from many sources. In chapter three, I indicated a number of possible sources for Traven's own inspired creation. Westermann may have drawn upon these as well as Albert Pinkham Ryder's painting *The Flying Dutchman* (1887) which is in the National Museum of American Art in Washington D.C., powerfully depicting a foundering boat being borne down by the ghostly ship. Ryder's own words could also have affected him, "neath the waters he shall ever sleep, and Ocean will the secret keep" (Brown 1989, 317). Winslow Homer's painting *The Gulf Stream* is one other possible inspiration (Adrian 2001, 44).

Westermann shares with Traven a sense of loss and the insecurity of never finding a safe haven. He also enjoyed covering his tracks and was almost willfully obscure about the sources and meanings of his sculpture. And like Traven he had empathy with subjects who cannot accept or be accepted by society (Barrette 1988, 12-13). One of his letters has the legend "Every year 15 ships of over 500 tons vanish without a trace & no survivors. True!" (Westermann, 153).

Mexico

In Mexico Traven was friendly with the two greatest Mexican artists of their generation, Diego Rivera (1886-1957) and David Alfaro Siqueiros (1896-1974) even though he didn't share their political views. Rivera was for a while a Trotskyist, and later a Stalinist, while Siqueiros was also a communist and did prison time because of his involvement in Trotsky's assassination.

In the early sixties, Traven wrote a scenario about Siqueiros, whilst the painter included Traven in a mural he painted in The National Museum of History in Chapultepec Castle – formerly the Palacio

Nacional in Mexico City (Raskin 1980, 134). Igal Maoz, the Israeli painter and collaborator of Siqueiros also dined at Traven's. Traven offered a public tribute to Siqueiros in *Siempre* (8 February, 1967) (cited Guthke 1991, 462n389).

One reason why Traven could remain friends with Siqueiros, the assassin, and Rivera, the Trotskyist turncoat, is that Traven as an anarchist would never forgive Trotsky for his responsibility for the massacre of the striking ship yard workers and seamen at Kronstadt in 1921. And even in his most fervent Trotskyist phase Rivera still said "you know I am a bit of an anarchist" (Herrera, 247).

The most enduring memorial to the Mexican Revolution is not so much in the large and very respectable body of literature inspired by it (with the exception of course of Traven!) but of the frescoes. George Biddle (1885-1973) the painter of the frescoes in the Department of Justice building in Washington D.C., and an important art administrator under President Roosevelt, went so far as to say that "the Mexican artists have produced the greatest national school of mural painting since the Italian Renaissance" (Williams, 277n10).

Rivera was the most notable creator of these murals of Mexican history and culture, popular uprisings and industrial life - those at the RCA building in New York – The Radio City Mural - being destroyed in 1934 by the managing agents because of an offending head of Lenin, before he had completed it. He was very controversial both as man and artist, and not universally liked; his work was dismissed by D. H. Lawrence as "Bah, imitations of Gauguin" (cited Charlot, 161).

However, on the left Trotsky said that Rivera was the greatest interpreter of the October Revolution (Wolfe 1990, 238). And a leading art expert Louis Gilet said of the frescoes in the Chapel of Chapingo (now the School of Agriculture), "this is a work of which one will seek in vain for an equivalent not only in the rest of America, but also in Europe, and in Russia" (Wolfe 1990, 212). Albert Einstein was also very appreciative of Rivera: "it would be difficult to name an artist at the present time whose work has moved me so profoundly" (*Workers Age* 15 March 1934, 7).

Rivera was an anarchist as a young man (Egbert 1970, 325). He then ran the leftist gauntlet from Communism through Trotskyism and back again to the Party. He mixed with a very cosmopolitan, liberated, and radical set, and at the same time was a proponent of the *indigenista* theory that the cradle of mankind was in Mexico; he may have introduced this idea to Traven.

José Clemente Orocozo was the third man of the most famous trio of Mexican muralists all of whom studied at the San Carlos Academy and became the most distinguished and active leaders of The Syndicate of

Revolutionary Painters, Sculptors and Engravers of Mexico (1922-1924). It has been said that no one has illustrated the tragedy of the Mexican Revolution like Orozco; that his murals are the pictorial analogue of Mariano Azuela's *Los de Abajo*. And like Azuela he is cynical, but not disillusioned and was infused with pity, charity and love of the Indian and downtrodden (Wolfe 1990, 160-161).

Oroczo knew Alma Reed (1889-1966), who was also the lover of Felipe Carrillo Puerte governor of Yucatán until he was martyred in Merida with ten comrades in the civil war. However, Orozco has left no record of any contact with Traven.

Frida Kahlo in recent years has become recognized as an even more important artist than Rivera – a man she married twice. She is now a major icon, and indeed her life and work has become an inspiration to millions. The last entry in her diary is especially brave, "I hope the leaving is joyful-and I hope never to return" (Kahlo 1995, 285). She does not appear to have commented on Croves/Traven.

Miguel Covarrubias (1904-1957) was not only a multi-talented man – a very famous caricaturist, illustrator, writer, collector, stage and costume designer, anthropologist and archeologist – but he was also a life long socialist, and on McCarthy's black list. He marched in support of Tom Mooney (1882-1942) in San Francisco in 1938. Mooney, a trade union leader had been framed on the charge of planting a bomb. "M. C." and his wife Rosa's house, number 5, Calle Reforma, became the center of social life for artist, intellectuals and show business people. Traven certainly visited them there (Williams, 141).

Jean Charlot (born 1898) assisted Rivera in, and sketched him at, his Herculean task toiling on the scaffold while he painted the murals in the auditorium of the Preparatoria for fifteen hours a day (Charlot, 142). He was born in France of Mexican stock and after serving in the 1914-1918 war migrated to Mexico. He does not comment on Traven.

According to the web site "voice of the slug" Traven was familiar with *El Machete* a newspaper that began life as the organ of the Syndicate of Painters in 1924 and ended in 1938 as the official paper of the *Partido Communista Mexicana* (PCM). It is probable that Traven read, subscribed to, or even contributed (under a pseudonym of course) to this magazine. It was normally printed in the anarchist colors of red and black. Of the several ironies about this paper one is that its selling price of ten centavos put it out of the reach of most workers – many rural *peones* did not earn more than thirty centavos a day. Another was that its language and theory was of the middle class. But the illustrations and the masthead with its motto were hugely popular:

El machete sirve para cortar la caña...y humillar la soberbia de los ricos impíos – The machete serves to cut the cane and to humble the pride of arrogant rich. (Wolfe 1990, 153)

Alberto Beltrán (born 1943) did the greatly acclaimed illustrations to the *Creation of the Sun and Moon* published in New York (Hill and Wang). He has illustrated numerous other important books. A founder of the conservative newspaper *El Día* he was nevertheless a good friend in Traven's final years and witnessed Traven's signing of his final will (Guthke 1991, 380).[6]

Traven's novels appeared in Spanish for the first time in the 1930s and it is probable that they influenced some Mexican writers of the 1940s and 1950s (Steele, 307). He has been described as "*auténtico novelista mexicano*" whose influence is perceptible in works such as: *La selva encantada* (1945) by Alba Sandoiz; *La escondida - the woman held hostage* (1947) by Miguel Nicholás Lira (1905-1961); *El callado dolor de los tzotziles* (1948) by Ramón Rubín, and others (Gonzalez 1951, 316-321).

However, in a comprehensive bibliography of novels of the Mexican Revolution published in 1972 (Rutherford) and a thorough discussion of "Mexico in its novel" published in 1966 (Brushwood) Traven does not merit a footnote, let alone any discussion of his novels or their influence on the men and women who followed him.

Miguel Nicholás Lira was a close friend of Frida Kahlo from their high school days. They engaged in high spirited and often criminal activities and were known among themselves as *cachuchas* (a vulgar term equivalent to cunts). He became a lawyer and also wrote verse and two novels about the Revolution. *La escondida* centers on the personal and sexual rivalry between two revolutionary leaders in the immediate post *Porfiriato* period. It received the Lamz Duret prize in 1947 and was made into a film. The other is *Mientras la muerte llega* (1958); it is set during the Maderista revolt in the Tierra Grande region (Rutherford 1972, 62).

José Revueltas' *El luto humano* (1943) is a powerful tale by a man who was a Communist at the time, of people who have been through the Revolution and political upheaval without being committed to any ideal (Brushwood, 27). In 1968 although as old a man as Traven he protested publicly at the army's massacre of the university students and was imprisoned (Raskin 1980, 101).

Ramón Rubín's *El callado dolor de los tzotziles* (1948) is one of the few novels to deal with the life of the Indian – and involves the same groups and area that Traven devoted himself to for so many years.

Carlos Fuentes' *La muerte de Artemio Cruz* (1962) is an allegorical novel on a large scale. Artemio's death bed is an opportunity to look back at his life and discover how both Cruz and Mexico have adopted false values. In Cruz's case it is the accumulation of wealth and power that started with his rise to the top of *Carrancismo*, and for Mexico, acceptance of the influence and imitation of the United States. (Brushwood, 40-41). In *La región más transparente – Where the Air is Clear* (1958) his central character is an old revolutionary turned financial tycoon; the novel is mainly about his ruin. It can be seen as an indictment of the Revolution and its ability to change institutions but inability to change men (Brushwood, 38).

Carlos Fuentes is a writer to whom Traven's dark and often surreal humor would appeal. He writes about the Mexican Revolution: "any revolution whose hymn celebrates a cockroach spaced out on marijuana has [humor] inherently" (Carlos Fuentes 1992, 140).

> The little cockroach, the little cockroach
> Will not travel any more
> Because it wants some, because it has no
> Marihuana smoke to blow! (Brenner 1970, 209)

> *La cucaracha, la cucaracha*
> *ya no puede caminar,*
> *porque no tiene, porque le falta*
> *mariguana que fumar*

Juan Rulfo's, masterpiece is *Pedro Páramo* (1955). It shows evidence of a wide reading distilled into a most distinctive novel. Pedro Páramo is a *cacique*, and his hate and obsessive love has been seen as a metaphor on the state of Mexico at that time (Brushwood, 31). *El Llano en llamas – The Burning Plain*, was published two years earlier; it is a collection of short stories about rural life. It has been said that Faulkner was his teacher (Brushwood, 31n13). The lead story is titled "Macario".

Agustín Yáñez's *Al Filo Del agua - The Edge of the Storm* (1947) is another highly praised novel. It recreates the reality of Mexico just before the beginning of the Revolution. He shows that revolution has changed a small isolated town and the people's lives but not remade them. After writing this he entered politics becoming the governor of Jalisco state. He started publishing again in 1959. In *La creación* (1959) he follows the fortunes of some of his characters from *Al Filo Del agua* during the Revolution (with less success) (Sommers1968, 195n9).

La tierra pródiga (1960) is about the subjugation of land. *Las tierras flacas* (1962) revolves around a modern patriarch (*cacique*) and the one woman he wants but cannot have. One of his many sons rebels and brings change to the people.

One of Traven's most important friends and one with whom he an intense relationship was Esperanza López Mateos (died 1951) who became his business agent in the 1940s. She was a writer, lawyer, the sister of a future Mexican President, and eventually translator of eight of Traven's novels into Spanish. Like Tina Modotti she was a communist and bisexual – she was married to Antonio Figueroa, the brother of the brilliant cameraman Gabriel Figueroa. She was confined to a wheelchair after an accident, and in 1951, after she was told that she was terminally ill, and could only expect increasingly racking pain, committed suicide (Johnson 1969, 12).

She is the author and publisher of *La carta y el recuerdo* (1943), a novel set in Saigon. Incidentally, Marut in 1914 sent an unnamed publisher the typescript of a novel set in Saigon based on his experiences there from about 1899-1900. It was called *Die Fackel des Fürsten – The Torch of the Prince* (Guthke 1991, 97). Antonio Rodríguez concluded that the style of Esperanza's book was the same as that of the Traven novels, and at the very least she could have written "Traven's" *El Puente en la selva* (Rodríguez cited by Humphrey 1965, 126-127). As it is a matter of record that she translated most of Traven's books, the resemblance between her novel and Traven's may not be so surprising. When she died Traven said that the world had "lost one of the most wonderful and extraordinarily highly gifted women with dear Esperanza" (cited Raskin 1980, 174).

Rosario Castellanos' (1925-1974) novel *Oficio de Tiniebras* (1962) is based upon an actual revolution – that occurring in San Cristóbal de las Casas from 1867-1870 (Sommers 1964, 53). It deals powerfully with the Mayan dream that one day they will be free from *caxlane* (white) rule. She hopes that the two cultures can meet but does not suggest any way that this might be achieved. As a girl in the 1930s she grew up on her parent's ranch in Comitán, Chiapas. In an earlier novel *Balúm Canán* (1957) she goes back to this childhood, and looks at a dispute between Indians and whites from the viewpoint of a white child.

The Castellanos' holding was greatly diminished by President Lázaro Cárdenas' (1895-1970) land reform and the family moved to Mexico City. Her parents died soon after, and she started to associate with a group of writers. She contracted an unhappy marriage at the age of thirty-three, and later became ambassador to Israel. She died of an electric shock in 1974 at the too early age of forty-nine (Guillermoprieto 1996, v-xii). If she had lived her comments on Traven's greater acceptance would have been interesting. Manuel Castellanos (whom I think is her brother) became a major defender of the Indians from the 1930s. In 1946 he assisted voter registration of Chamula Indians.

César Bezares Coutiño's *La simiente del corsario* (1958) is set in Chiapas. In the prologue to the book (dated 1953) the author says that he had no first hand experience of the Revolution (Rutherford 1971, 44-45). However, it is difficult to imagine that he had not read Traven as three of the jungle cycle novels in Esperanza López Mateos' translation were readily available in Spanish translations by 1953.

Traven's indictment of the treatment of the Indian still has relevance in today's world. Writing in 1963, Pablo González Casanova wrote that much of the Mexican population was marginalized, for example over fifty percent of the rural population was illiterate. He could see no improvement coming in the lot of the marginalized Indian without significant and profound reform, social revolution and development (Casanova 1966, 227).

Traven's friend the sculptor Federico Canessi completed a very striking bust of him just before he died (Recknagel, 312). He carried the urn carrying Traven's ashes and cast them over the Lacandón forest (Stone 1977, 87).

The Rest of Central and Southern America

Whilst he was working in Tampico in 1924 Traven met Augusto Sandino (1895-1934) the Nicaraguan patriot and anarchist (Guthke, 184). Sandino – an Indian-American - became the model for General Juan Mendez in *General from the Jungle*. Raskin maintains that Traven bought arms for Sandino (Raskin 1977, 77).

Sandino chose the traditional anarchist red and black flag for his "army of madmen" and proved to be a supreme strategist. He was killed by the national guard of Anastasio Somoza García – which was surely tipped off by the Mexican Communist party acting under Stalin's orders. The colors red and black also comprise the flag of the Mexican labor unions. Traven is not mentioned in Gregorio Selser's major biography of Sandino (1981).

Rómulo Gallegos' (1884-1968) celebrated epic novel of the *selva*, *Canaima*, was published in 1935. Canaima is the forest God of evil and Gallegos shows the fascination the forest has always had for the explorer, and depicts it at the beginning of the twentieth century as the site for exploitation of man and natural resources. We do not know if Traven had read it but he must have been aware of its author. Gallegos was elected President of Venezuela in 1948 but after only four months he was deposed in a military coup. He spent the next ten years in exile – mostly in Mexico and inspired by the Mexican Revolution he wrote his last novel, *Tierra Bajo los Pies – Earth Underfoot* (1971) (Gallegos 1996, xiii-xiv).

Other Reverberations

The postmodern debt to Traven has not been acknowledged properly. He was decades ahead of his time. In "A Writer of Serpentine Shrewdness" (published first in German in 1919) an author produces on one page of paper a best selling novel which sells like hotcakes when it is stretched to book-length with one "priceless" word per page. The skill as we now have learnt to our cost is to string together as few words as possible and make them appear to be the sublime crystallization of genius (*To the Honorable Miss S*, 35).

In "The Art of a Painter" academic critics go crazy over a painting that is substituted at random for another. In "Originality" an actor who is expecting to lose his job tears up the script and performs the play at random. He had discerned what the times wanted, and consequently the audience and the critics greet it with rapture. In "My visit to the Writer Pguwlkschrj Rnfajbzxlquy" the prodigious writer, genius and innovator PR whose work was impossible to understand and therefore criticize, is seen to be interned in a hospital for the criminal insane. In one of his longest stories "The Night Visitor" Gales' friend Doc. Cranwell is a post-modernist's dream; he is the writer of eighteen books, none of them published because as soon as he had finished one he would destroy it (*To the Honorable Miss S*, 19).

There is something of Traven in Doc. Cranwell; John Huston recalls that Traven in a letter to Paul Kohner says "quite a number of books I wrote never reached a printer's shop and were burned before they could harm any publisher or reader" (Huston 1980, 138-139). Huston was very intrigued by Traven, and more affected by him than he realized. They share a love for the male loner and underdog who are either abandoned by society or who choose to break away from it (Engell 1993, 92). Although he was a very wealthy man, Huston's last house was a beach shack in Mexico near the Chacala Indian community (Stone 1997, 671). His screen play is in print (Naremore, 1979).

Traven's filmography is as follows.

Compiling this has not been as easy as it might seem. There are numerous discrepancies in the major sources, and many disagreements among them. So I am not claiming absolute infallibility in this section.

The Treasure of the Sierra Madre (1948): (Warner Brothers: Producer, Henry Blanke).

Directed by, and screen play written by, John Huston; with music by Max Steiner (1888-1971). Director of Photography: Ted McCord. Traven as Hal Croves acted as advisor on the set. It was the first major Hollywood Picture to be shot on location outside the USA. Over a two-month period it was filmed in the rugged country surrounding the village of Junapeo nearby the town of San Jose de Purua in Mexico. Paul Kohner an actor's agent in Hollywood negotiated the script and film rights (Hagemann 1959, 39). The shooting was not without its problems; a local newspaper said that the film was anti-Mexican so the local population and the Mexican government forced a temporary cessation of filming. Miguel Covarrubias and Diego Rivera assured President Miguel Alemán that the report was untrue and shooting resumed (Williams, 272n61).

It is noticeable that none of Traven's comments on movie making in *The Treasure of the Sierra Madre* found their way into the dialog of Huston's finished film (Kaminsky 1978A, 59). However, he appears on screen as an extra for about two seconds. If you are alert you can see him just before Howard starts to talk about prospecting for gold in the Hotel Oso Negro in right profile, sitting front left on the screen dressed, as one might expect in a natty suit.

Erich Von Stroheim's epic film *Greed* may have had some influence on Traven and Huston. Frank Norris' *McTeague* certainly influenced Von Stroheim.

Time said of the book when it came out in the United States in 1935 that "it had the kind of moral that Hollywood likes". It is "an adventure story that is not only dramatic but makes good sense" (*Time* 1935, 74-75). The movie was an instant success with film critics and the public alike (Nolan 1965, 68). John Huston won two Academy Awards (1948) for directing and writing and Walter Huston won as best supporting actor. The picture was also nominated for best picture but was beaten by Lawrence Olivier's *Hamlet*. John Huston received a Golden Globe Award (1948) for Best Director; the film was voted Best Drama and Walter Huston, Best Supporting Actor. At the Venice Film Festival of 1948, Max Steiner received Best Music Award. The Writers Guild of America/Screen Writers Guild of America gave Huston the 1948 Best-Written American Western Award.

The film was named Fourth Best Film of the Year in 1948 by the National Board of Review, and John Huston got Best Script and Walton Huston Best Actor D. W. Griffiths Awards. The *New York Times* named it the Best Film of 1948. Huston also won the New York

Film Critics Award for best picture of the year and best direction and was voted Best Director of 1947-1948 by *Film Daily*. In the monumental guide to references and resources about Huston, there are five pages of citations of books, articles and film reviews about *The Treasure of the Sierra Madre* (Cohen and Lawton 1997, 376-380).

It continues to appeal to all audiences and The American Film Institute "Best Ever Survey" (1977) rated it the fiftieth best American Film ever. In 1972 the USC Performing Arts Council "Most Significant American Films Survey" rated it the eleventh most significant. And it has one of the most famous lines of dialogue in film. Alfonso Bedaya as "Gold Hat" claiming to be a *federale* is asked by Bogart to show his badge:

> Badges? We ain't got no badges! We don't need no badges! I don't have to show you any stinking badges.

Now there is even a web site devoted to the topic of the extraordinary large number of times the phrase has been used and adapted in film radio and television shows up to the present day.

In March 1973 the movie was finally issued in VHS format for video players thus ensuring exposure to a new generation.

One of the many ironies about the film and its iconographic status is the attitude of the production company. It was supposed to begin and end with another famous quote from the book: "Gold, Mister, is worth what it is because of the human labor that goes into the finding and getting of it". Warner Brothers told John Huston to delete it "all on account of the word 'labor'" (Kanfer 1973, 87).

Blago Sierra Madre was shot later in Belgrade (Humphrey, 141). Jovan Popoćić made the first translation into Serbo-Croat in 1952. The screen play was published in 1953 (Treverton, 117).

During the forty-five years the movie has been out there have been some obvious spin offs. Martin Rubin reminds us of Anthony Mann's 1953 Western *The Naked Spur* and how its few characters also struggle to the death in the wilderness spurred on by avarice (Rubin 1993, 155n10). Rubin also highlights some of the reasons why *The Treasure of the Sierra Madre* continues to fascinate new generations of film lovers; Huston constantly keeps the issue of the heroic in constant question, presenting numerous false leads, unresolved feints and teasing delays (Rubin 1993, 143).

In Robert Stone's novel *The Children of Light* (1986), one of the main characters is an alcoholic screenwriter who goes to Mexico to see how the film production of a script of his is working out. The leading actress takes him to what she believes to be a religious shrine. He recognizes it as the abandoned movie set of an old B. Traven remake that the Mexican government was going to turn into a museum but was now being used to store feed for a pig farm (Alarcón 1997, 75-78).

La Rebelión de los Colgados - *The Rebellion of the Hanged* (1954).

Production: José Kohn. Director: Alfred Crevenna with screenplay credited to Traven. The cameraman was Gabriel (Gabby) Figueroa who was the first cousin of Esperanza López Mateos and President Adolfo López Mateos and a good friend of Traven. Traven was Godfather to Gabriel Figueroa junior (Guthke 1993, 120). Pedro Armendariz and Carlos Lopez Moctezuma starred. The film was issued in both English and Spanish versions and was the Mexican government's choice for best film at the Venice Film Festival in 1954 – where it did not get an award. Its release in the U.S. coincided with the execution of the Rosenbergs and the beginning of the McCarthy witch hunt so despite good reviews it failed at the box office. Traven had a high opinion of José Kohn, a Czech Jew who arrived penniless in Mexico having survived the Nazi concentration camps (Stone 1977, 59-60).

Recently it came to light that Traven under the name of Hal Croves was merely the front man for the screenplay. The final version was written (in English and Spanish) by the well-known American screenwriter John Bright who was living in exile in Mexico having been blacklisted in the USA. Treverton says Rosa Elena Luján was responsible for the Spanish version. However, John Bright says that she was his secretary, and the Spanish translator was Carlos Ortigoza. Bright took over as screen writer from Emilio Fernandez whose script horrified Croves/Traven. Some seven weeks were spent on location in Chiapas and five days into the shooting Fernandez who was also the initial director was fired. Croves was on location claiming to be the emissary of Traven who was in a sanitarium in Switzerland (Bright 2002, 216-217).

Figueroa became the cameraman for John Huston's *Night of the Iguana* (1964) set in Mexico and *Under the Volcano* (1984) made from Malcolm Lowry's novel. Huston changed the ending of *Under the Volcano*, and the film resonates with the *Treasure of the Sierra Madre* as three *mestizos* kill the ex-Consul on a deserted road (Zogbaum, 223n55).

Figueroa also became a big name producer in Mexico. The Mexican government arranged with M-G-M to mount a co-production about General Emiliano Zapata. Dalton Trumbo wrote the script as his last job in Mexico. Later, the studio sold the entire project to Twentieth Century Fox where it became *Viva Zapata* with the screenplay by John Steinbeck (Cook 1977, 197).

Una Canasta de Tres Cuentos Mexicanos – A Basket of Mexican Stories (1956).

Production and Direction José Kohn y cia. Camera: Gabriel Figueroa. Premiere in Mexico City. This is a series of three short films based on the stories: "An Unexpected Solution"; Assembly Line"; and "The Tigress" ("Submission") (Ponick, 212). Hal Croves is credited with the screen play. It was in fact written by John Bright (Ceplair, 29). Pedro Armendariz, Arturo De Cordoba and Maria Félix were the stars. Adriana Williams says that Julio Bracho was involved and the backdrop in one scene is one of Miguel Covarrubias' mural maps in the Hotel Prado (Williams, 283n58).

Pedro (Pete) Armendariz played a leading role in many films; his most famous roles being Kino in *The Pearl* (1948) from a screen play by John Steinbeck. He also played the Lieutenant in John Ford's *The Fugitive* made from Graham Greene's *The Power and the Glory* and Pedro in Buñuel's *El Bruto* (1952). He also starred in two other films made from Traven's work.

Das Totenschiff - The Death Ship (1959).

Co-production UFA, Hamburg/José Kohn, Mexico; Director Georg Tressler; Camera, Heinz Pehlke; Screenplay by Hans Jacoby; Starring Horst Bucholz and Elke Sommer. Traven wrote several screen play versions but none of them were used. Ponick says that Traven was unhappy about the insertion of a painfully contrived romance between Gales (Horst Bucholz) and the young pulchritudinous Elke Sommer. In the end it is *The Yorikke* and not *The Empress of Madagascar* that is scuppered (Ponick, 212). Hans Jacoby was a very experienced screen writer. His first credit was in 1930; he worked in Hollywood until the mid 1950s; his scripts included three *Tarzans* and *Phantom of the Opera*.

The film had been a long while coming. Ernst Preczang in the 1920s brought up the idea, and the German production company UFA announced in 1931 that it was interested in acquiring the film rights. But Traven declined all offers until the 1950s (Guthke 1991, 330).

Another version was shot in Rome: *La Nave Morta* (1970). The first translation into Italian was by Teresa Pintacuda in 1950. Treverton refers to an English version released in 1970 but he is the only one to mention it (Treverton, 118). An English screen play was published in 1987.

Macario (1959).

Production: Clasa Films Mundiales. Director: Roberto Galvadón. Film title: *The Third Guest*. Screenplay by Traven. Ignacio López Tarso played his first major role as Macario. This film was nominated for Best Foreign Film Oscar. It was presented with a Cannes Film Festival Award for Superior Technical Achievement. The director said categorically that Traven had very little voice in the script, and very little to do with the filming (Barrow 1987, 137). Traven sent a five page film scenario to James Wong Howe in 1950 (Guthke 1991, 345). Recently it came to light that Emilio Carballido re wrote Traven's screen play, received an award for the adaptation and is now usually credited with it. A textbook, "based on the film script by B. Traven" was published in 1973 (Treverton, 117). It frequently appears on the Film Festival circuit.

Días de otōno (1962) based on "Frustration" – ***Dennoch eine Mutter***.

The screenplay of Julio Alejandro and Emilio Carballido was used and not Traven's. Carballido was a well known and respected playwright and the author of a number of stories and novels. *El norte* (1958) is a doom-ladened love affair between a middle aged woman and a young boy. The similarity in theme between his novel and Traven's bitter sweet short story may be one reason why Carballido was attracted to the story. He was dialogue supervisor for Buñuel's *Nazarin* (1958).

Under the title *Mercedes Ortega Lozano* Traven had reworked the story in 1945 and sent a five hundred page treatment of it to Lupita Tovar. He also wrote about it to Axel Holmström in Sweden, and his English agent, Curtis Brown (Guthke 1991, 345, 347-348).

La Rosa Blanca (1963).

Director and leading actor: Reinhold Olschewsky. Traven wrote a screenplay in 1960 but Philip Stevenson's script was finally used. One of the stars was Christine Martell, a former Miss France and then the wife of Miguel Alemán Jr. son of a former President (Irsfeld, 182). He was offended by his wife's nude scenes so these were cut; however, because of Mexican government censorship the film was still not released until 1975 (Guthke 1991, 387). It had been shown privately in the USA for the first time at the B. Traven Conference in Tucson in April 1974 (Ponick, 213).

El Puente en la Salva - The Bridge in the Jungle (1971).

United Artists. Directed by Francisco (Pancho) Kohner. Starring Charles Robinson, Katy Jurado, John Huston and Elizabeth Guadalupe Chauvet. Traven wrote a screenplay in 1957 but in the end that of Kohner's was used (Guthke 1991, 385-386). Treverton refers to an English screen play by Albert Maltz (Treverton, 117). A copy of this screen play is available in the John Huston Collection at the Academy of Motion Picture Arts and Sciences (AMPAS), Beverley Hills as is Kohner's first draft with blue revisions (Cohen and Lawton, 524). Huston read Traven's script in 1947 and found it fascinating in its diversity and digression into such areas as the philosophy of the camera (Pratley 1977, 59-60). Another version was shot in Paris (1970).

Not surprisingly, John Huston got top billing; he played Sleigh – the largest part he ever essayed. Charles Robinson was Gales, and Elizabeth Guadalupe Chauvet, Carmelita. However, in his autobiography published in 1980 Huston makes no mention of his part in filming *The Bridge in the Jungle*; he only recounts the unsuccessful negotiations that took place earlier in 1956 with Gregory Peck and Allied Artists (Huston, 258-259).

Pancho Kohner is the son of the Mexican actress Lopita Tovar - of whom Traven was an obsessive fan, and Paul Kohner, the go-between for Traven and Huston in the negotiations about *The Treasure of the Sierra Madre*. Paul Kohner contacted Traven for the first time in 1932 regarding rights for *The Death Ship*. He came to a conclusion that Traven had two personalities, one a shrewd and mischievous man intent on constructing an aura of mysterious mythology, the other a bona fide eccentric recluse who harbored paranoid delusions. For years after an argument Kohner and Traven never communicated but were reconciled at the end of Traven's life (Kohner 1977, 134-137).

Just before his death Clasa Films commissioned Traven to write a script for a documentary on the new MilPaso Dam in Chiapas (Miller 1967, xiii).

Baumann comments probably correctly on the "hopelessly Germanic English" of several of Traven's unsuccessful film scripts, and how Traven employed a number of Americans, including Charles Miller, to polish his English prose (Baumann 1987, 34; 43n6). Traven spent most of his creative energies during his declining years on writing film scripts and polishing up short stories. He was more successful in the latter enterprise as half a dozen or more were published in the mass circulation pulp magazines. In the Special Collections at The University of California Riverside there is a Screenplay entitled "The

Midnight Visitors" based on Traven's "Midnight Call." I am not aware of the author.

Luis Buñuel (1900-1983) settled in Mexico 1947. Traven with his passion for the cinema may have met him. Gabriel Figueroa was Buñuel's cameraman on *Los Olivados - The Young and the Damned* (1950), *El* (1952), *Nazarin* (1958), *La Fievre Monte a El Pao* (1959) and *El Angel Exterminador* (1962). Buñuel hated Catholicism, even though Figueroa describes Buñuel as an essentially "religious" man (Durgnat 1967, 10).

Traven may also have met the Soviet filmmaker Sergei Mikhailovich Eisenstein when he was in Mexico for fifteen months from 1930-1932 shooting *Qué Viva México! - Thunder over Mexico*. Eisenstein had certainly read Traven in German when the books started to come out in the 1920s. Moreover, he met Rivera in Moscow in 1927 and developed a close friendship with him.

Traven's powerful scene in *The General of the Jungle* of the rebels being buried in the ground up to their shoulders and their heads smashed by the hooves of galloping horses may have been taken from the film, some rushes of which the director had shown him (Zogbaum, 199-200). An approximation to Eisenstein's vision can be seen in *Time in the Sun* (Seton 1978, 205n1).

Television, Radio and Audio

In May 1967 *Westdeutscher Rundfunk* broadcast a five evening documentary based on Gerd Heidemann's years of research into Traven A TV documentary about Traven, written, narrated and directed by Will Wyatt called "The Secret of the Sierra Madre" was aired for the first time in England on 19 December 1978.

Audio recordings of *Seele eines Hundes* and *Das Lied der Baumwollpflücker in Mexiko* read in German, and *The Treasure of the Sierra Madre* in English have been produced (Treverton, 117). The latter was first broadcast on the Lux Radio Theater, 18 April 1949 starring Humphrey Bogart and Walter Huston with William Keighley as the mandatory host.

The short story "Assembly Line" was adapted for television in Germany in the mid 1950s. It was also made into an Opera at the same time (Guthke 1991, 457n345).

Traven and Rosa Elena Luján produced a play version for radio of *The Death Ship* (1955) but by 1991 it was still unpublished (Guthke 1991, 356).

Theater

Totenschiff: Play in Four Acts by Hal Croves and Rosa Elena Luján. Premiere in Zurich in August 1955.

The Creation of the Sun and Moon was staged by Seki Sano in Mexico City in the 1950s (Miller 1968, 130).

La Rebelión de los Colgados was staged by Seki Sano in Mexico City in 1953 (Beck et al, 177-180). Émigré Germans were used and Traven blackballed the event still sticking to his desire for privacy and also because he remained suspicious of their political motives.

10,000 Baskets was adapted from the short story *Assembly Line*, and published in 1995. Written by Lonnie Burstein Hewitt and Penny Bernal it was specifically designed for the ESOL (English as a Second Language) classroom. The play remains true to the spirit of Traven's work and was performed in San Diego.

The Treasure of the Sierra Madre (Director Herb Rollins) was scheduled to be performed in a World Premiere by the San Jose Stage Company in California from 14 April - 9 May 2004. It was quite a triumph to get permission from Traven's widow who stubbornly held onto the copyright and had refused all other prior requests.

Robert B Olafson whose most significant publications on Traven are in my bibliography wrote *The Great Traven Hunt or Erica's Dream* in 1977. A copy is in the Klein archive at Stanford University.

Theses and Doctoral Dissertations

Over the years there has developed a thriving cottage industry in a number of universities turning out learned, and not so learned, tracts on Traven. Among those I have read are:

Charles Humphrey: "Traven: An Examination of the Controversy over His Identity with an Analysis of His Major Work and His Place in Literature." Ph. D. dissertation, Austin: University of Texas, 1965. This was a path-breaking study and deals with German and Spanish secondary sources as well as the usual British/American. It has a valuable bibliography of reviews of many of the novels. Much of it consists of a straightforward detailed account of the main works.

Dee L. Ashliman: "The American West in Nineteenth Century German Fiction," Ph. D. Dissertation: Rutgers University, 1969. This is a thorough piece of work and briefly discusses Traven's possible borrowings from his German forebears.

John Irsfield: "The American as a Symbol of the Conflict between Industry and Nature in the First Five Novels of B. Traven," Ph. D. Dissertation. Austin: University of Texas, 1969. A short workmanlike account but now overtaken by more substantive criticism and findings.

Michael L. Baumann: "A Discussion of Four B. Traven Questions with Particular Attention to *The Death Ship*." Ph. D. dissertation: University of Pennsylvania, 1971. This was transformed without much amendment into his important book; *B. Traven: An Introduction* (1976).

Joseph Addison Davis: "Rolling Home: The Open Road as Myth and Symbol in American Literature, 1890-1940," Ph. D. dissertation: The University of Michigan: 1974. Apart from some now seriously outdated literary theory this is an entertaining account of the rich American literature on the gentlemen of the road.

Ronald Gary Walker: "Blood, Border, and Barranca: The Role of Mexico in the Modern English Novel". Ph. D. dissertation: University of Maryland: 1974. He turned this into *Infernal Paradise: Mexico and the Modern English Novel* (1978). He makes just one passing mention of Traven in the thesis. It is a thorough examination and exhumation of Lawrence, Greene, Huxley, Waugh and Malcolm Lowry's use of Mexico in their fiction as well as an account of their usually short and uncomfortable visits to the country. The chapters on Lowry are the most stimulating.

Shiela Wood Navarro: "An Analysis of B. Traven: Focusing on His 'Jungle Novels'". M. A. thesis: University of Tennessee, 1974. At only forty pages generously double spaced it doesn't add much to our knowledge.

Sheryl, Pearson: "The Anglo-American Novel of the Mexican Revolution, 1910-1940," Ph. D. dissertation: The University of Michigan, 1976. This is a thorough, if largely non comparative, study of Graham Greene, D. H. Lawrence and Traven's novels about Mexico. The bibliography is large, but I was unable to see it as it had been ripped out of the copy of the thesis I borrowed – presumably by another unscrupulous researcher.

Terrence Lee Ponick: "The Novels of B. Traven: Literature and Politics in the American Editions." Ph. D. dissertation: University of South Carolina, 1976. A useful account with some material not found in other works of the period. Ponick was also the editor of a short lived *B Traven Newsletter* of which two issues were published in 1975 and 1976; they are available in UCR special collections.

George Steven Hanson: "The Short Stories of B. Traven." Ph. D. dissertation: University of California San Diego, 1980.

Thomas Louis Benjamin: "Passages to Leviathan: Chiapas and the Mexican State, 1891-1947." Ph. D. dissertation: Michigan State University, 1981. Using mainly archival material and primary sources Benjamin has produced an impressive and detailed study of the formation of a new political order in Chiapas from 1891 until 1947. He clearly shows how labor unions were co-opted by the state – the modern Leviathan.

Lynn Katherine Risser: "The Mexican Setting in the Contemporary American Novel." Ph. D. dissertation: University of Arkansas, 1985 is an interesting account of fashionable and not so fashionable American novelists of the period. Only a perfunctory and not especially illuminating treatment of one of Traven's novels is attempted.

They are all in my bibliography and I have cited them in the text when, and if, useful.

Archives

In addition to the Powell collection in the Young Research Library (YRL) at UCLA Los Angeles there are other collections of interest to Traven fans scattered around the USA, Europe and Mexico.

The William Weber Johnson archives, the James Goldwasser, Marut archive, and the Hagemann collection are all at the library of University of California at Riverside (UCR). That of John Huston is in the library of the AMPAS in Beverley Hills Southern California and occupies some sixty-three feet of shelves; it contains correspondence between Huston, Paul Kohner and Traven. It covers the years 1932-1981 but is especially strong from the 1940s-1970s.

The Frederick Thompson I.W.W. collection at Wayne State University has material relating to Traven's connections with the wobblies. The George McCrossen (1898-1983) and his wife, Dora Malet's archive in the University of New Mexico library in Santa Fe contains a number of letters written by Irene Mermet from 30 July 1924 to 28 March 1925 (Wyatt, 238-240). They are to be found Box 5, folder 19. Although a successful businessman, McCrossen was a liberal and member of the John Reed Club.

In Austin, the State University of Texas library holds the "Treasure of the Sierra Madre" archive (Farmer, 1968). Anita Brenner's papers are also held by the Humanities Research center in Austin. Traven's folder (no.1) is in Box 51. The University of Wisconsin holds the Warner Film Library which comprises the bulk of their films, files and screen plays from the 1930-1950 "Golden Age of Hollywood," including *The Treasure of The Sierra Madre* (Balio 1979, 7).

The Klein papers of Herbert and Mina Klein are in the Department of Special Collections at Stanford University in Palo Alto, California. They cover the period of 1933-1989 and occupy some six feet of shelves. They are a mine of information about the reception of Traven in the United States, and the labors of all of the most significant Traven scholars and researchers. Klein was born in New York City but went to Berlin in 1930 first as a newspaper man and then to teach English at the *Marxistische Arbeiter Schule*. A student introduced him to the work of Traven sparking an interest that stayed with him for fifty years. He left Berlin in 1933 (Klein 1991, 1).

On the same campus at Stanford University is the Hoover Institution, which although it has a formidable conservative reputation has a remarkably eclectic and non ideological collection of material and is staffed by some of the most helpful people you could wish to meet. It has an unparalleled archive on the left in the USA and Europe.

The Charles Miller collection at the University of California in Berkeley (UCB) includes a number of letters exchanged with Ethel Duffy Turner concerning one of their mutual passions, Traven. Also in Berkeley is Peter Howard's Serendipity Books. A vast warehouse contains among other treasures and dross, many Traven first editions in a number of European languages.

The Augustin Souchy archives in the International Institute of Social History in Amsterdam possess a file on Souchy's relations with Traven. There is a Traven Archive in Cuernavaca.

The Internet

How Traven would have loved the internet. It would have given him an unparalleled opportunity to lay false trails, devise new identities and throw researchers off the scent. And he would have reveled in the anonymity of the chat rooms to try out new personae.

The general comment about trawling the web in search of Traven is that the material is often out of date, endlessly repetitive, and by no means near to being complete; many webmasters merely copy previous material very carelessly. Therefore no hit is free from errors, some laughable, and some more serious. However, a number of web sites have been diverting, if not always accurate or useful, in my labors. These include (with the prefix www and all with the suffix: .com unless otherwise indicated):

Anarchist Librarians
Angelfire

Biblio: contains Edward Treverton's unparalleled inventory of Traven titles in many languages and editions.

Dreamgarden: translates *Der Ziegelbrenner* as "Brickthrower".

ezln.org : the website of EZLN.

Endplay: has the full text of Marut's "In the Freest State".

Hal Croves

Helsinki.fi/hum: this website is Tapio Helen's and is devoted to her *Historiallista Papereita* 12 (last updated 10 July 2001). It is the longest site, and the most scholarly.

Miskatonic.org/rara-avis is full of erudite, wacky and misguided questions and answers about an eclectic range of literary matters.

noleaders.net/anok: this one has color photos of the covers of many of Traven's books.

Popsubculture: translates *Der Ziegelbrenner* as "Brickburner".

recollection books: sponsors *The Anarchist Encyclopedia: a Gallery of Saints and Sinners*. It is a professional looking production but must be carefully scrutinized for bias, humor and mistakes.

Voice of the Slug: this is one of the most professionally designed sites, and has a lot of useful and readily digestible information about Traven's life and acquaintances, and reasonably intelligent reviews of some of the novels.

Notes

1. In 1917 he feigned epilepsy to avoid being sent again to the western front (McCloskey 1997, 32-33). He supported the Spartacists and was a member of the KPD from 1921-1932. Later he abandoned most of his social radicalism apart from a general affiliation to the U. S. anti-Stalinist Left (McCloskey, 149). Like many other progressives he protested against the judicial murder (execution) of Sacco and Vanzetti (Lewis 1971, 116).
2. She was the mistress of Vittorio Vidali also known as Enea Sormenti and Carlos Contreas. Vidali was Stalin's agent, and was responsible for a number of assassinations in Spain and elsewhere. After the war he represented Trieste in the Italian Senate as a Communist (Hope, 12).
3. In the action movie *Speed*, Keanu Reeves plays Jack Traven an LAPD SWAT cop. This highly rated film gets almost as many hits on the web as Traven/Croves. Once again I do not know if the screen writer was a fan of B. Traven
4. Another famous blacklisted author, Ring Lardner Jr. (born 1915) also moved to Mexico for two years after he was released from jail after serving ten months of his sentence for contempt of court. Robert Tasker (1898-1944) was a writing partner of John Bright and a fellow communist, but unlike Bright was a former convict who served five years in San Quentin. He was also married to a

Mexican and fled to Mexico to avoid the draft. He died there in mysterious circumstances.

5. Julie Garfield was a big star and died of a heart attack probably brought on by stress before he could appear again before the committee (McGilligan and Buhle, 726). Unlike several others (such as Elia Kazan, Clifford Odets and Lee J. Cobb) he did not name names (McGrath 1993, 149).

6. I realized the other day that I have published in *El Día*. In 1986 the journal ran my article "Una Lucha en Muchos Frentes" about the liberation war being fought in Eritrea, I had just returned to the U. S. after two months in the battle zone. (15 and 21 April 1986).

Epilogue: A Tale of Two or More Men

> Spit death in the face and turn the other way. (Traven cited by Raskin 1977, 81)

Croves at numerous points in his life (lives) denied he was Traven and maintained that Traven was the writer while he was merely the literary agent.[1] Playing this role he traveled to Germany with his wife for the opening of the film *The Death Ship* (1959). In the Berlin Hilton he signed the register: "Torsvan, also known as Croves." He had appeared earlier as Croves on the set of *The Treasure of the Sierra Madre*.

He once told his wife she was married to at least four men. Of course a number of other authors have disguised the fact that they were female rather than male, black rather than white, or not a single individual, but rather a team, syndicate or partnership of writers by using pseudonyms, aliases and pen names. Just one instance is the poetical identity, "Michael Field" under which soubriquet sheltered two late Victorian Irish ladies of the Lesbian persuasion.

Even when he was tracked down in Acapulco by the Mexican journalist Luís Spota in 1948 where he was living a quiet life as Torsvan "El Gringo", he still maintained he was Croves, and that Traven was really several writers. He said that he had contributed only anecdotes to Traven's work (*Time* 16 August 1948, 36).

Croves had written to *Time* earlier that year in the wake of the revived interest in Traven's work engendered by the premiere of the movie *The Treasure of the Sierra Madre*. He once again iterated that he was not Traven. Huston made a brief riposte to this sally saying that if Croves wanted to keep his privacy let him remain mysterious (*Time* 15 March 1948). He (Hal Croves) wrote from San Antonio Texas, an almost similar letter to *Life* and in it he categorically stated that Huston would never again be given authority to direct another film based on Traven's books (*Life* 15 March 1948, 23).

There are three popular and competing/conflicting biographies: two major claimants to the title "Traven"

In reading this short but intense chapter I would advise readers to keep referring back to my chapter three where I give a detailed chronology of Traven's life, work and times without making any editorial comment on which man he really was. Three men keep reappearing in Traven's stories of his life.

1. Otto Feige was born in East Prussia in 1882; his birth is recorded. His parents were not married at the time.

2. Ret Marut was born in San Francisco in 1882. There is no record of his birth. The San Francisco 1906 fire destroyed all documents. His parents were not married at his birth and he may not have known who his father was or never met him.

3. Berrick Torsvan was born in Chicago in 1890. His birth was not registered. Sometimes Traven said his parents were married and sometimes like the given biography of baby Traven 1 and 2 above, that they wed after his birth.

Feige was apprenticed to a locksmith but ran away from home in 1904.

There is no record of Marut until 1905 when he talks to Westphalia miners.

Torsvan ran away from home to the sea at the age of ten in 1900.

According to Will Wyatt Feige became an actor, publisher and writer under the names of Richard Maurhut and Ret Marut (1907-1919).

Marut was an individualist anarchist and a member of the Bavarian Soviet. Later he was on the run for several years from the police in Austria and Germany. In Berlin in 1920 he claimed to be B. Traven and joined Rocker's anarcho-syndicalist circle. In 1923 with Rocker's help he sailed to Canada. He was refused asylum and deported to England. Jailed in London (1923-1942) he claimed to be Feige. Feige's parents received a letter from Otto in 1924. Deported again Marut sailed to Mexico. He arrived in Tampico in 1924. Never again did he admit to being Otto Feige. Only at his death bed did Traven admit to being Marut.

Torsvan remained a sailor and first visited Mexico in 1913. He witnessed the aftermath of the revolution against President Díaz first hand. On his return to the USA he became active in I.W.W. circles until 1920 when as a result of anti-anarchist activities by the American police he sought sanctuary in Mexico. Torsvan was in Chiapas 1926 as Torsvan. Torsvan claimed to be Traven.

In 1953 Croves (Traven's alter ego from 1941) was identified by Frans Blom as the man he knew as Torsvan in 1926. Tina Modotti identified Croves in 1939 as the man she knew as Torsvan in Mexico in 1929. Humphrey Bogart also made a positive ID.

In later life Traven often gave his name as Torsvan-Croves; probably because by then so many people had connected the two aliases. It is possible though to make a conjecture that there really were two men: Feige (born in Poland) and Torsvan (born in the USA), who in 1924 or shortly after met and became very close friends.[2] Guthke mentions that *Der Ziegelbrenner* had one subscriber in Mexico; what would be more natural than that Marut would make contact with him on his landing on the shores of Mexico, and what would be more likely than that they became close friends.

It is possible that if Feige went to sea at some period from 1904-1907 he could have messed with Torsvan. They then could have really been the prototypes of Gales and Stanislaus. No one ever saw the two men together so in order for this theory to make any sense one must have become an almost complete recluse, died much earlier than the other, or have been sequestered in a very secure institution. From 1926 to 1969 there was only one man in Mexico variously known as Torsvan and Croves who was indisputably Traven.

Torsvan had scribbled several stories set in the various exotic locations he had visited while a sailor, and sent several of them off to a number of U. S. publishers – we do not know to whom as he did not keep a record. All of these manuscripts were returned and he only managed to earn a few dollars from his pen; they all seem to have been destroyed, rotted away or disappeared.

The Death Ship could have been written jointly by Feige and Torsvan. Both men would have had some fluency in two languages, Torsvan was more comfortable in English (although if he was the subscriber to *Der Ziegelbrenner* he would have had to possess a passable reading ability in German) whilst Feige wouldn't have had much time to perfect his English while on the run in Europe from 1919-1924.

Torsvan naturally took on the persona of Gales the American hobo, and Feige that of Stanislaus the German/Pole. They pooled their experiences. Torsvan wrote in English. Feige translated it into German. There were several rewritings of the subsequent books as they were translated from English to German and back again by various hands. In the 1940s Esperanza López Mateos translated some of the books into Spanish. There is no evidence that she dealt with two men or had any doubts that Traven existed as a single (and presumably, virile) individual.

It is possible that the two friends went gold prospecting (1924-1926). In the film *The Treasure of the Sierra Madre* a newspaper dated 14 February 1925 is shown as Dobbs buys the winning lottery ticket. Two weeks later he cashes in his prize, and the three men start for the Sierra Madre. I presume Croves told Huston that the action of the plot was supposed to take place in 1925 and I assume the story bears some resemblance at least to his/Traven's personal experiences at that precise time.

The result of his/their labors: *The Treasure of the Sierra Madre* was written in English. There could then have been a fatal break in the relationship, and one of the two men (Feige) disappeared possibly after a serious fight just as Dobbs and Curtin's friendship ended in conflict and death. Feige was left for dead. *The White Rose*, and *The Cotton-pickers* were written by Torsvan.

In *The Treasure of the Sierra Madre* Curtin saves Dobbs life who then tries to murder him. Traven said that Stanislaus (Feige) saved his life. Did he then as Torsvan (Gales) try to murder Feige or perhaps succeed in the attempt, or was there some accident where he failed to save his friend.

A further gloss is to posit that the six Jungle novels were written in English by Torsvan and translated into German by Feige. For this theory to work Feige would have to die in 1940 and not in 1924-1926. It is possible that he had been so seriously injured either in a pit fall or brawl that he was confined to a nursing home. However, no one has found a record of Feige/Traven's stay in a nursing home, insane asylum or prison in Mexico, Europe or the USA during the years 1924-1969. Croves under pressure would sometimes say Traven was in a sanitarium in Switzerland – possibly remembering his reading of Thomas Mann's *The Magic Mountain*.

Only two Traven stories were published from 1940 to 1960 and these were by Marut/Feige and originally written in German in the 1920s. *Aslan Norval* was probably drafted by Feige in the late 1930s lost or put aside, and topical allusions and some eroticism/soft core sex put in later by Torsvan. *Macario* presents a problem as it was written in English in 1950; however, it is perfectly possible for Torsvan to have written it.

Before his death Croves/Torsvan/Traven said he had been Marut but never admitted to having been Feige – possibly because no one had raised the issue until Wyatt some years after Traven's death. It is possible that he was Feige but also took on Torsvan's persona after 1924 and adapted his writings to send off to Germany. It is possible that he convinced himself it was better to blot out all record of Feige;

however, I must admit that I can think of no cogent reason why he would want to do this.

It is impossible to reconcile the Feige/Marut/Torsvan stories of into a watertight, totally consistent and credible biography. The old trickster has fooled us again.

A Red Herring?

If the above were not confusing enough, I recently discovered the work of a German American writer called Hans Otto Storm (1895-1941). I was immediately interested in the word association: Storm-Marut-Gales as well as: Otto Feige-Otto Storm and decided to add this tid bit of research to an already bubbling pot of intrigue.

Storm was born in Bloomington, Southern California and was a descendant of German refugees fleeing from the anti-socialist persecution that followed the failure of nationalist revolutions in Europe from 1848-1849. He was an engineer by training and led a very active life including long spells in Peru and Nicaragua. He spent two years in American Army hospitals during WW I. He died of electric shock on 11 December 1941 while rushing to complete a large radio transformer in the laboratory. On a number of occasions Traven when posing as Torsvan put down his profession as engineer.

Like Traven he wrote of the sea from personal long experience. See in particular: *Made in U. S. A.* (1939). There are some remarkable similarities between his life and literary style and Traven's. The eminent literary critic Edmund Wilson said of Storm: "his style has always been hampered by an uncertainty about idiomatic English and a proclivity for German locutions" (Wilson 1941, 36). We have seen the same sort of reaction to Traven's written and spoken English.

His last and best book *Pity the Tyrant* (1937) is about an American technician who becomes involved in a revolution in Peru. It has the same air of "that peculiar foreboding often noted by outsiders in a Spanish-American town". "People die here I tell you" the engineer writes home, "it's a place of endings" (Storm 1937, 136). There is an uncanny echo of Traven right at the beginning of the book: a bank clerk is trying to place a customer:

> "he's German." "No, he's English." "But he has a German name." "But he speaks English." "German Accent, though." That's no accent; he's
>
> English-maybe American. Look at the papers." (Storm 1937, 1)

Storm made a number of trips to Mexico. His notebooks show that on 5th April 1931 he left Los Angeles by sea en route to Nicaragua. He stopped off at Mazatlán (Storm 1948, 228-230). Storm's short story, "The Well-worn Mantle" was probably written on this first visit to Mexico; it is very Travenesque and one wonders if at the very least the two men met. In December 1938 Storm flew to Lima, and during four days in the air passed through Mexicali, Hermosillo, Guayamas, Mazatalán, Guadalajara and Tapachula, the last port before Guatemala (Storm 1948, 289-291). Traven also trained for his pilot's license. He acquired a half share in a small aircraft and in the 1930s spent much time in San Antonio Texas learning to fly (Zogbaum, 98-99).

Storm's other novels are also worth looking at. *Full Measure* (1929) is about industrial expansion and could only have been written by an engineer. It is very long at nearly 400 pages but not without humor. In its infancy the radiotelegraph required "power equal to that of a fair-sized locomotive to produce, at the receiving end, a sound similar in pitch and volume to that issued by a somewhat undernourished cricket" (Storm 1929, 390). His last book, *Count Ten* (1940) is far too long at 623 pages but again shows his technical skill and expertise. Like Traven he creates art from experience. He is a possible name to add to the list of candidates vying for the mantle of "Traven".

Vale

I cannot end without coming back to Traven's often strident complaint that people worry too much about the man and not enough about what he has achieved. Like Wagner, of whom I have also written at length, his achievement in his art is what really matters, and speculation about his life, no matter how intriguing, is incidental (Pateman, 2002). It seems unlikely that the enigma of Traven's origins will ever be solved; he has been so adept at hiding his traces and laying so many plausible false trails; so perhaps we should stop ferreting away and let his ashes blow away in peace.

But Traven's life is important in its steadfast commitment to the ideals of anarchism. Zola on being asked to define an anarchist said, "*un anarchiste, c'est un poète*". Conversely, the poet is more or less of an anarchist (Sanborn, 361). It has been said that the present-day revolution in Chiapas rose from the ashes of a dead mahogany forest. It is also symbolically important as well as literally and poetically true to end with a comment that it has risen from the ashes of a dead anarchist– those of Traven were scattered over the forest in 1969.

Notes

1. It is ironic to note that the number of hits recorded by Hal Croves on the major search engines, google.com and yahoo.com exceed those of B. Traven; Rosa Elena Luján is not far behind him.

2. One source suggests that Traven had experienced a number of homosexual affairs. Gales and Stanislaus were lovers (Raskin). No one else has raised this possibility but I suppose someone will be bound to do so eventually.

Glossary and Acronyms

abajo	underdog
abbarotero	merchant
acasillados	resident *peones*
agrarista	supporter of land reform, post-1915
aguacero	heavy downpour of rain
águila	eagle
alcalde	important village official
alguacil	a constable
amarillos	"Yellows"
AMPAS	Academy of Motion Picture Arts and Sciences
angelitos	little angels; dead babies
Anschluss	the annexation of Austria
arrieros	mule drivers
ayuntamiento	municipal government
balseros	rafters
Banditos	bandits
El Barco de los Muertos	*The Death Ship*
barranca	a ravine or canyon
Die Baumwollpflücker	*The Cotton pickers*
bayadère	Indian female temple dancer
BBC	British Broadcasting Corporation
La bellísima	Tina Modotti
boga	to guide a log into the river
Bola	local political skirmish
bonito	good or beautiful
borrachales	drunkards
boyeros	ox drivers

bracero	field hand
Die Brücke im Dschungel	*The Bridge in the Jungle*
brujo	sorcerer
Büchergilde	book club
Burros	donkeys
Caballeros	gentlemen
cabildo	jail
cabrón	cuckold
caca	excrement
Cachuchas	cunts
Caciques	local unofficial political bosses
caciquismo	leadership
cafetero	laborer on a coffee plantation
callejoneros	path cutters
calpulli	mounds of ancient pueblos
Camarilla	political clique
Camino Real	the King's Highway
campesinos	peasants
cangaceiro	social bandit
caoba	mahogany
capataces	foremen
caracajadas	belly laughs
carasapo	frog-face; Diego Rivera to Frida Kahlo
carrancismo	the ideology surrounding Carranza
carrancista	supporter of Venustiano Carranza
The Carreta	*The Cart*
carretero	cart driver
cartucho	cartridge
Casa Del Obrero Mundial	House of the Workers of the World
caucho	rubber
Caudillo	supreme boss, charismatic leader
caxlane	white (corruption of *castellano*)
cayuqueros	canoe-men
CCRI	Clandestine Revolutionary Indian Committee
Centaur of the North	Pancho Villa
Central	logging camp headquarters
CGT	*Confederacion General de Trabajadores* (General Confederation of Workers) "*rojos*" "Reds"
charros	landlords
Chelana	pet name of Rosa Elena Luján

Glossary and Acronyms 169

chicleros	*chicle* gatherers
chingada	the violated one
chisme	malicious gossip
cholo	half-breed
chozas	huts
chulel	the soul dwelling within an animal
científicos	nickname of Díaz's ruling clique
Ciudad	city
civilizado	live, dress and speak like a *Ladino*
cochino	pig
coloradors	Pascual Orozco's troops
comiteco	locally made brandy
commandante	police chief
compadres	buddies
confradía	a confraternity
Conquistador	conqueror
contralistas	contractors
corridos	popular ballads
cortes	national parliament
costumbre	Indian customary law
coyotes	overseers or smugglers of wetbacks
criollos	of pure Spanish descent born in Mexico
Cristeros	reactionary religious bandits
CROM	*Confederacion Regional Obrera Mexicana* (Regional Confederation of Mexican Labor) Yellows, *amarillos*
cuadrilla	team on coffee plantations
El cuartel	barracks
Cuauhtémoc	sweeping eagle
cura	parish priest
cursi	vulgar
DDR	German Democratic Republic
Deacena Trágica, la	Ten Days that Shattered the Nation
decente	respectable
El Desierto de la Soledad	the wilderness of solitude
desorejamiento	cropping of ears
Dia de los muertos	November 2nd
dieguitos	assistants of Rivera
dorados	Pancho Villa's golden boys
ejidatarios	possessors of land rights
ejido	individual piece of communal land

enganchadores	contractors of migrant labor
entrada	expedition or raid
Erlebensträger	carrier of experiences
ESOL	English as a Second Language
EZLN	*Ejército Zapatista de Liberación Nacional*- (Zapatista Army of National Liberation)
FBI	Federal Bureau of Investigation
federales	federal troops under Díaz
FEME	*Femgericht*, pre-Nazi political killer squads
filbustero	soldier of fortune
finca	landed estate
finqueros	ranchers
Frijoles	black beans
Gachupín	rude word for Spaniard
Gañanes	ox driver's assistants
Ein general kommt aus dem Dschungel	The General from the Jungle
gente de razon	white men
Gobierno	Government
golfo	good for nothing
Graf	Count
Gringo	white man; American
Guardia blanca	a private militia used to prevent land reform
Guerra de castas	War of the Castes (1867-1870)
hacendado	owner of a hacienda
hachero	axeman
Hacienda	estate
heimat	home
HUAAC	House Un-American Activities Committee
huacaleros	carriers
Huaraches	sandals
Huitzilopochtli	God of War
!Huy¡	wow!
indigenismo	recognition of the worth of Indian ethnicity
indigenista	indigenously created, or about Indians
indios	Indians
indulto	pardoning the bull at the bullfight
ingeniero	university trained engineer
los ingenios	sugar refineries

I.W.W.	Industrial Workers of the World
Jefe máxima	Calles after his Presidency officially ended
jefe politico	principal civilian officer
journalero	temporary day worker
Junta	military dictatorship
KPD	*Kommunistiche Partei Deutschlands* (German Communist Party)
Der Karren	*The Cart*
Ladino	Spanish settler
Land des Frühlings	*Land of Springtime*
LAPD SWAT	Los Angeles Police Department Special Weapons Action Team
lektor	foreign language assistant
leperadas	four letter words
licienciado	attorney
Llano	the plain
los de abajo	the underdogs
macheteros	jungle clearers
Machismo	manliness
Maderista	supporter of Francisco I. Madero
Maestro	rural schoolteacher
Maguey	*Agave americana*
maíz	corn
Majordomo	*hacienda* foreman
malpaíz	badlands
mapaches	reactionary landowners in Chiapas
máquina loca	locomotive packed with dynamite
marrano	pig or (abusively) a poor Jew
Der Marsch ins Reich der Caoba	*March to Caobaland*
Maximato	the rule of puppet presidents
mescal	distilled *pulque*
mestizaje	blending of Indian and European
mestizo	of mixed race
mexicanismos	Mexican turns of phrase
milagros	miracles; amulets
milpa	a plot of maize
modernismo	literary regeneration; modernization
monteador	scout searching for mahogany

montería	mahogany logging camps
monteros	tree fellers
mordida	bribe; bite
moscas	flies; hangers on
moza	guide
m'tito	little son
muchacho	boy
nahual	fearsome night-time spirit
negrero	slave dealer
niña	girl or white woman
nordismo	dominance of the North during the Revolution
norteamericanos	from the USA
Nouveaux riches	the newly rich
"Okies"	migrant workers from Oklahoma
orozquistas	followers of General Orozco
pachucos	urban Mexican gang members in the U. S.
pampa	grassland
paraje	camp site
El Parque Cachú	Cashew Park
Patria chica	hometown
patrón	the owner; chief; boss
PCM	*Partido Communista Mexicana* (Mexican Communist Party)
pendéjo	dumb
peón	slave or peasant
peónism	slavery
petate	rush mat
pícaro	the picaresque
pistoleros	bandits
PNR	*Partido Nacional Revolucionário* (National Revolutionary Party)
Porfiriato	the age of Porfirio Díaz
Posada	stopping place or inn
precursora	forerunner of The Revolution
PRI	*Partido Revoluciónario Institucional* (Institutional Revolutionary Party)
Pueblo	a small independent village or town
Puente en la Selva	*The Bridge in the Jungle*
Pulpería	a run-down bar

Glossary and Acronyms

pulque	alcoholic drink made from *agave* juice
putas	whores
Quetzalcoatl	The Plumed Serpent
Radix malorum est Cupiditas	avarice is the root of all evil
ranchería	where the peons live on a hacienda
Ranchero	a farmer
Rancho	a small or medium size farm
Räterepublik	Republic of Councils
La Raza	race
La Rebelión de los Colgados	The Rebellion of the Hanged
Die Rebellion der Gehenkten	The Rebellion of the Hanged
Regierung	Government
Reichstag	Parliament, Congress
retablos	painted and ornamented altarpieces
La Révolte des pendus	The Rebellion of the Hanged
rojos	Reds
La Rosa Blanca	The White Rose
rurales	federal mounted police
Der Schatz der Sierra Madre	The Treasure of the Sierra Madre
secretario de municipalidad	town secretary
selva	forest
semaneos	small forest logging camps
Serapes	blankets
seringueiros	rubber-tappers
simpático	sympathetic
Sindicato	a labor union or grouping of unions
soldaderos	female camp followers
Sonnen-Schöpfung	Creation of the Sun and Moon
Sugi-Mugi	deck hand on a ship
Tata/taita	daddy
tejones	badgers, false *maderistas*
Tepozteko	God of Drunkenness
El Tesoro de la Sierra Madre	The Treasure of the Sierra Madre

tienda de raya	the company store
tierra caliente	hot country
tierra fría	cold country
tierra y libertad	land and liberty
Tlaloc	God of Rain
TLS	Times Literary Supplement
Das Tottenschiff	*The Death Ship*
trozas	logs
tumbo	dump
UCB	University of California Berkeley
UCLA	University of California Los Angeles
UCR	University of California Riverside
UCSD	University of California San Diego
USC	University of Southern California
Vaqueros	cowboys, mounted troops
vendidos	sell outs
venta	an inn
viejo	old man
Villista	a supporter of Pancho Villa
völkisch	folk nationalism
Die Weisse Rose	*The White Rose*
WFM	Western Federation of Miners
Xochiquetzal	Goddess of Flowers
YRL	Young Research Library
Zapatismo	the active political philosophy of Zapata
Der Ziegelbrenner	*The Brick Maker*
zócala	marketplace or square
zopilotes	vultures

Bibliography

Aaron, Daniel. *Writers on the Left: Episodes in American Literary Communism.* New York: Harcourt Brace & World, 1961.
Abreu Gómez, Ermilo. *Canek* translated by David Heft. Washington D.C.: Williams and Heintz, 1940.
Acken, Edgar L. "Revolt in the Jungle." *The New York Herald Tribune Book Review* (20 April 1952): 8.
Adrian, Dennis. "H. C. Westermann's Sculptures, 1954-1981: Fragments of a Critical Introduction." *Exhibition Catalogue.* Chicago: Museum of Contemporary Art, 2001, 34-49.
"Adventure Unglossed." *Time* (17 June 1953): 74-75.
Agee, James. *Agee on Film: Criticism and Comment on the Movies.* New York: Modern Library, 2000.
Alarcón, Daniel Cooper. *The Aztec Palimpsest: Mexico in the Modern Imagination.* Tucson: The University of Arizona Press, 1997.
Alexander, Robert J. *Trotskyism in Latin America.* Stanford: Hoover Institution Press, 1973.
Allsop, Kenneth. *Hard Travellin': The Hobo and His History.* New York: New American Library, 1967.
"Also Out this Week: Fiction." *New Yorker* (28 April 1934): 102.
Anaya A. Rudolfo. *The Silence of the Llano: Short Stories.* Berkeley: Tonatiuh-Quinto Sol International, 1982.
Ashliman, Dee L. "The American West in Nineteenth Century German Fiction." *Ph. D. Dissertation.* Rutgers University: 1969.
Avant, John Alfred. "The Carreta." *Library Journal* 95 5 (1 March 1970): 915.
Azuela Mariano. *Los caciques.* Mexico: Talleres Editoriales de la Compañía Periodísta Nacional, 1917.
_____ *Domitilo quiere ser diputado.* Mexico: A. Carranza e Hijos, 1918.

_____ *Las moscas*. Mexico: A. Carranza e Hijos, 1918.

_____ *Las tribulaciones de una familia decente*. Tampico: Biblioteca de El Mundo, 1918.

_____ *Two Novels of Mexico: The Flies; The Bosses* translated by Lesley Byrd Simpson. Berkeley: University of California Press, 1956.

_____ *Three Novels: The Trials of a Respectable Family; The Underdogs; The Firefly* translated by Francis Kellam Hendricks and Beatrice Berler. San Antonio: Trinity University Press, 1979.

_____ *The Underdogs* translated by Frederick H. Fornoff. Pittsburgh: University of Pittsburgh Press, 1992.

Balio, Tino. "Foreword." *The Treasure of the Sierra Madre* edited by James Naremore. Madison: University of Wisconsin Press, 1979, 7-8.

Bang, Herman. *Denied a Country* translated by Marie Busch and A. G. Chater. New York: Alfred A. Knopf, 1927.

Barber, Michael. "Paperbacks." *Books and Bookmen* 337 (October 1983): 36.

Barrette, Bill. "Foreword." Westermann, Horace Clifford. *Letters*. New York: Timken Publishers, 1988.

Barrow, Leo L. "Still another Definition of Jazz Literature." *B. Traven: Life and Work* edited by Ernst Schürer and Phillip Jenkins. University Park: The Pennsylvania University Press, 1987, 137-140.

Baumann, Friederike. "B. Traven's *Land des Frühlings* and the Caoba Cycle as a Source for the Study of Agrarian Society." *B. Traven: Life and Work* edited by Ernst Schürer and Phillip Jenkins. University Park: The Pennsylvania University Press, 1987, 245-257.

Baumann, Michael Leopold. "A Discussion of Four B. Traven Questions with Particular Attention to the Death Ship." *Ph. D. Dissertation*. University of Pennsylvania: 1971.

_____ *B. Traven: An Introduction*. Albuquerque: University of New Mexico Press, 1976.

_____ "B. Traven: Realist and Prophet." *The Virginia Quarterly Review* 50 (Winter 1977): 73-85.

_____ "Review of *To the Honourable Miss S....*" *Small Press Review* 14 (June-July 1982): 32.

_____ "Some Problems with *The White Rose*." *B. Traven: Life and Work* edited by Ernst Schürer and Phillip Jenkins. University Park: The Pennsylvania University Press, 1987, 25-43.

Beals, Carleton. *Brimstone and Chili: A Book of Personal Experiences in the Southwest and in Mexico.* New York: Alfred A. Knopf, 1927.

Bechofer Roberts, C. E. "Some New Novels." *The New English Weekly* IV (1 February 1934): 249.

Beck, Johannes, Klaus Bergmann, and Heiner Boehncke, eds. *Das B. Traven-Buch.* Reinbek bei Hamburg: Rowohlt Taschenbuch Verlag, 1976.

Beevers, John. "All Abroad." *Time and Tide* XV (15 September 1934): 1143-1144.

Bek-Gran, Robert. *Vom Wessen der Anarchie.* Nürnberg: Verlag Der Bund, 1920.

Benjamin, Thomas Louis. "Passages to Leviathan: Chiapas and the Mexican State, 1891-1947." *Ph. D. Dissertation.* Michigan State University: 1981.

Beresford, J. D. "Four Good Stories." *The Manchester Guardian Weekly* XLII (15 March 1940): 215.

Berkhofer, Robert. F. Jr. *The White Man's Indian: Images of the American Indian from Columbus to the Present.* New York: Vintage Books, 1979.

Berler, Beatrice. "Introduction." Mariano Azuela, *Three Novels: The Trials of a Respectable Family; The Underdogs; The Firefly* translated by Francis Kellam Hendricks and Beatrice Berler. San Antonio: Trinity University Press, 1979, xv.

Berman, Paul. "B. Traven I Presume." *Michigan Quarterly Review* 17 1 (Winter 1978): 82-96.

_____ "Weimar in the Sierra Madre." *New Republic* 184 9 (Winter 1978): 24-27.

Bernfeld, Siegfried. "Letter." *New York Times Book Review* (1970): 10.

Betz, Albrecht. *Hanns Eisler: Political Musician.* Cambridge: Cambridge University Press, 1982.

Birbeck, George, ed. *Boswell's Life of Johnson, ii.* Oxford: Clarendon Press, 1934.

Bishop, Morchard. "Rough Stuff in Novels." *John O'London's Weekly* LXI (1 February 1952): 111.

Blom, Frans and Gertrude Duby. *La Selva Lacandona.* Mexico, D.F.: Editorial Cultura, 1955.

Blom, Gertrude. *Bearing Witness* edited by Alex Harris and Margaret Sartor. Chapel Hill: University of North Carolina Press, 1984.

_____ "The Jungle is Burning." *Mexico through Foreign Eyes, 1859-1990* edited by Carole Naggar and Fred Ritchin. New York: W.W. Norton & Company, 1993, 145-148.

Blom, Gertrude and Frans Blom. "Lacondon." *The Handbook of Middle American Indians: Ethnology Part One* edited by Robert

Wauchope and Evon Z. Vogt. Austin: The University of Texas, 1969, 276-297.

Blume, Mary. "Review." *Los Angeles Times* (10 July 1970).

Bonney, Mary Anne. "Review of *The Night Visitor and Other Stories*." *Punch* 285 (30 November 1983): 72.

Book List. "Review of *The Cotton Pickers*." 65 (15 July 1969): 1261.

_____ "Review of *The General from the Jungle*." 69 (15 July 1973): 1050.

The Bookman. "Review of *Die Weisse Rose*." LXXX 477 (June 1931): 162.

Bourget-Pailleron, Robert. "Souvenirs et Romans (1)." *Revue des Deux Mondes* 45 (May 1938): 313-224.

Brandenburg, Frank, *The Making of Modern Mexico*. Englewood Cliffs: Prentice-Hall, 1964.

_____ "Revolutionary Achievements in Economic Life." *Is the Mexican Revolution Dead?* edited by Stanley R. Ross. New York: Alfred A. Knopf, 1966, 228-245.

Braybrooke, Neville. "The Hero without a Name: Some Notes on B. Traven's *The Death Ship*." *Texas Quarterly* 6 4 (Winter 1963): 140-144.

_____ "Reassessment: The Hero without a Name, B. Traven's *The Death Ship*." *The Spectator* (13 August 1965): 212.

Brenner, Anita. *Idols behind Altars: the Story of the Mexican Spirit*. Boston: Beacon Press, 1970.

_____ *The Wind that Swept Mexico; The History of the Mexican Revolution, 1910-1942*. Austin: University of Texas Press, 1971.

Breton, André. *La Révolution Surréaliste 8*. Paris: Editions Surréalistes, 1926.

_____ "Frida Kahlo and Mexican Art." *Catalogue of Exhibition*. London: Whitechapel Art Gallery, 1982, 35-36.

"Briefly Noted Fiction." *New Yorker* (10 May 1952): 137-138.

Bright, John. *Worms in the Winecup: A Memoir*. Lanham: The Scarecrow Press, 2002.

Brissenden, Paul F. *The I.W.W.: A Study of American Syndicalism*. New York: Russell & Russell, 1957.

Britton, John. A. *Carleton Beals: A Radical Journalist in Latin America*. Albuquerque: University of New Mexico Press, 1987.

Brooks, Frank H. *The Individualist Anarchist: An Anthology of Liberty (1881-1908)*. New Brunswick: Transaction Books, 1994.

Brown, Elizabeth. *Albert Pinkham Ryder*. Washington: Smithsonian Institution Press, 1989.

Browne, Wynard. "Fiction-I." *The London Mercury* (March 1934): 462-464.

Brushwood, John S. *Mexico in its Novel: A Nation's Search for Identity.* Austin: University of Texas Press, 1966.
Buber, Martin. *Between Man and Man* translated by Ronald G. Smith. New York: Macmillan Company, 1965.
Buchan, William. "Fantasy Perhaps." *The Spectator* 219 7254 (7 July 1967): 23-24.
Die Büchergilde. 11 (November 1931).
Büchner, *Georg. Woyzeck* translated by Geoffrey Motton. London: Nick Hern Books, 1996.
Bunyan, John. *The Pilgrim's Progress: From This World to That Which is to Come* (Part I first published in 1678; Part II in 1684). London: Paradine, 1978.
Burdett, Oscar. "Fiction." *The English Review* LX (June 1935): 755-756.
Byam, Milton S. *"Rebellion of the Hanged." Library Journal* 77 8 (15 April 1952): 717.

Cacucci, Pino. *Tina Modotti: A Life* translated by Patricia J. Duncan. New York: St. Martin's Press, 1999.
Calder-Marshall, Arthur. "The Novels of B. Traven." *Horizon* 1 7 (July 1940): 522-528.
Calderón de la Barca, Marquise Fanny (Frances Erskine Inglis). *Life in Mexico, during a Residence of Two Years in that Country.* Garden City: Doubleday, 1966.
Campobello, Nellie. *Cartucho: Relatos de la Lucha en el Norte de Mexico.* México, D. F.: Ediciones Integrales, 1931.
"Candido and the Capitalists." *Time* 59 (21 April 1952): 114.
Capitanchik, Maurice. "Identity Card." *The Spectator* 222 (28 June 1969): 856-857.
Capouta, Emile. "Bookmarks." *The Nation* 221 (29 November 1975): 569-570.
Carey, James C. *The Mexican Revolution in Yucatan, 1915-1924.* Boulder: Westview, 1984.
Carroll, John. *Breakout from the Crystal Palace: the Anarchopsychological Critique: Stirner, Nietzsche, Dostoevsky.* London: Routledge, 1974.
Cartano, Tony. *After the Conquest* translated by Steve Cox. London: Secker & Warburg, 1988.
Carter, Boyd. "The Mexican Novel at Mid-Century." *Prairie Schooner* XXVIII 2 (Summer 1954): 143-156.
Casanova, Pablo González. "The Mexico Which Has and the Mexico Which Has Not." *Is the Mexican Revolution Dead?* edited by Stanley R. Ross. New York: Alfred A. Knopf, 1966, 217-227.

Castaneda, Carlos. *The Teachings of Don Juan: a Yaqui Way of Knowledge*. Berkeley: University of California Press, 1968.

_____ *Journey to Ixtlan: The Lessons of Don Juan*. New York: Simon & Schuster, 1971.

Castellanos, Rosario. *Balúm Canán*. México, D. F.: Fondo de Cultura e Económica, 1957.

_____ *The Book of Lamentations* translated by Esther Allen. New York: Marsilio Publishing, 1996.

Céline, Louis Ferdinand. *Bagatelles pour un massacre*. Paris: Denoël. 1937.

_____ *Death on the Installment Plan* translated by Ralph Mannheim. New York: New Directions, 1966.

_____ *Journey to the End of the Night* translated by Ralph Mannheim. London: Calder, 1988.

"Central American Anecdote." *Time* (18 July 1938): 50-51.

Ceplair, Larry. *Hollywood Blacklist: John Bright*. Los Angeles: Oral History Program, UCLA, 1991.

Cerruto, Oscar. "Bruno Traven, El Escritor Incognito." Introduction to *El Barco de Los Muertos*. Mexico: no publisher indicated, 1945, 7-14.[1]

Chamberlain, John. "The World in Books." *Current History* XLII (August 1935): xii.[2]

_____ *New York Times* (11 June 1935): 19.

Changing Times. "The Bookshelf: Fiction." 33 (December 1979): 31.

Chankin, Donald O. *Anonymity and Death: the Fiction of B. Traven*. University Park: Pennsylvania State University Press, 1975.

_____ "Review of *B. Traven: Life and Work* edited by Ernst Schürer and Phillip Jenkins. *Modern Fiction Studies* 43 2 (Summer 1988): 233-234.

Charlot, Jean. *The Mexican Mural Renaissance, 1920-1925*. New Haven: Yale University Press, 1963.

Charques, R. D. "Fiction." *The Spectator* CLXXXVIII (25 January 1952): 122.

Cheuse, Alan. "Leftist, Didactic and Inspired." *The Nation* 216 (8 January 1973): 56-58.

_____ "Review of *General from the Jungle*." *New York Times Book Review* (26 August 1973): 24-25.

_____ "The Treasure of the Calle Mississippi." *Los Angeles Times* (15 February 1974): 3.

_____ "Eight Short Travens: *The Kidnapped Saint*." *New York Times Book Review* (19 October 1975): 34, 36.

_____ *Listening to the Page: Adventures in Reading and Writing*. New York: Columbia University Press, 2001.

Choice. "English and American: Traven, *The Night Visitor.*" III (July 1966): 413.

―――――― "English and American: Traven, *The Cotton Pickers.*" VI (January 1970): 1579.

―――――― "Germanic: Traven, *The Carreta.*" VIII (July 1971): 680.

―――――― "Review of *The Rebellion of the Hanged.*" 9 (February 1973): 1586.

―――――― "Review of *The Death Ship.*" 10 (September 1973): 968.

―――――― "Review of *The General from the Jungle.*" 10 (September 1973): 969.

―――――― "Review of *The Kidnapped Saint and Other Stories.*" 13 (July/August 1976): 656.

Christensen, Peter Glenn. "Legend, Story and Flashback in *The Treasure of the Sierra Madre* and *Nostromo.*" *B. Traven: Life and Work* edited by Ernst Schürer and Phillip Jenkins. University Park: The Pennsylvania University Press, 1987, 326-336.

Cicora, Mary A. *From History to Myth: Wagner's Tannhäuser and its Literary Sources.* Bern: Peter Lang, 1992.

Cinquemani, Frank L. "Review of *Government.*" *Library Journal* 96 (1 May 1971): 1639.

Coblentz, Stanton A. *Avarice: A History.* Washington, D.C.: Public Affairs Press, 1965.

Cohen, Allen and Harry Lawton. *John Huston: a Guide to References and Resources.* New York: G.K. Hall & Co., 1997.

Cohn, Norman. *The Pursuit of the Millennium.* London: Palladin, 1970.

Colcord, Lincoln. "A Powerful Book Unfettered, Wild." *The New York Herald Tribune Books* (13 May 1934): 5.

Collier, George A. with Elizabeth Lowery Quaratiello. *Basta!: Land and the Zapatista Rebellion in Chiapas.* Oakland: Institute for Food and Development Policy, 1994.

Connolly, Cyril. "New Novels." *The New Statesman-Nation* (27 April 1935): 593-594.

Conrad, Joseph. *Nostromo: A Tale of the Seaboard.* New York: Holt, Rinehart & Winston, 1961.

―――――― *The Shadow Line: a Confession "Worthy of Undying Regard."* Oxford: Oxford University Press, 1985.

―――――― *Typhoon and Other Stories.* New York: Knopf, 1991.

―――――― *The Heart of Darkness with The Congo Diary.* Harmondsworth: Penguin Books, 1995.

Constantine, Mildred. *Tina Modotti: A Fragile Life.* New York: Paddington Press, 1975.

Cook, Bruce. "The Great B. Traven Mystery...Is He the Kaiser's Illegitimate Son?" *The National Observer* VI (27 November 1967): 1, 11.

_____ *Dalton Trumbo*. New York: Charles Scribner's Sons, 1977.

Cooper, James Fennimore. *The Last of the Mohicans: A Narrative of 1757*. New York: Signet, 1962.

Coper, Rudolf. *Failure of a Revolution: Germany in 1918-1919*. Cambridge: Cambridge University Press, 1955.

Cordan, Wolfgang. *Secret of the Forest: on the Track of Maya Temples* translated by Basil Creighton. Garden City: Doubleday & Company, 1964.

Countiño, César Bezares. *La simiente del corsario*. Mexico: Editoria Libro Americana, 1958.

Cowell, Pattie. "'Sailing with Sealed Orders': Herman Melville's *White-Jacket* and B. Traven's *The Death Ship*." *B. Traven: Life and Work* edited by Ernst Schürer and Phillip Jenkins. University Park: The Pennsylvania University Press, 1987, 316-325.

Creighton, Basil. *An Edwardian Romance*. London: Fairfax Hall, 1976.

Dahlhaus, Carl and John Deathridge. *The New Grove Wagner*. New York: Norton & Company, 1984.

Dana, Richard Henry. *Two Years before the Mast: A Personal Narrative of Life at Sea*. New York: Penguin, 1981.

Davis, Joseph Addison. "Rolling Home: The Open Road as Myth and Symbol in American Literature, 1890-1940." *Ph. D. Dissertation*. The University of Michigan: 1974.

De Lara, L. Guiterrez and Edgcumb Pinchon. *The Mexican People: Their Struggle for Freedom*. Garden City: Doubleday, Page & Co., 1914.

Deathridge, John, ed. *Family Letters of Richard Wagner* translated by William Ashton Ellis. Ann Arbor: University of Michigan Press, 1991.

_____ "Wagner and the post-modern." *Cambridge Opera Journal* 4 2 (1992): 143-161.

DeLeon, David. *The American as Anarchist: Reflections on Indigenous Radicalism*. Baltimore: John Hopkins Press, 1978.

Dickens, Charles. *Hard Times: For These Times* (first published in 1854). New York: W.W. Norton, 2001.

Doerflinger, William. "Review of *The Death Ship*." *The Saturday Review of Literature* (5 May 1934): 677.

Dos Passos, John. *The 42nd Parallel*; *Nineteen Nineteen*; *The Big Money*. London: J. Lehman, 1950.

Dubofsky, Melvyn, *We Shall Be All: A History of the Industrial Workers of the World.* Chicago: Quadrangle Books, 1969.
Dugrand, Alain. *Trotsky in Mexico* translated by Pierre Broué. Manchester: Carcanet, 1992.
Dulsey, Bernard M. "Foreword." Icaza, Jorge. *Huasipungo: The Villagers* translated by Bernard M. Dulsey. Carbondale: Southern Illinois University Press, 1973, xi-xv.
Dunn. H. H. *The Crimson Jester: Zapata of Mexico.* New York: Robert M. McBride, 1933.
Durant, Jack D. "Review of B. Traven's *The Night Visitor and Other Stories.*" *Studies in Short Fiction* VI (Fall 1967): 92-94.
Durgnat, Raymond. *Luis Buñuel.* London: Studio Vista, 1967.

Eagleton, Terry. *Exiles and Émigrés: Studies in Modern Literature.* London: Chatto & Windus, 1970.
Edberg, George J. "Review of *El Tesoro de la Sierra Madre* edited by Mario B. Rodríguez." *Modern Language Journal* XLVIII 5 (May 1964): 393.
Edwards, Stewart. "Introduction." *Selected Writings of Pierre-Joseph Proudhon.* London: Macmillan, 1970.
Egbert, Donald D. *Social Radicalism and the Arts: Western Europe.* New York: Knopf, 1970.
Emerson, Ralph W. *Society and Solitude.* Boston: Houghton Mifflin, 1904.
Engell, John. "*The Treasure of the Sierra Madre*: B. Traven, John Huston and Ideology in Film Adaptation." *Literature/Film Quarterly* 17 4 (1989): 245-252.
_____ "Traven, Huston, and the Textual Treasures of the Sierra Madre." *Reflections in a Male Eye: John Huston and the American Experience* edited by Gaylyn Studlar and David Desser. Washington D.C.: Smithsonian Institution Press, 1993, 79-95.
Essbach, Wolfgang. "Language without a Master: Max Stirner's Influence on B. Traven." *B. Traven: Life and Work* edited by Ernst Schürer and Phillip Jenkins. University Park: The Pennsylvania University Press, 1987, 101-119.
Etulain, Richard W. ed. *Jack London on the Road: The Tramp Diary and Other Hobo Writings.* Logan: Utah State University Press, 1979.
Eyman, Scott. *Five American Cinematographers: Interviews with Karl Strauss, Joseph Ruttenberg, James Wong Howe, Linwood Dunn, and William H. Clothier.* Metuchen: The Scarecrow Press, 1987.

Fadiman, Clifton. "The Great Traven Mystery." *The New Yorker* XI (15 June 1935): 66-67.

Farmer, David John. *A Catalogue of the Collection of B. Traven's Treasure of the Sierra Madre*. Austin: The University of Texas, Humanities Research Center, 1968.

Fehervary, Helen. *Anna Seghers: The Mythic Dimension*. Ann Arbor: The University of Michigan Press, 2001.

Ferguson, Otis. "Action Stuff." *The New Republic* (27 July 1938): 340-341.

Flandrau, Charles Macomb. *Viva Mexico*. Urbana: University of Illinois Press, 1964.

Flandrau, Grace. "A Drama of Simple People." *The Saturday Review of Literature* XVIII (30 July 1938): 6.

Flantz, Richard. "A Sane Protagonist in *Extremis*: B. Traven's Gay Imaging of Participation and Suffering in *The Bridge in the Jungle* and *The Death Ship*." *B. Traven: Life and Work* edited by Ernst Schürer and Phillip Jenkins. University Park: The Pennsylvania University Press, 1987, 120-136.

Fraser, John, "The Novels of B. Traven." *The Graduate Student of English* I 1 (Fall 1958): 7-15.

_____ "Rereading Traven's *The Death Ship*." *The Southern Review* IX (January 1963): 69-92.

_____ "Splendor in the Darkness: B. Traven's *The Death Ship*." *The Dalhousie Review* 44 1 (Spring 1964): 35-43.

Friedrich, Paul. *Agrarian Revolt in a Mexican Village*. Englewood Cliffs: Prentice-Hall, 1970.

Frohock, W. M. *The Novel of Violence in America*. Dallas: The Southern Methodist University Press, 1957.

Fuentes, Carlos. *La región más transparente*. Mexico: Fondo de Cultura e Económica, 1958.

_____ *The Death of Artemio Cruz* translated by Sam Hileman. New York: Farrar, Strauss and Giroux, 1962.

_____ "The Barefoot *Iliad*." *The Underdogs* (*critical edition*) translated by Frederick H. Fornoff. Pittsburgh: University of Pittsburgh Press, 1992, 123-140.

Gallegos, Rómulo. *Canaima* translated by Will Kirkland. Pittsburgh: University of Pittsburgh Press, 1996.

Garland, Peter. *Americas: Essays on American Music and Culture, 1973-80*. Santa Fe: Soundings Press, 1982.

Geismar, Maxwell. "Peons in Agony." *The Saturday Review* XXV (26 April 1952): 15-16.

Geller, Stephen. "*The Cotton Pickers*." *The Saturday Review* (19 July 1969): 40.

Georg, Eugen. *The Adventure of Mankind* translated by Robert Bek-Gran. New York: E.P. Dutton & Company, 1931.[3]
Georg, Manfred. "Do You Know B. Traven?" *Die Weltbühne* XXV (24 September 1929): 484-487.
_____ "B. Traven's Identity." *New Republic* CXVI (24 March 1947): 35.
Gilly, Aldofo. *The Mexican Revolution* translated by Patrick Camiller. London: Verso, 1983.
Goldman, Emma. *Anarchism and Other Essays.* New York: Dover, 1969.
Gonzalez, Manuel Pedro. *Trayectoria de la Novela en México.* México D. F.: Botas, 1951.
Gonzalez, Mike. *Diego Rivera: The Man Who Painted Walls.* London: Redwords, 1992.
Goss, Robert T. "From Ret Marut to B. Traven: More than a Change in Disguise." *B. Traven: Life and Work* edited by Ernst Schürer and Phillip Jenkins. University Park: The Pennsylvania University Press, 1987, 44-55.
Gott, Richard. *Punch.* (18 June 1980): 982.
Graf, Oskar Maria. *Prisoners All* translated by Margaret Green. New York: Alfred A. Knopf, 1928.
Green, Martin. *Dreams of Adventure, Deeds of Empire.* London: Routledge & Kegan Paul, 1980.
Greene, Graham. *Nineteen Stories.* London: William Heinemann, 1947.
_____ *The Power and The Glory.* New York: Viking, 1962.
_____ *Another Mexico.* New York: Viking, 1964.
Gregory, Horace. "In the Mexican Mountains." *The New York Herald Tribune Books* (9 June 1935): 5.
Grimm Jacob and Wilhelm Grimm. *German Folk Tales* translated by Francis P. Magoun, Jr., and Alexander H. Krappe. Carbondale: Southern Illinois University Press, 1960.
Gruber, Helmut. "The Political-Ethical Mission of German Expressionism." *The German Quarterly* XL 2 (March 1967): 186-203.
Gruening, Ernest. *Mexico and its Heritage.* London: Stanley Paul and Company, 1928.
Guillermoprieto, Alma. "Introduction." *The Book of Lamentations* translated by Esther Allen. New York: Marsilio Publishing, 1996, v-xii.
Guillory, Daniel L. "Review of *The Treasure of the Sierra Madre.*" *Reprint Bulletin Book Review* 25 (February 1980): 22.
Güiraldes, Ricardo. *Don Segundo Sombra* translated by Patricia Owen Steiner. Pittsburgh: University of Pittsburgh Press, 1995.

Guiteras-Holmes, Calixta. *Perils of the Soul: The World View of a Tzotzil Indian*. New York: Free Press of Glencoe, 1961.

Gunn, Drewey Wayne. *American and British Writers in Mexico, 1556-1963*. Austin: University of Texas Press, 1974.

―――――― *Mexico in American and British Letters: A Bibliography of Fiction and Travel Books, Citing Original Editions*. Metuchen: The Scarecrow Press, 1974A.

Guthke, Karl S. "Was There Another Man? B. Traven as Author of his own Works." *B. Traven: Life and Work* edited by Ernst Schürer and Phillip Jenkins. University Park: The Pennsylvania University Press, 1987, 12-24.

―――――― *B. Traven: Biographie eines rätsels*. Frankfurt am Main: Büchergilde Gutenberg, 1987A.

―――――― *B. Traven: the Life behind the Legends* translated by Robert C. Sprung. New York: Lawrence Hill, 1991.

―――――― *Trails in No-Man's Land: Essays in Literary and Cultural History*. Columbia, S.C.: Camden House, 1993.

Guzmán Martin Luís y Franco. *The Eagle and the Serpent* translated by Harriet de Onis. New York: Alfred A. Knopf, 1930.

Hagemann, E. R. "A Checklist of the Work of B. Traven and the Critical Estimates and Biographical Essays on Him; together with a Brief Biography." *The Papers of the Bibliographical Society of America* 53 (First Quarter 1959): 37-67.

―――――― "¡Huye! A Conjectural Biography of B. Traven." *Inter-American Review of Bibliography: Revista InterAmericana de Bibliografía* 12 (December 1960): 370-386.[4]

―――――― "Correspondence." *Powell Collection*. Los Angeles: Special Collections, Folio 12.

Hale, Edward Everett. *The Man without a Country and Other Naval Writings*. Annapolis: Naval Institute Press, 2002.

Halperin, Maurice (M. H.) "Books in Various Languages." *Books Abroad* X (Winter 1936): 101.

―――――― "Books in Spanish: Fiction." *Books Abroad* XV (Summer 1941): 336-337.

Hamsun, Knut. *Hunger* translated by Robert Bly. New York: Farrar, Strauss and Giroux, 1998.

Hanley, James. "Sugi-Mugi." *The Spectator* CLII (26 January 1934): 131.

Hanson, George Steven. "The Short Stories of B. Traven." Ph. D. Dissertation. San Diego: University of California San Diego, 1980.

Hart, John Mason. *Anarchism and the Mexican Working Class, 1860-1931*. Austin: University of Texas Press, 1978.

Hazera Lydia de León. *La novela de la selva hispanoamericana: nascimiento, desarrollo, y transformacion.* Bógata: Publicaciones del Instituto Caro y Cuervo, 1971.

_____ "The Making of Two Guerrilla Generals in Azuela's *The Underdogs* and Traven's Jungle Novels." *B. Traven: Life and Work* edited by Ernst Schürer and Phillip Jenkins. University Park: The Pennsylvania University Press, 1987, 345-355.

Heidemann, Gerd. "Das Rätsel Traven gelöst." *Stern* (25 August 1963): 8-11.

_____ "Wer ist der Mann, der Traven Heisst?" *Stern* (7 May 1967): 58-71, 170-173.

_____ *Postlagernd Tampico: Die abenteurliche Suche nach B. Traven.* Munich: Blanvalet Verlag, 1977.

Hemingway, Ernest. *The Fifth Column and the First Forty-Nine Stories.* New York: Charles Scribner's Sons, 1938.

Hendricks, Frances Kellam. "Introduction." *Three Novels: The Trials of a Respectable Family; The Underdogs; The Firefly* translated by Francis Kellam Hendricks and Beatrice Berler. San Antonio: Trinity University Press, 1979, xvii-xxiv.

Hergesheimer, Joseph. *Tampico, a Novel.* New York: Alfred A. Knopf, 1936.

Herndon, James. "How to Survive in the Jungle." *New York Times Book Review* (31 October 1971): 52-53.

Herrera, Hayden. *Frida: A Biography of Frida Kahlo.* New York: Harper & Row. 1983.

Hetmann, Frederick. *Der Mann der sich verbarg: Nachforschungenüber B. Traven.* Stuttgart: Ernst Klett, 1983.

Hewitt, Lonnie Burstein and Peggy Bernal. *10,000 Baskets.* Boston: McGraw Hill, 1995.

Hicks, Granville. *The Great Tradition: An Interpretation of American Literature since the Civil War.* New York: The Macmillan Company, 1935.

_____ "Proletarian Mystery." *New Masses* XVI (16 July 1935): 23.

_____ "Romancers of the Left." *New Masses* XXVIII (23 August 1938): vi.

Hill, Lawrence. "Letter to the Editor." *New York Times Book Review* (27 December 1970): 10.

Hillerman, Tony ed. *The Best American Mystery Stories of the Century.* Boston: Houghton Mifflin, 2000.

Hilton, James. "Review of *The Treasure of the Sierra Madre*." *The Daily Telegraph* (11 September 1934).

_____ *Good-Bye Mr. Chips.* Boston: Little, Brown, 1962.

_____ *Lost Horizon*. New York: Morrow, 1963.
Hollinghurst, Alan. "Rambunctious?" *The New Statesman* 98 (14 December 1979): 948.
Hollinrake, Roger. *Nietzsche, Wagner, and the Philosophy of Pessimism*. London: Allen & Unwin, 1982.
Hooks, Margaret. *Tina Modotti: Radical Photographer*. New York: Da Capo Press, 2000.
Hope, Warren ed. *Who Killed Carlo Tresca?* Harrisburg P.A.: Mountain Laurel Publications, 1983.
House, Roy Temple (R. T. H.) "Books in German: Fiction." *Books Abroad* VI (April 1932): 238.
Houissa, Ali. "Review of *Trozas*." *Library Journal* 119 (1 April 1994): 135.
Howard, Peter. *B. Traven: A Collection*. Berkeley: Serendipity Books, 1987.
Hulton, Clara. "Review of *Creation of The Sun and Moon*." *Library Journal* 84 (15 October 1969): 3824.
Humphrey, Charles R. "B. Traven: An Examination of the Controversy over His Identity with an Analysis of His Major Work and His Place in Literature." *Ph. D. Dissertation*. Austin: University of Texas, 1965.
Hunter, Clyde O. "Winner Lose All." *The New Republic* LXXXIII (31 July 1935): 342.
Huston, John. "Letter." *Time* (16 March 1948).
_____ *An Open Book*. New York: Alfred A. Knopf, 1980.
Hutton, John G. *Neo-Impressionism and the Search for Solid Ground: Art, Science, and Anarchism in Fin-de-Siècle France*. Baton Rouge: Louisiana State University Press, 1994.
Huxley, Aldous. *Eyeless in Gaza*. New York: Alfred A Kopf, 1936.
_____ *Beyond the Mexique Bay: A Traveller's Journal*. London: Chatto & Windus, 1949.

Icaza, Jorge. *Huasipungo: The Villagers* translated by Bernard M. Dulsey. Carbondale: Southern Illinois University Press, 1973.
Irsfield, John Henry. "The American as a Symbol of the Conflict between Industry and Nature in the First Five Novels of B. Traven." *Ph. D. Dissertation*. Austin: University of Texas, 1969.

James, Earle K. "Foreword." José Eustasio Rivera. *The Vortex* translated by Earle K. James. New York: G.P. Putnam's Sons, 1935, vii-x.
Janik. Allan and Stephen Toulmin. *Wittgenstein's Vienna*. New York: Simon and Schuster. 1973.

Jannach, Hubert. "The B. Traven Mystery." *Books Abroad: An International Quarterly* 35 1 (1961): 28-29.
_____ "B. Traven: *Aslan Norval.*" *Books Abroad: An International Quarterly* 35 1 (1961): 59.
_____ "B. Traven – An American or German Author?" *German Quarterly* 36 4 (November 1963): 459-468.
_____ "A Literary Curiosity." *German Quarterly* 38 (1965): 404-406.
Jay, Martin, *The Dialectical Imagination: A History of the Frankfurt School and the Institute of Social Research 1923-1950.* London: Heinemann, 1974.
Jenkins, Phillip. "B. Traven and the Wobblies." *B. Traven: Life and Work* edited by Ernst Schürer and Phillip Jenkins. University Park: The Pennsylvania University Press, 1987, 199-215.
Johnson, William Weber. "Who is Bruno Traven?" *Life* XXII (10 March 1947) 13-16.
_____ "A Literary Legend Who Prefers Anonymity." *Los Angeles Times* (8 October 1967): 37-38.
_____ "A Noted Novelist Who Lived and Died in Obscurity." *Los Angeles Times* (13 April 1969): 12.
_____ "B. Traven: His Secrets and His Passion for Anonymity." *New York Herald Tribune* (*Book Week*) (25 May 1969A): 9.
_____ *Heroic Mexico: The Violent Emergence of a Modern Nation.* Garden City: Doubleday & Company, 1969B.
_____ "Review of *The Carreta.*" *The New York Times Book Review* (19 March 1970): 5
_____ "The Many Faces of B. Traven." *Los Angeles Times Book Review* (8 August 1970): 8.
_____ "Solving the Mysterious Puzzle of a Man who Wrote and Ran." *Los Angeles Times* (14 September 1980): 3.
_____ "Trying to Solve the Enigma of the *Sierra Madre.*" *Smithsonian* 13 12 (March 1983): 156-175.

Kafka, Franz. *The Diaries of Franz Kafka* translated by Mark Brod. New York: Schocken, 1965.
_____ *The Metamorphosis and Other Stories* translated by Donna Freed. New York: Barnes and Noble, 1996.[5]
_____ *The Castle* translated by Mark Harman. New York: Schocken, 1998.
_____ *The Trial* translated by Breon Mitchell New York: Schocken, 1998.
_____ *Amerika: the Man who Disappeared* translated by Mitchell Hofman. New York: New Direction, 2002.

Kahlo, Frida. *The Diary of Frida Kahlo: an Intimate Self-Portrait.* New York: Harry N. Abrams, 1995.

Kahlo, Frida and Tina Modotti. *Catalogue of Exhibition.* London: Whitechapel Art Gallery, 1982.

Kaminsky, Stuart M. *John Huston: Maker of Magic.* Boston: Houghton Mifflin, 1978.

———— "Gold Hat, Gold Fever, Silver Screen." *The Modern American Novel and the Movies* edited by Gerald Peary and Roger Shatzkin. New York: Frederick Ungar, 1978A.

Kanfer, Stefan. *A Journal of the Plague Years.* New York: Atheneum, 1973.

Kaufmann, Walter. "Introduction." Friedrich Nietzsche. *The Portable Nietzsche.* London: Chatto & Windus, 1971, 1-19.

Kazin, Alfred. *"The Bridge in the Jungle." The New York Times Book Review* (24 July 1938): 6.

Keeney, Willard. "'Ripeness is All': Late, Late Romanticism and Other Recent Fiction." *The Southern Review* III 4 (October 1967): 1050-1061.

Kennedy, Milward. "Novels." *The National and English Review* CXXXVIII (March 1952): 183-186.

Kerouac, Jack. *On the Road.* New York: Viking Press, 1959.

———— *Lonesome Traveler.* New York: McGraw Hill, 1960.

———— *Tristessa.* New York: McGraw Hill, 1960.

Keune, Manfred. "Being as Adventure: *The Death Ship* and *The Treasure of the Sierra Madre* as Novels of Adventure." *B. Traven: Life and Work* edited by Ernst Schürer and Phillip Jenkins. University Park: The Pennsylvania University Press, 1987, 83-100.

Keyes, Evelyn. *Scarlett O'Hara's Younger Sister: My Lively Life In and Out of Hollywood.* Secaucus: Lyle Stuart, 1977.

Kidder, Frederick E. *"The Night Visitor." Library Journal* 91 1 (9 May 1966): 2367.

Kirby, Thomas A. "The Pardoner's Tale and *The Treasure of the Sierra Madre." Modern Language Notes* LXVI (March 1951): 260-270.

Kirsch, Robert. "Traven: I-Man Who's Who." *Los Angeles Times* (18 February 1977): 11.

Klein, Herbert Arthur (writing as Arthur Heller). "A Great Unknown: *The Death Ship." The New Masses* (12 June 1934): 24.

Klein, Herbert Arthur. "Hell Afloat: *The Death Ship." New Republic* (13 June 1934).

———— "Correspondence and Ephemera." *Powell Collection.* Special Collections UCLA Research Library, Box 1, Folio 12.

———— "Papers, 1933-1989." *Special Collection.* Stanford: Stanford University, 1991.

Klein, Mina Cooper. "Correspondence with M. L. Martinez." *Powell Collection.* Special Collections UCLA Research Library, Box 1, Folio 8.

Knight, Alan. "Peasant and caudillo in revolutionary Mexico 1910-1917." *Caudillo and Peasant in the Mexican Revolution* edited by D. A. Brading. Cambridge: Cambridge University Press, 1980, 17-58.

_____ "Mexican Peonage: What was it and Why was it?" *Journal of Latin American Studies* 18 1 (May 1986) 41-74.

Knopf, Alfred A. *The Borzoi Broadsheet* (September 1935).

Koepke, Wulf. "B. Traven and the German Exiles in Mexico." *B. Traven: Life and Work* edited by Ernst Schürer and Phillip Jenkins. University Park: The Pennsylvania University Press, 1987, 290-306.

Kohner, Frederick. *The Magician of Sunset Boulevard: the Improbable Life of Paul Kohner, Hollywood Agent.* Palos Verdes: Morgan Press, 1977.

Kohner, Pancho. *Screenplay of B. Traven's The Bridge in The Jungle.* Switzerland: Capricorn Productions, 1969.

Krim, Seymour. "The Passion of the Peons." *The Commonweal* LVI (13 June 1952); 250.

Küpfer, Peter. *Aufklären und Erzählen: Das literarische Früwerk B. Travens.* Zurich: Zentralstelle der Studentenschaft, 1981.

Kutt, Inge. "Facts and Guesses: The Difference between the First German and American Editions of B. Traven's *The Treasure of the Sierra Madre.*" *The Papers of the Bibliographical Society of America* 73 3 (1979): 315-331.

La Farge, Oliver. *Laughing Boy.* Cambridge: The Riverside Press, 1929.

La Farge, Oliver and Frans Blom. *Tribes and Temples: A Record of the Expedition to Middle America Conducted by the Tulane University of Louisiana in 1925, Volume I.* New Orleans: Tulane University, 1926.

_____ *Volume II.* 1927.

Labor, Earle ed. *The Portable Jack London.* New York: Penguin Books, 1994.

Lange, Victor. "Introduction." Georg Kaiser, *Gas I* translated by Herman Scheffauer. New York: Frederick Ungar Publishing Co., 1963, 1-7.

Langford, Walter M. *The Mexican Novel Comes of Age.* Notre Dame: Notre Dame University, 1971.

Larder, Ring Jr. *The Lardners: My Family Remembered.* New York: Harper & Row, 1976.
Lawrence, D. H. *The Plumed Serpent.* New York: Knopf, 1931.
_____ *Mornings in Mexico and Etruscan Places.* London: Heinemann, 1956.
_____ *The Woman Who Rode Away, and Other Stories.* Cambridge: Cambridge University Press, 1995.
Le Boutillier, Peggy. "Who is Traven? What Is He?" *Modern Mexico* XI (January 1948): 14-15.
Levi, Primo. *If This is a Man* translated by Stuart Woolf. London: Folio Books, 2000.
Lévi-Strauss, Claude. *Tristes Tropiques* translated by John and Doreen Weightman. New York: Athenaeum, 1974.
_____ *Structural Anthropology, Volume II* translated by Monique Layton. New York: Basic Books, 1976.
Lewis, Beth I. *George Grosz: Art and Politics in the Weimar Republic.* Madison: University of Wisconsin Press, 1971.
Lewis, Oscar. *Life in a Mexican Village: Tepotzlán Restudied.* Urbana: University of Illinois Press.
Library Review. "Books for Young Readers: *The Creation of the Sun and Moon.*" 23 (Spring 1972): 206.
Lipson, Charles. *Standing Guard: Protecting Foreign Capital in the Nineteenth and Twentieth Centuries.* Berkeley: University of California Press, 1985.
Lira, Miguel Nicholás. *La escondida.* México, D.F.: E.D.I.A.P.S.A., 1948.
_____ *Mientras la muerte llega.* Mexico: Libro-Mex, 1958.
London, Jack. *The Night-Born* (including "The Mexican".) New York: The Century Co., 1913.
_____ *The Iron Heel.* New York: Bantam, 1971.
_____ *The Call of the Wild.* Chicago: Nelson-Hall, 1980.
_____ *John Barleycorn 'Alcoholic Memoirs'.* Oxford: Oxford University Press, 1989.
_____ *The Sea Wolf.* Oxford: Oxford University Press, 1992.
López y Fuentes, Gregorio. *Campamento.* Madrid: Espana-Calpe, 1931.
_____ *Tierra: La Revolución Agraria en Mexico.* Mexico: Talleres de El Universal, 1932.
_____ *¡Mi general!* Mexico: Botas, 1934.
_____ *Los peregrinos inmóviles.* Mexico: Ediciones Botas, 1944.
_____ *El Indio* translated by Anita Brenner. New York: Frederick Ungar, 1961.
Lowry, Malcolm. *Under the Volcano.* Philadelphia: Lippincott, 1965.

———— *Dark as the Grave Wherein My Friend Is Laid*. New York: World Publishing, 1968.
Lübbe, Peter. "Utopian Elements in the Novels of B. Traven." *B. Traven: Life and Work* edited by Ernst Schürer and Phillip Jenkins. University Park: The Pennsylvania University Press, 1987, 149-155.
Ludszuweit, Christoph. *B. Traven: Über das Problem der "inner Kolonisierung" im Werk von B. Traven*. Berlin: Karin Kramer Verlag, 1996.
Luján, Rosa Elena. "Remembering Traven." *The Kidnapped Saint and Other Stories* edited by Rosa Elena Luján, Mina C. Klein and H. Arthur Klein. Brooklyn: Lawrence Hill, 1981, vi-xi.
Lunn, Eugene. *Prophet of Community: the Romantic Socialism of Gustav Landauer*. Berkeley: University of California Press, 1973.
Lürbke, Anna. *Mexikovisionen aus dem Deutschen Exil: B. Traven, Gustave Regler und Anna Seghers*. Tübingen: Francke Verlag, 2000.
Lynn, D. "*The Works of B. Traven*." Arena 1 (1950): 89-94.

McAlpine, William Reid. "B. Traven: The Man and His Work." *Tomorrow* VII (August 1948): 43-46.
McCarren, Felicia. *Dance Pathologies: Performance, Poetics, Medicine*. Stanford: Stanford University Press, 1998.
Maclaren, Hamish. "Selected Fiction." *Fortnightly Review* CXCI (March 1934): 382-383.
McCloskey, Barbara. *George Grosz and the Communist Party: Art and Radicalism in Crisis, 1918 to 1936*. Princeton: Princeton University Press, 1997.
Macdougall, Robert B. "An Ironic Story of the Greed for Gold." *The Saturday Review of Literature* XII (22 June 1935): 14.
McDougall, Stuart Y. *Made into Movies: From Literature to Film*. New York: Holt, Rinehart and Winston, 1985.
McGilligan, Patrick, and Paul Buhle. *Tender Comrades: A Backstory of the Hollywood Blacklist*. New York: St. Martin's Press, 1997.
McGrath, Patrick J. *John Garfield: the Illustrated Career in Films and on Stage*. Jefferson, N.C.: McFarland and Company, 1993.
McLynn, Frank. *Villa and Zapata: A History of the Mexican Revolution*. New York: Carroll & Graf Publishers, 2001.
MacNamarra, Desmond. "Mystery Man." *New Statesman* (23 June 1967): 880.
Machinek, Angelika. *B. Traven und Max Stirner: Die Einflus Stirners aur das Werk von Ret Marut/B. Traven*. Frankfurt: Verlag Davids Drucke, 1986.

Magdeleno, Mauricio. *Sunburst* translated by Anita Brenner. New York: The Viking Press, 1944.

_____ *La Tierra Grande*. Buenos Aires: Espasa-Calpe, 1949.

Magee, Elizabeth. *Richard Wagner and the Nibelungs*. Oxford: Clarendon Press, 1990.

Mair, John. "New Novels." *New Statesman* (9 March 1940): 338-340.

Mallan, Chicki. *Yucatán Handbook*. Chico: Moon, 1990.

Malraux, André. *Man's Hope* translated by Stuart Hope and Alistair Macdonald. New York: The Modern Library, 1941.

Malthaner, I. "Books in German Fiction. *Books Abroad* VII (January 1933): 76.

Manges, Dayle. "Review of *The White Rose*." *Library Journal* 104 (15 December 1979): 2666.

Mano, D. Keith "Review of *The Rebellion of the Hanged*." *New York Times Book Review* (27 August 1972): 2.

Manrique, Jorge Alberto. *Orozco: Mural Painting*. Mexico: Fondo Editorial de la Plastica Mexicana, 1991.

Mansur, Carole. "Reviews." *Punch* 287 (21 November 1984): 287.

Marks, John. "New Novels." *The Spectator* CLVIV (22 March 1940): 424.

Marsh, Fred T. "*The Treasure of the Sierra Madre*." *The New York Times Book Review* (9 June 1935): 6.

Marshall, Peter. *Demanding the Impossible: a History of Anarchism*. London: Fontana, 1993.

Martin, Stoddard. *Wagner to "The Waste Land": a Study of the Relationship of Wagner to English Literature*. Totowa: Barnes and Noble, 1982.

Mathews, J. H. *Benjamin Péret*. Boston: G.K. Hall & Co., 1975.

Mateos, Esperanza López. *La carta y el recuerdo*. 1943.

Maurer, Charles B. *Call to Revolution: the Mystical Anarchism of Gustav Landauer*. Detroit: Wayne State University Press, 1971.

Melling, Philip. "*The Death Ship*: B. Traven's Cradle." *The Twenties: Fiction, Poetry, Drama* edited by Warren G. French. Deland: Everett, 1975, 139-156.

Melville, Herman. *White Jacket or The World in a Man-of-War*. London: John Lehman, 1952.

_____ *The Confidence-Man: His Masquerade*. New York: New American Library, 1964.

_____ *Moby Dick: or, the Whale*. Oxford: Oxford University Press, 1999.

Memmi, Albert. *Dominated Man: Notes towards a Portrait*. New York: Orion Press, 1968.

Mencken, H.L. "Introduction." *The Nietzsche-Wagner Correspondence* edited by Elizabeth Foerster-Nietzsche and translated by Caroline V. Kerr. New York: Liveright, 1921, xi-xvii.

Menotti, Gian Carlo. "Libretto and Programe Notes to Compact Disc." *The Consul*. Berkshire Opera Company and Cooperata: New York, 1998.

Mezo, Richard E. *A Study of B. Traven's Fiction: the Journey to Solipaz*. San Francisco: Mellen Research University Press, 1993.

Michaels, Jennifer E. *Anarchy and Eros: Otto Gross' Impact on German Expressionist Writers*. New York: Peter Lang, 1983.

Miller, Charles Henry. "B. Traven, American Author." *Texas Quarterly* 6 4 (Winter 1963): 162-168.

———. "B. Traven in the Americas." *Texas Quarterly* 6 4 (Winter 1963): 208-211.

———. "Traven no es misterio," translated by Rosa Elena Luján. *Siempre!* 565 (22 April 1964): 44-45.

———. "B. Traven." *New York Times Book Review* (20 November 1966): 84.

———. "¿Cuál misterio?, dejen en paz a Traven." *Siempre!* 701 (30 November 1966): 14, 70.

———. "Introduction." *The Night Visitor and Other Stories*. London: Sphere, 1967, vii-xiii.

———. "Our Great Neglected Wobbly." *Michigan Quarterly Review* VI I (Winter 1967A): 57-61.

———. "B. Traven, Pure Proletarian Writer." *Proletarian Writers of the Thirties* edited by David Madden, Carbondale: Southern Illinois University Press, 1968, 114-133.

———. "B. Traven's Anarchistic Treasures: Reflections on *The Treasure of the Sierra Madre*." *B. Traven: Life and Work* edited by Ernst Schürer and Phillip Jenkins. University Park: The Pennsylvania University Press, 1987, 73-82.

Mitchell, Allan. *Revolution in Bavaria, 1918-1919: The Eisner Regime and the Soviet Republic*. Princeton: Princeton University Press, 1965.

Moeller, Bernard, ed. *Latin American and the Literature of Exile: a Comparative View of the 20th Century European Refugee Writers*. Heidelberg: C. Winter, 1983.

Molina, Cristóbal. "War of the Castes: Indian Uprisings in Chiapas, 1867-70, as told by an eye-witness," translated by Ernest Noyes and Dolores Morgadanes. *Studies in Middle America 5* edited by Maurice Ries. New Orleans: Tulane University of Louisiana, 1934, 353-395.

Monteath Peter. "B. Traven's Discovery of America and Native Americans." *Columbus and the Consequences of 1492* edited by Anthony Disney. Melbourne: La Trobe University, 1994, 80-88.

Morrison, Theodore ed. *The Portable Chaucer*. New York: Penguin Books, 1977.

Mulvey, Laura and Peter Wollen. "Frida Kahlo and Tina Modotti." *Catalogue of Exhibition*. London: Whitechapel Art Gallery, 1982, 6-27.

Muñoz, Rafael Felipe. *Memorias de Pancho Villa*. Mexico: S. El Universal Gráfico, 1923.

_____ ¡*Vámonos con Pancho Villa*! Madrid: Espasa-Calpe, 1931.

_____ *Si me han de matar mañana*. Mexico: Ediciones Botas, 1933.

_____ *El feroz cabecilla*. México, D.F.: Ediciones Botas, 1936.

_____ *Se llevaron el canon para Bachimba*. Buenos Aires: Espasa-Calpe, 1941.

Murphy, Patrick D. "Anarcho-primitivism in the Jungle Novels." *B. Traven: Life and Work* edited by Ernst Schürer and Phillip Jenkins. University Park: The Pennsylvania University Press, 1987, 216-225.

Müssener, Helmut. "B. Traven in Sweden." *B. Traven: Life and Work* edited by Ernst Schürer and Phillip Jenkins. University Park: The Pennsylvania University Press, 1987, 277-295.

"Mystery Man." *Newsweek* (21 April 1952): 124.

Nabokov, Vladimir. *Ada, or Ardor, a Family Chronicle*. New York: Vintage Books, 1990.

Naggar, Carole and Fred Ritchin eds. *México through Foreign Eyes, 1850-1990*. New York: W.W. Norton & Company, 1993

Naremore, James, ed. *The Treasure of the Sierra Madre*. Madison: University of Wisconsin Press, 1979.[6]

Navarro, Shiela Wood. "An Analysis of B. Traven: Focusing on His 'Jungle Novels'." *M. A. Thesis*. University of Tennessee: 1974.

Neville, Helen. "The Noble Savage." *The Nation* (6 August 1938): 133-134.

"New Books: A Selected List." *London Mercury* XXXII 188 (June 1935): 194.

The New English Weekly. "Reviews." VII (20 June 1935): 197-198.

New York Times Book Review. "Reviews." (29 April 1934): 21

_____ "Paperbacks of the Month." (14 July 1974): 31-32.

_____ "Paperbacks: New and Noteworthy." (3 July 1977): 19.

_____ "New and Noteworthy." (8 July 1984): 30.

New Yorker. "Also Out This Week." (28 April 1934): 102.

_____ "Review of *The Bridge in The Jungle.*" (23 July 1938): 59.
Newby, Eric. *The Last Grain Race*. London: Folio Society, 2001.
Newman, Ernest. *The Life of Richard Wagner, Volume Four: 1866-1883*. New York: Alfred A. Knopf, 1946.
Neyman, Mark. "*The Cotton Pickers.*" *Library Journal* 77 8 (15 May 1969): 2003.
_____ "Review of *March to the Montería.*" *Library Journal* 96 (15 September 1971): 2794.
Nichols, Lewis. "American Notebook, B. Traven Again." *New York Times Book Review* (11 June 1967): 51.
Nietzsche, Friedrich Wilhelm. *On the Genealogy of Morals* translated by Walter Kaufmann and R. J. Hollingdale. *Ecce Homo* translated by Walter Kaufmann. New York: Vintage Books, 1969.
_____ *The Portable Nietzsche* translated by Walter Kaufmann. London: Chatto & Windus, 1971.
_____ *The Portable Nietzsche* translated by Walter Kaufmann. New York: Viking Penguin, 1982.
Nolan, Robert. "Review of *The Kidnapped Saint.*" *Library Journal* 100 (1 December 1975): 2266.
Nolan, William F. *John Huston: King Rebel*. Los Angeles: Sherbourne Press, 1965.
Nordhausen, Frank. "B. Traven's Anfänge: Die 'Urfassung" Des Totenschiffs." *The German Quarterly* 65 3-4 (Summer-Fall 1992): 378-395.
Norris, Frank. *The Octopus*. New York: Doubleday & Co., 1901.
_____ *The Pit: A Story of Chicago*. New York: Grove Press, 1956.
_____ *McTeague: A Story of San Francisco*. New York: Penguin Books, 1994.
Nukanen, Ernest Jr. "Letter Disputes Review by D. K. Mano of *The Rebellion of the Hanged.*" *New York Times Book Review* (17 September 1972): 51.

Olafson, Robert B. "Keeping Those Cotton-Picking Hands out of the Unions! A Sequel to 'Traven Hunt'." *Organon* 3 1 (Spring 1972): 55-59.
_____ "B. Traven's *Norteamericanos* in Mexico." *The Markham Review* IV (October 1973): 1-5.
_____ "B. Traven and *The Death Ship* as High Culture." *A Question of Quality: Popularity and Value in Modern Creative Writing* edited by Louis Filler. Bowling Green: Bowling Green University Popular Press, 1976, 160-171.

_____ "B. Traven's Six-Novel Epic of the Mexican Revolution." *B. Traven: Life and Work* edited by Ernst Schürer and Phillip Jenkins. University Park: The Pennsylvania University Press, 1987, 141-147.

Onyeama, Dillibe. "Cosmopolitan Fiction." *Books and Bookmen* 25 (June 1980): 28-29.

Orwell, George. *The Road to Wigan Pier*. San Diego: Harvest Hill/HBJ Books, 1958.

Osterle, Heinz. D. "Review of *B. Traven: Life and Work* edited by Ernst Schürer and Phillip Jenkins." *German Quarterly* 63 2 (Spring 1990): 310-313.

Painter George. "New Novels." *The New Statesman and Nation* XLIII (9 February 1952): 160-161.

Parmenter, Ross. "*The Creation of the Sun and Moon* by B. Traven." *New York Times Book Review* (2 February 1969): 26.

Pateman, Roy. "Una Lucha en Muchos Frentes." *El Día* (15, 21 April 1986).

_____ *Eritrea: Even the Stones are Burning* 2nd edition. Lawrenceville, N.J.: The Red Sea Press, 1998.

_____ *Chaos and Dancing Star: Wagner's Politics, Wagner's Legacy*. Lanham: University Press of America. 2002.

Payne, K. "Americans and Indians: Cultural Commentary in B. Traven's *The Treasure of the Sierra Madre*." *Dutch Quarterly Review of Anglo-American Letters* 18 1 (1988): 46-58.

Paz, Octavio. *The Labyrinth of Solitude: the Other Mexico*; *Return to the Labyrinth of Solitude*; *Mexico and the United States*; *The Philanthropic Ogre* translated by Lysander Kemp, Yara Milos and Rachel Phillips Belash. New York: Grove Press, 1985.

Pearce, Roy Harvey. *The Savages of America: A Study of the Indian and the Idea of Civilization*. Baltimore: The John Hopkins Press, 1995.

Pearson, Sheryl M. S. "The Anglo-American Novel of the Mexican Revolution, 1910-1940: D. H. Lawrence, B. Traven, Graham Greene." *Ph. D. Dissertation*. University of Michigan: 1976.

Perez, Betty L. "Steinbeck's *In Dubious Battle* (1936)." *A Study Guide to Steinbeck: a Handbook to His Major Works* edited by Hayashi Tetsumaro. Metuchen: The Scarecrow Press, 1972, 47-68.

Pier, Florida. "New Fiction." *Time and Tide* XV 5 (3 February 1934): 148-149.

Pippett, Roger. "New Hands and Old." Review of *The Best American Short Stories of 1954* edited by Martha Foley. *New York Times Book Review* (22 August 1954): 5.

Plomer, William. "Fiction" *The Spectator* CLIII (28 September 1934): 454.

_____ "Fiction" *The Spectator* CLIV (26 April 1935): 705.

Poniatowska, Elena. *Tinísima: Novela*. México, D.F.: Ediciones Era, 1992.

Ponick, Terrence Lee. "The Novels of B. Traven: Literature and Politics in the American Editions." *Ph. D. Dissertation*. University of South Carolina: 1976.

Porter, Katherine Anne. *Flowering Judas and Other Stories*. New York: The Modern Library, 1935.

_____ *Ship of Fools*. Boston: Little, Brown and Company, 1962.

Powell, Lawrence Clark, "Who Is B. Traven?" *New Masses* (2 August 1935): 22-23.

_____ "Mystery Man of Mexico." *Typescript* in Powell Collection, Young Research Library, UCLA, no date indicated.

Pozas, Ricardo Arciniegas. *Juan the Chamula: an Ethnological Recreation of the Life of a Mexican Indian* translated by Lysander Kemp. Berkeley: University of California Press, 1962.

Pratley, Gerald. *The Cinema of John Huston.* South Brunswick: A.S. Barnes and Company, 1977.

Prescott. William Hicking. *The Conquest of Mexico*. New York: H. Holt and Company, 1922.

Pritchett, V. S. "New Novels." *The New Statesman and Nation* (8 September 1934): 296.

_____ "The Fortnightly Library." *The Fortnightly Review* CXLII n. s. (November 1934): 638-639.

Proudhon, Pierre-Joseph. *The General Idea of the Revolution in the Nineteenth Century* translated by John B. Robinson. London: Freedom Press, 1923.

_____ *What is Property? An Inquiry into the Principle of Right and of Government* translated by Benjamin R. Tucker. London: William Reeves, 1969.

Publishers' Weekly. "Review of *The Bridge in the Jungle*." 191 (9 January 1967): 59.

_____ "Review of *The Cotton Pickers*." 195 (24 February 1969): 64.

_____ "Review of *Government*." 199 (15 March 1971): 72.

_____ "Review of *March to the Montería*." 200 (30 August 1971): 273.

_____ "Review of *The Carreta*." 203 (14 May 1973): 48.

_____ "Review of *Trozas*." 241 (10 January 1994): 42.

Punch. "Sea Life - the Seamy Side." (31 January 1934): 140.

Quercus, P. E. G. "Trade Winds." *The Saturday Review Of Literature* (28 April 1934): 671.

Raskin, Jonah. "In Search of Traven." *The Radical Reader* edited by Stephen Knight and Michael Wilding. Sydney: Wild and Woolley, 1977, 73-89.
_____ "Afterword." *Assembly Line*. Somerville, Mass.: New England Free Press, 1977.
_____ *Underground: In Pursuit of B. Traven and Kenny Love*. Indianapolis: Bobbs Merrill, 1978.
_____ *My Search for B. Traven*. New York: Methuen, 1980.
Recknagel, Rolf B. *B. Traven: Beiträge zur Biografie*. Franfurt am Main: Röderberg-Verlag G.m.b.H., 1983.
Reed, John. *Insurgent Mexico*. New York: International Publishers, 1969.
Regler, Gustav. *A Land Bewitched: Mexico in the Shadow of the Centuries* translated by Constantine Fitzgibbon. London: Putnam, 1955.
_____ *The Owl of Minerva: The Autobiography of Gustav Regler* translated by Norman Denny. New York: Farrar, Strauss and Cudajhy, 1959.
Reilly, John M. "The Voice of *The Death Ship*." *The Minnesota Review* 9 (Summer 1977): 112-115.
Renn, Ludwig (pseudonym of Vieth von Golssenau). *Warfare: the Relation of War to Society* translated by Edward Fitzgerald. New York: Oxford University Press, 1939.
Renshaw, Patrick. *The Wobblies: the Story of Syndicalism in the United States*. Garden City: Doubleday & Company, 1967.
"Reviews." *Life and Letters* XII 64 (April 1935): 98-102.
Revueltas, José. *El luto humano*. Mexico: Editorial Mexico, 1943.
_____ "Crisis and Destiny of Mexico." *Is the Mexican Revolution Dead?* edited by Stanley R. Ross. New York: Alfred A. Knopf, 1966, 142-151.
Rexroth, Kenneth. "Disengagement: the Art of the Beat Generation." *New Writing #11*. New York: New American Library, 1957.
Rheingold, Joseph C. *The Mother, Anxiety, and Death: The Catastrophic Death Complex*. Boston: Little, Brown & Co., 1967.
Richter, Armin. *Der Ziegelbrenner: Das individualanarchistische Kampforgan des frühen Traven*. Bonn: Bouvier Verlag Herbert Grundmann, 1977.
Richter, Horst. *Anton Räderscheidt*. Recklinghausen: Verlag Aurel Bongers, 1972.

Rideout, Walter B. *The Radical Novel in the United States, 1900-1954*. Cambridge: Harvard University Press, 1956.
Risser, Lynn Katherine. "The Mexican Setting in the Contemporary American Novel." *Ph. D. Dissertation*. Fayetteville: University of Arkansas, 1985.
Rivera José Eustasio. *The Vortex* translated by Earle K. James. New York: G.P. Putnam's Sons, 1935.
Robinson, Cecil. *Mexico and the Hispanic Southwest in American Literature*. Tucson: The University of Arizona Press, 1977.
Rochfort, Desmond. *Mexican Muralists: Orozco, Rivera, Siqueiros*. San Francisco: Chronicle Books, 1993.
Rocker, Rudolf. *Nationalism and Culture* translated by Ray E. Chase. New York: Covici Friede, 1937.
Rodriguez, Antonio, *Siempre*! 200 (24 April 1957): 24-25, 69-70.
_____ "Esperanza López Mateos fue B. Traven." *Siempre*! 562 (1 April 1964): 26-27, 86.
Rosmer, Alfred. *Trotsky and the Origins of Trotskyism* translated by Ted Crawford. London: Francis Boutle Publishers, 2002.
Rubin, Martin. "Heroic, Antiheroic, Aheroic: John Huston and the Problematical Pragmatist." *Reflections in a Male Eye: John Huston and the American Experience* edited by Gaylyn Studlar and David Desser. Washington D.C.: Smithsonian Institution Press, 1993, 137-156.
Rubin, Ramón. *El Callado Dolor de los Tzotiles*. México, D.F.: Impressara Insurgentes, 1949.
Rühle, Jürgen. *Literature and Revolution: A Critical Study of the Writer and Communism in the Twentieth Century* translated by Jean Steinberg. New York: Frederick A. Praeger, 1969.
Rulfo Juan. *The Burning Plain and Other Stories* translated by George D. Schade. Austin: University of Texas Press, 1967.
_____ *Pedro Páramo* translated by Margaret Sayers Peden. Austin: University of Texas Press, 2002.[7]
Rus, Jan and Robert Wasserstrom. "Civil-Religious Hierarchies in Central Chiapas: a Critical Perspective." *American Ethnologist* 7 3 (August 1980): 466-478.
Russell, W. Clark. *The Death Ship: being an Account of a Cruise in "The Flying Dutchman." Collected from the Papers of the Late Geoffrey Fenton of Poplar, Master Mariner*. London: Chatto & Windus, 1901.
Rutherford, John. *Mexican Society during the Revolution: A Literary Approach*. Oxford: Clarendon Press, 1971.

_____ *An Annotated Bibliography of the Novels of the Mexican Revolution of 1819-1917 in English and Spanish*. Troy, N.Y.: Whitson Publishing Company, 1972.

S. W. "Mexican Adventure." *The Manchester Guardian Weekly* XXXI (5 October 1934): 275.

Sale, Roger. "Review: Good Servants and Bad Masters." *Hudson Review* XX 4 (Winter 1967-1968): 666-674.

Salzman, Jack. *Albert Maltz*. Boston: G.K. Hall & Co., 1978.

Sanborn, Alvin F. *Paris and the Social Revolution: a Study of the Revolutionary Elements in the Various Classes of Parisian Society*. London: Hutchinson, 1905.

Sanciprián, Nancy. *B. Traven en México*. San Angel, D.F.: Consejo Nacional para la Cultura y las Artes, 1991.

Sandoiz, Alba. *La selva encantada*. México, D.F: Ediciones Bota, 1945.

Scherret, Felix. "Das Werk B. Traven's" *Die Literatur* 32 (1930-1931): 389.

Schürer, Ernst and Phillip Jenkins eds. *B. Traven: Life and Work* University Park: The Pennsylvania University Press, 1987.

Schwartz, Harry W. *This Book Collecting Racket*. Chicago: Normadie House, 1937.

"A Seaman's Story." *The New York Times Book Review* (29 April 1934): 21.

Seibert, Peter. "Traven's *White Rose*: Regressive Idyll or Social Utopia?" *B. Traven: Life and Work* edited by Ernst Schürer and Phillip Jenkins. University Park: The Pennsylvania University Press, 1987, 156-180.

Seigel, Jerome. *Bohemian Paris: Culture, Politics and the Boundaries of Bourgeois Life*. New York: Viking, 1986.

Selser, Gregorio. *Sandino: general de hombres libres* translated by Cedric Belfrage. New York: *Monthly* Review Press, 1981.

Serge, Victor. *Memoirs of a Revolutionary: 1901-1941* translated and edited by Peter Sedgwick. London: Oxford University Press, 1963.

Seymour, Jim. *Hellaloo Pete O'Reno*. Pasadena: Upton Sinclair, 1919.

_____ "A Hobo on Mexico." *GALE'S International Monthly* (March 1920).

Shakespeare, William. *Hamlet*. New York: The Macmillan Company, 1913.

_____ *The Taming of the Shrew*. New York: The Macmillan Company, 1923.

_____ *The Tragedy of King Lear*. Boston: Ginn and Company, 1940.

Shattuck, Roger. *The Banquet Years: the Origins of the Avant-Garde in France, 1885 to World War I*. Freeport: Books for Libraries Press, 1972.
Sheppard, Richard F. "End Papers," *The New York Times* CXVI (24 April 1967): 31.
Silone, Ignazio. *Fontamara* translated by Eric Mosbacher. London: Everyman, 1994.
Simpson, Lesley Byrd. *Many Mexicos*, 4th edition. Berkeley: University of California Press, 1966.
Sinclair, Andrew, "Introduction." Louis-Ferdinand Céline, *Death on the Installment Plan* translated by John Marks. London: Panther, 1968, 7-13.
Sinclair, Upton. *American Outpost: A Book of Reminiscences*. New York: Farrar & Rinehart, 1932.
_____ *The Jungle*. New York: New American Library, 1990.
_____ *Oil*. Berkeley: University of California Press, 1997.
Siqueiros, David Alfaro. *Art and Revolution* translated by Sylvia Calles. London: Lawrence and Wishart, 1975.
Skow, John. "End of the Chase." *Time* (11 April 1977): 93-94.
Small Press Review. "Review of *The White Rose*." 12 (May 1980): 8.
Smith, Bernard. "Speaking of Books; B(ashful) Traven." *The New York Times Book Review* (22 November 1970): 2, 56-57.
_____ *A World Remembered, 1925-1950*. New Jersey: Humanities Press, 1994.
Sommers, Joseph. "Changing View of the Indian in Mexican Literature." *Hispania* XLVIII (March 1964): 47-55.
_____ *After the Storm: Landmarks of the Modern Mexican Novel*. Albuquerque: The University of New Mexico Press, 1968.
Soskin, William. "Mysterious B. Traven." *The New York Herald Tribune Books* (14 August 1938): 5.
Spell, Jefferson Rea. *Contemporary Spanish-American Fiction*. New York: Biblo and Tannen, 1968.
Spitzegger, Leopold. "Who is B. Traven?" *Plan*. I 8 (August 1946): 668-671.
Spoer, Ben (pseudonym of Ernst Preczang). "10 Jahre Traven" translated by F.A. Ebner. *Büchergilde* 4 (April 1936): 8-21.
Spota, Luís. "Mañana descubre la identidad de B. Traven," *Mañana* 258 (7 August 1948): 10-26.
_____ *Casi el paraíso*. México: Fondo de Cultura Economía, 1956.
Steele, Cynthia. "The Primitivist as Anarchist: Two Novels by B. Traven in the Mexican Literary and Political Context of the 1930s." *B. Traven: Life and Work* edited by Ernst Schürer and Phillip

Jenkins. University Park: The Pennsylvania University Press, 1987, 307-315.

Steinbeck, John. *In Dubious Battle*. New York: The Modern Library, 1936.

────────── *The Pearl*. New York: Viking Press, 1947.

Stent Ronald. *A Bespattered Page?: the internment of His Majesty's most loyal aliens*. London: Andre Deutsch, 1980.

Stirner, Max. *The Ego and Its Own: the Case of the Individual against Authority* translated by Stephen T. Byington. New York: Libertarian Book Club, 1963.

Stone, Judy, "The Mystery of B. Traven." *Ramparts* 6 2 (September 1967): 31-60.

────────── "Conversations with B. Traven." *Ramparts* 6 3 (October 1967): 55-70.

────────── "Review." *Los Angeles Times* (20 May 1973): 4, 11, 13.

────────── *The Mystery of B. Traven*. Los Altos: William Kaufmann, 1977.

────────── "Second Thoughts about the Mystery of B. Traven." *B. Traven: Life and Work* edited by Ernst Schürer and Phillip Jenkins. University Park: The Pennsylvania University Press, 1987, 66-72.

────────── *Eye on the World: Conversations with International Filmmakers*. Los Angeles: Silman-James Press, 1997.

────────── *The Mystery of B. Traven*, 2nd edition. iUniverse.com September 2001.

Storm Hans Otto. *Full Measure*. New York: The Macmillan Company, 1929.

────────── *Pity the Tyrant*. New York: Longman's Green and Co., 1937.

────────── *Made in U. S. A*. New York: Longman's Green, 1939.

────────── *Count Ten*. New York: Longman's Green and Co., 1940

────────── *Of Good Family: Stories and Observations about Spanish America* edited by David Greenhood. New York: Swallow Press, 1948.

"Stumbling." *Times Literary Supplement* (5 June 1969): 601.

Suárez, Luis. "y Presenta al mundo a B. Traven." *Siempre!* 695 (19 October 1966): 4-9. 70.

Sullivan, Mary. "Fiction: Gerontophile." *The Listener* 78 (6 July 1967): 25.

Sutton, Marilyn. *An Annotated Bibliography, 1900-1995 to Geoffrey Chaucer, The Canterbury Tales: The Prologue and The Pardoner's Tale*. Toronto: University of Toronto Press, 2000.

Swift, Jonathan. *A Modest Proposal: for Preventing the Children of Poor People from being a Burden to Their Parents, or the Country, and for Making Them Beneficial to the Public.* (First published 1729). New York: Dover, 1946.

Sylvester, Hary. "The Snapping of Chains in the Mahogany Forest." *The New York Times Book Review* (20 April 1952): 4-5.

Tambling, Jeremy. *Opera: Ideology and Film.* Manchester: Manchester University Press, 1987.

Tannenbaum, Frank. "Some Reflections on the Mexican Revolution." *Is the Mexican Revolution Dead?* edited by Stanley R. Ross. New York: Alfred A. Knopf, 1966, 185-209.

_____ *Mexico: The Struggle for Peace and Bread.* New York: Alfred A. Kopf, 1968.

Tanner, Michael. *Wagner.* Princeton: Princeton University Press. 1996.

Thatcher, David S. *Nietzsche in England, 1890-1914.* Toronto: Toronto University Press, 1970.

Thompson, Ralph. "Books of the Times." *New York Times* (18 July 1938).

_____ "Outstanding Novels." *Yale Review* (Autumn 1938).

Thoreau, Henry D. *Walden, or Life in the Woods.* New York: Signet, 1960.

_____ *Collected Essays and Poems.* New York: Literary Classics of the United States, 2001.

Time. "Adventure Unglossed." (17 June 1935): 74.

_____ "Review of *The Bridge in the Jungle.*" (18 July 1938): 51.

_____ "Review of *The Rebellion of The Hanged.* (21 April 1952): 114.

The Times Literary Supplement. "Uncivilization." XXXIX (2 March 1940): 109.

_____ "A Choice of Ten Good Entertainments." (19 March 1940): vii.

_____ "Who Is Traven?" (22 June 1967): 553.

Tobler, Hans Werner. "Conclusion: Peasant Mobilization and the Revolution." *Caudillo and Peasant in the Mexican Revolution* edited by D. A. Brading. Cambridge: Cambridge University Press, 1980, 245-255.

Toller, Ernst. *I Was a German* translated by Edward Crankshaw. New York: William Morrow, 1934.

_____ *Look through the Bars: Letters from Prison, Poems, and a New Version of "The Swallow Book"* translated by R. Ellis Roberts. New York: Farrar & Rinehart, 1937.

Tomlinson, Henry Major "The Death Ships." *The Manchester Guardian Weekly* XXX (26 January 1934): 215.

Torres-Ríoseco, Arturo. *The Epic of Latin American Literature*. Berkeley: University of California Press, 1970.

Tozzi, Romano. *John Huston: Hollywood's Magic People*. New York: Falcon Enterprises, 1971.

Traven, B. *Der Ziegelbrenner* 1 (1 September 1917).

_____ 9/14 (15 January 1919): 93.

_____ 23/25 (20 March 1920): 40.

_____ 26/34 (30 April 1920).

_____ "My Novel: *The Death Ship*." *Büchergilde* (March 1926).

_____ "Indianische Kunst von B. Traven." *Typographische Mitteilungen* 26 (1929): 71-74.

_____ "Dichter und Lesser" translated by F. A. Ebner. *Gutenberg Book Magazine* (9 September 1934): 144-147.

_____ *Land Des Frühlings*. Zürich: Büchergilde Gutenberg, 1938.

_____ *La rebellion de los colgados* translated from German by Pedro Geoffroy Rivas. México, D.F.: Ediciones Insignus (pirated), 1938 with an introduction by Rivas.

_____ *La Rosa Blanca* translated from German by Pedro Geoffroy and Lis Kostakowsky. México, D.F.: Editorial Cima, 1940.

_____ "La tercera Guerra mundial." *Estudies Sociales* 1-12 (1945): 9-16.

_____ "Dónde y cuándi perdió Alemania la Guerra." *Mañana* (9 November 1946): 19-23.

_____ "To Frame or Not to Frame," *Selected Writings* 5 (1946): 101-104.

_____ "Letter." *Life* (15 March 1948): 23.

_____ "Letter." *Time* (16 August 1948): 36.

_____ "A Legend of Huehuetonoc," translated by Esperanza López Mateos. *California Quarterly* 1 2 (Winter 1952): 56-65.

_____ "A Customer Broke a Tooth." *Modern Reading* 20 (Winter 1951-1952): 44-55.

_____ "Effective Medicine." *Manhunt* 2 (August 1954): 31-42.

_____ *Canasta de Cuentos Mexicanos* translated from English by Rosa Elena Luján. México, D.F.: Compañia General de Ediciones, S.A., 1956.

_____ "How to Tame Them." *Short Stories* 218 2 (New York) (November 1956): 59-82.

_____ "His Wife's Legs." *Accused* 1 4 (1956): 116-120.

_____ "Indian Trading." *Short Stories* (March 1957): 115-127.

_____ "An Unexpected Solution." *Short Stories* 219 (New York) (June 1957): 62-67.

_____ "Ceremony Slightly Delayed." *The Saint Detective Magazine* 8 (October 1957): 88-104.

_____ "Burro Trading." *Short Stories* 220 4 (New York) (August 1958).

_____ *The Death Ship: the Story of an American Sailor.* London: Jonathan Cape, 1959.

_____ *Stories by the Man Nobody Knows: Nine Tales by B. Traven.* Evanston: Regency Books, 1961.[8]

_____ *The Treasure of the Sierra Madre.* London: Mayflower, 1961.

_____ *Khundar.* Egnach: Clou Verlag, 1963.

_____ "Foreign Correspondent." *Texas Quarterly* 6 4 (1963): 173-175.

_____ "Sun Creation." *The Magazine of Fantasy and Science Fiction* VI (April 1964): 16-27.

_____ "Midnight Call." *Argosy* 26 (May 1965).

_____ "Submission." *Argosy* 26 (November 1965): 62-81.

_____ "The Quarter." *Fling* (March 1966).

_____ "Love, Justice, and a Bomb." *Argosy* 27 (February 1966): 82-93.

_____ *The Night Visitor and other Stories.* London: Sphere, 1967.[9]

_____ "Tribute to Siqueiros." *Siempre* (8 February, 1967): 5

_____ *The Bridge in the Jungle.* London: Jonathan Cape, 1969.

_____ *The Cotton Pickers.* New York: Hill & Wang, 1969.

_____ "When the Priest is not at Home." *Fourteen for Now: A Collection of Contemporary Short Stories* edited by John Simon. New York: Harper & Row, 1969.

_____ *The Carreta.* New York: Hill & Wang, 1970.[10]

_____ "Tin Can." *Adam Bedside Reader* # 43 (June 1970): 66-98.

_____ *The Creation of the Sun and Moon."* London: Frederick Muller, 1971.

_____ *Government.* New York: Hill & Wang, 1971.

_____ *Macario* edited by Sheilah R. Wilson. Boston: Houghton Mifflin Company, 1971.

_____ *March to Caobaland.* Harmondsworth: Penguin, 1971.

_____ *The Rebellion of the Hanged* translated by Charles Duff. Harmondsworth: Penguin, 1971.

_____ *General from the Jungle* translated by Desmond I. Vesey. Hill & Wang, 1972.

_____ "Las Pulquerías." *Siempre* (3 July 1974): 40-45.

_____ "El niño mexicano como artista y creador." *Siempre* (3 July 1974): 118.

_____ "A New God was Born." *The Ancient Mysteries Reader* edited by Peter Haining. New York: Doubleday, 1975.

_____ *The Kidnapped Saint and Other Stories* edited by Rosa Elena Luján, Mina C. Klein and H. Arthur Klein. Brooklyn: Lawrence Hill, 1981.

_____ "An Introduction to the Jungle Novels." *Praxis* 3 (1976):113-114.

_____ *Aslan Norval*. Frankfurt and Main: Büchergilde Gutenberg, 1978.

_____ *The White Rose* translated by Donald J. Davidson. Westport, Lawrence Hill, 1979.

_____ *To the Honorable Miss S. and Other Stories* translated by Peter Silcock. Westport, Lawrence Hill, 1981.

_____ *Trozas* translated by Hugh Young. Chicago: Ivan R. Dee, 1994.

_____ "Death Songs of Hyotamore of Kyrene," translated by Clark A. Dissmeyer. *The Free Press Death Ship* 3 (2003): 7.[11]

Treverton, Edward N. *B. Traven: A Bibliography*. Lanham: The Scarecrow Press, 1999.

Troy, William. "Radix Malorum." *The Nation* (17 July 1935): 79.[12]

Trumbo, Dalton. *Johnny Got His Gun*. Secaucus: Citadel, 1970.

_____ *Time of The Toad.* New York: Harper & Row, 1972.

Tschörtner, H. D. "Unknown Letters of Ret Marut from 1914." *B. Traven: Life and Work* edited by Ernst Schürer and Phillip Jenkins. University Park: The Pennsylvania University Press, 1987, 56-65.

Tucholsky, Kurt (Peter Panter). "B. Traven." *Die Weltbühne* 26 2 (1930): 793-800.

Tully, Jim. *Beggars of Life*. New York: Albert & Charles Boni, 1924.

_____ *Shadows of Men.* New York: Doubleday, Doran, 1930.

Turner, Ethel Duffy. *Writers and Revolutionists: an Interview conducted by Ruth Teiser*. Berkeley: University of California Press National Oral History Office, 1967.

_____ *Revolution in Baja California: Ricardo Flores Magón's High Noon*. Detroit: Blaine Ethridge Books, 1981.

Turner, John Kenneth. *Barbarous Mexico*. Chicago: Charles H Kerr & Company, 1910.

Urquizo, Francisco L. *Recuerdo que Visiones aisladas de la Revolución*. Mexico: Botas, 1934.

_____ *Tropa vieja*. Mexico: Talleres Gráficos del Departamento de Publicidad de la Secretaria de Educación Pública, 1943.

Valensi, Frances. "The Rubber Tappers." *The New Republic* LXXXIII (19 June 1935): 174-175.

Van Cleeve, John. *Sebastian Brandt's The Ship of Fools in Critical Perspective, 1800-1991*. Columbia, S.C.: Camden House, 1993.

Van Den Berg, Hubert. "Free Love in Imperial Germany: Anarchism and Patriarchy 1870-1918." *Anarchist Studies* 4 1 (1996): 3-26.

Van Doren, Mark. "Men without Countries." *The Nation* (16 May 1934): 569-570.

Van Hejenoort, Jean. *With Trotsky in Exile: From Prinkipo to Coyoacán*. Cambridge: Harvard University Press, 1978.

Vápeník, Rudolf. "B. Traven from a Czech Point of View." *B. Traven: Life and Work* edited by Ernst Schürer and Phillip Jenkins. University Park: The Pennsylvania University Press, 1987, 270-276.

Vogt, Evon Z. "The Chiapas Highlands." *The Handbook of Middle American Indians: Ethnology Part One* edited by Robert Wauchope and Evon Z. Vogt. Austin: The University of Texas, 1969, 133-151.

Wagner, Richard. *Richard Wagner's Prose Works* translated by William Ashton Ellis. New York: Broude, 1966.

Wain, John. "The Insulted and the Injured." *The New York Review of Books* 7 1 (18 July 1966): 22-24.

Waite, Robert G. L. *Vanguard of Nazism: the Free Corps Movement in Post War Germany, 1918-1923*. Cambridge: Harvard University Press, 1952.

Walker, Ronald Gary. "Blood, Border, and Barranca: The Role of Mexico in the Modern English Novel." *Ph. D. Dissertation*. University of Maryland: 1974.

_____ *Infernal Paradise: Mexico and the Modern English Novel*. Berkeley: University of California Press, 1974.

Walter, Nicholas. *The Spectator* (21 June 1980): 17-18.

_____ *The Times Literary Supplement* (1 January 1982): 13.

Warner, John H. "Tragic Vision in B. Traven's *The Night Visitor*." *Studies in Short Fiction* VII 3 (Summer 1970): 377-384.

Wasserstrom, Robert. *Class and Society in Chiapas*. Berkeley: University of California Press, 1983.

Waugh, Evelyn. *Robbery under Law: The Mexican Object-Lesson*. London: The Catholic Book Club, 1940.

Wedekind, Frank. *Franziska* translated by Philip Ward, adapted by Eleanor Brown. London: Oberon Books, 1998.

West, John Anthony. "Review of *The Treasure of the Sierra Madre*: On Caviar." *Books and Bookmen* 12 6 (March 1967): 38.

―――――― "The Great Traven Mystery. *New Yorker* (22 July 1967): 82-87.

―――――― "Traven's 'Death Ship'-Authentic, Hypnotic, and Maybe Alchemical." *The New York Times Book Review* (10 November 1985): 62.

West, Rebecca. *Survivors in Mexico* edited by Bernard Schweizer. New Haven: Yale University Press, 2003.

Westermann, Horace Clifford. *Letters* edited by Bill Barrette. New York: Timken Publishers, 1988.

―――――― *Exhibition Catalogue.* Chicago: Museum of Contemporary Art, 2001.

Weston, Edward. *Daybooks* I edited by Nancy Newhall. New York: George Eastman House, 1961.

Whitman, Walt. *Leaves of Grass*. New York: Book League of America, 1931.

Whitmer, C. F. "Review of *Macario* edited by Sheilah Wilson." *Hispania* 56 (1 March 1973): 192-193.

Whitney, Dwight. "More about Traven." *Life* XXIV (2 February 1948): 66.

Widmer, Kingsley. "The Way Out: Some Life-Style Sources of the Literary Tough Guy and the Proletarian Hero." *Tough Guy Writers of the Thirties* edited by David Madden. Carbondale: Southern Illinois University Press, 1968, 3-12.

Wilde, Oscar. *The Soul of Man under Socialism and Other Essays*. New York: Harper & Row, 1970.

Willett, John. *The Theatre of Erwin Piscator: Half a Century of Politics in the Theatre*. London: Eyre Methuen, 1978.

―――――― *Art and Politics in the Weimar Period: The New Sobriety, 1917-1933*. New York: Da Capo Press, 1996.

Williams, Adriana. *Covarrubias*. Austin: University of Texas Press, 1994.

Wilson, Carter. *Crazy February.* Berkeley: University of California Press, 1974.

Wilson, Edmund. *The Boys in the Back Room: Notes on California Novelists*. San Francisco: The Colt Press, 1941.

Wilson, Henry Lane. *Diplomatic Episodes in Mexico, Belgium and Chile*. Garden City: Doubleday, Page & Company, 1927.

Wilson, Sheilah R. ed. *Macario.* Boston: Houghton Mifflin Company, 1971.

Wolf, Eric R. *Sons of the Shaking Earth*. Chicago: University of Chicago Press, 1959.

Wolfe, Bertram D. *A Life in Two Centuries*. New York: Stein and Day, 1981.

_____ *The Fabulous Life of Diego Rivera.* Chelsea, M.I.: Scarborough House, 1990.
Womack, John Jr. *Zapata and the Mexican Revolution.* New York: Alfred A. Knopf, 1969.
_____ *Rebellion in Chiapas: An Historical Reader.* New York: The New Press, 1999.
Woodcock, George. "Mexico and the English Novelists." *Western Review* 21 (Autumn 1956): 22-32.
_____ *To the City of the Dead: An Account of Travels in Mexico.* London: Faber and Faber, 1957.
_____ *Anarchism.* Harmondsworth: Penguin, 1963.
_____ "On the Track of B. Traven." *Times Literary Supplement* (17 August 1976): 1053.
Woodcock, George, and Ivan, Avakumovic. *The Anarchist Prince: a Biographical Study.* New York: Schocken Books, 1971.
Woodworth, Fred. "Anarchist: B. Traven." *The Match!* 5 (May 1974): 6.
Workers Age. "Rivera Supplement" (15 June 1933).
_____ "The Destruction of Rivera's Radio City Mural" (15 March 1934).
Wren, Percival Christopher. *Beau Geste.* New York: Grosset & Dunlap, 1926.
Wyatt, Will. *The Secret of the Sierra Madre: the Man Who was B. Traven.* Garden City: Doubleday & Company, 1980.

Yáñez, Agustín. *La creacíon.* México, D.F.: Fondo de Cultura Económica, 1959.
_____ *La tierra pródiga.* México, D.F.: Fondo de Cultura Económica, 1959.
_____ *Las tierras flacas.* México, D.F.: Editorial Joaqúin, Martiz, 1962.
_____ *The Edge of the Storm* translated by Ethel Brinton. Austin: University of Texas Press, 1963.
Yates, Donald A. "Review of *El Tesor de la Sierra Madre* edited by Mario B. Rodríguez." *Hispania* XLVII (May 1964): 442-443.

Zogbaum, Heide. *B. Traven: A Vision of Mexico.* Wilmington: Scholarly Resources Inc. Imprint, 1992.
Zola, Emile. *Travail* translated by Ernest Alfred Viztelly. London: Chatto & Windus, 1901.
_____ *Germinal* translated by Havelock Ellis. New York: Vintage Books, 1994.

Notes

1. This is I presume a pirated version.
2. As this was the month of my birth I must add in an indulgent mood that three years later I could well have read the review.
3. The translator's name could well be another alias of Traven's. See Recknagel, 263, 371n753.
4. "¡Huye!" does not appear in any Spanish dictionary I have seen. On the other hand, "¡Huy!" means "wow", an expression of excited surprise.
5. Including: "The Stoker" and "The Penal Colony."
6. This is the annotated Huston screen play and it is fascinating to compare it page by page with Traven's novel.
7. With fine photographs by Josephine Sacabo.
8. Wyatt says that the book was edited by the prolific and popular author Harlan Edison, with the authorization of Hal Croves. Edison also rewrote "considerably" three of the stories which were originals (Wyatt, 126). The three must be "Tin Can", "Frustration", and "When the Priest is not at Home".
9. There is a short introduction by Charles Miller but the translator is not named. I assume that any translation was carried out by Traven.
10. No translator is mentioned. It is assumed to be the work of Traven.
11. Finding Traven's works particularly the short stories and assembling a bibliography of the editions I have used has been daunting. We have seen that in later life he published in some obscure pulp adventure, detective and science fiction/fantasy magazines. I am sure that more published stories remain to be discovered just as there are surely more by Ret Marut to be unearthed from the German magazines. I have assumed that the stories "Taboo" and "Hunt for Hillary" that pop up on the web search engines Google.com and Yahoo.com and are of a startling pornographic nature are not by our man – I may of course be proved wrong. I wondered about "His Wife's Legs" (another decidedly suspicious title) as Rolf Recknagel's reference to it being found in *Accus[s]ed Detective Story Magazine* is wrong (Recknagel, 396). However, recently I discovered that Guthke has a more plausible reference for it, and a German equivalent; so I include it, although I have not been able to locate the journal, let alone the story (Guthke 1991, 460n361).
12. Troy obviously had a classical education. For the rest of us: the full citation reads *Radix malorum est cupiditas*. It means: "avarice (greed) is the root of all evil". The tag can be found on line 5 of the prologue to the "Pardoner's Tale" in Chaucer's *The Canterbury Tales*. Those of you with a Christian upbringing may see its derivation from 1 Timothy VI, 10: "money is the root of all evil". To which I say Amen.

Index

A Writer is He? 124
Academy Awards (Oscars), 135, 145, 149
Academy of Motion Picture Arts and Sciences (AMPAS), 150, 154
Acapulco, 5, 42, 120n25, 130, 136, 159
Accomplices, 114
Acken, Edgar, 109
Actor and the King, the, 7
Ada, 55
Adler, Alfred, 23
Adorf, Mario, 63
Adventure of Mankind, the, 117
Africans, 62
After the Conquest, 130
Agua Azul, 94
Ahasuerus, the Wandering Jew, 58, 79n15
Alba, Sandoiz, 140
Alejandro, Julio, 149
Alemán, President, 105, 145, 149
Ali Houissa, 107
All Fool's Day, 3, 17n4
Allied Artists, 150
Allsop, Kenneth, 66

Also Sprach Zarathustra, 24, 35n3
Amarillos, 167
American Film Institute, 146
Amerika, 60, 80n18
Amsterdam, 17n1, 43, 45, 112, 155
An Unexpected Solution, story and film, 114-115, 148
Anarchist Encyclopedia, the, 156
Anarcho-primitivism, 23
Anaya, Rodolfo A., 136
Andrés, Ugaldo, 95, 101, 104
Angelitos, 76, 167
Another Mexico, 87
Anti Christian, the, 35n6
Anti-Semitism, 60, 62, 79n16, 80n20
Anti-socialist laws, 37
Arabic, 1
Aragon, 131
Argosy, 116
Armendariz, Pedro, 134, 147-148
Army of Madmen, the, 143
Art and Revolution, 27
Art of the Painter, the, 7, 144

Art Work of the Future, the, 27
Artaud, Antonin, 72
Ashliman, Dee L., 152-153
Aslan Norval, 47, 91, 116-117, 162
Assembly Line, film, 74, 148
Assembly Line, play, 152
Assembly Line, story, 69, 74, 151-152
Atlantic Monthly, the, 58
Auden, W.H., 58
Aufbau, 11
Austin, 70, 80n25, 152-154
Australia, 243
Austria, 13, 15, 44, 123, 160
Avant, John, 102
Aztec, customs, 76; legends, 52, 104; order of the, 3; paradise, 29, 106-107; prince, 72
Azuela, Mariano, 93, 96-97, 108, 139

B. Traven: A Bibliography, viii
B. Traven: A Vision of Mexico, viii
B. Traven: an Introduction, viii, 153
B. Traven: Beiträge zur Biographie, viii, 121n35
B. Traven: Life and Work, viii
B. Traven: the Life behind the Legends, viii
B. Traven Newsletter, 153
Bachajón, uprising, 39, 95
Baja California, 15, 34, 94
Bakunin, Mikail, 119n4, 119n14
Ballard, J.G., 130
Balún Canán, 142

Bang, Herman, 22, 26
Barbarous Mexico, 94
Barber, Michael, 73
Barratry, 59
Barron, David, 133
Barstow: Eight Hitchhiker's Inscriptions, 133
Baruch, Hugo (Captain Jack Bilbo), 10
Bauer, Otto, 78n2
Baum, Vicki, 129
Baumann, Friederike, 83
Baumann, Michael, viii, 3, 5-6, 8, 11-12, 19n17, 64, 85, 89-90, 115, 121n35, 150, 153
Bavarian Revolution, the, (1919), 8, 10-11, 14, 20n25, 22, 25-27, 39-40, 78n1, 83, 117, 125, 160
Bay of Pigs invasion, 48
B-T Newsletter, the, 3, 46-47, 91
Beals, Carleton, 87, 131-132
Beau Geste, 69
Beck, Johannes, 117
Bedaya, Alfonso (Gold Hat), 146
Beefheart, Captain, 126
Beevers, John, 70
Before Sunrise, 29
Beggars of Life, 65
Beginning of a Novel, 89
Bek-Gran, Robert, 117
Belfrage, Cedric, 129
Belgium, 40
Belgrade, 146
Beltrán, Alberto, 48, 104-105, 140
Benjamin, Thomas Louis, 154
Beresford, J.D., 76
Berkhofer, Robert, 48, 84

Berkeley, 118
Berlin, 2, 7, 27-28, 38, 40, 46-47, 51, 83, 102, 123, 127, 155, 159-160
Berman, Paul, 27, 93
Bernal, Penny, 152
Bernfeld, Siegfried, 14
Best American Short Stories of 1954, 113
Between Man and Man, 27
Beyond the Mexique Bay, 87
Bibeljé, August, 11
Biddle, George, 138
Bierce, Ambrose Gwinet, 33
Biglier, Anton, 12
Birth of Tragedy, the, 24
Bishop, Morchard, 110
Bivouac, 98
Black Friday, 42
Blacklist, the, 61, 133-134, 136, 139, 147, 156n4, 157n5
Blago Sierra Madre, 146
Blanke, Henry, 145
Blind Boy Grunt, 67
Blood, Land, and Sex, 243
Blom Frans, 9, 18n14, 42, 47, 85, 161
Blom Gertrude Duby, 12, 35, 47, 106
Blue Sepeckled SParroW, the, 7, 18n10
Body and Soul, 135
Bogart, Humphrey, 9-10, 17n5, 47, 146, 151, 161
Bohemia, 11, 126
Bohnen, Uli, 118
Bolshevik Revolution, (1917), 20n27, 39, 90, 92, 138
Bonampak, 85

Book of Lamentations, the, 110, 120n28, 142
Book List, 66, 112
Bookman, the, 91
Bosses, the, 97, 108
Bourget-Pailleron, Robert, 111
Bracho, Julio, 148
Brandt, Sebastian, *The Ship of Fools*, 58, 79n14
Brave Bulls, the, (book and film), 134-135
Braybrooke, Neville, 53, 63, 78n8
Brazil, 110
Brecht, Bertholt, 43, 57, 123-124
Breisky, Arthur, 11, 126
Brenner, Anita, 132, 154
Breton, André, 125, 131
Bridge in the Jungle, the, book, 2, 28, 34, 42-45, 52, 63, 75-78, 124, 142
Bridge in the Jungle, the, film, 134, 150
Bright, John, 121n33, 134-135, 147-148, 156n4
Bright, Josefina Ferro, 134
Brissenden, Paul, *The I.W.W.*, 28
British Broadcasting Corporation (BBC), vii, 8, 151
Brixton Prison, 8, 41, 54
Brockett, Eleanor, 47, 64
Brook Farm Institute, 33
Brown, Curtis, 149
Browne, Wynard, 53-54
Brushwood, John S., 97, 140
Bruto, el, 148
Buber, Martin, 27, 36n8

216　Index

Buch Für Alles, das, 51
Büchergilde Gutenberg, 14, 32, 41, 43-44, 46, 51, 54, 56, 67, 73, 78n2, 79n13, 83, 89, 111-112
Bucheister Verlag, 41
Büchner, Georg, 29
Bucholz, Horst, 63, 148
Buenos Aries, 52, 56
Bulgarian, 1
Bulnes family, 118n1
Buñuel, Luis, 148-151
Bunyan, John, 63
Burdett, Oscar, 103
Burning Plain, the, 141
Burro Trading, 75, 114-115, 168
Busch, der, 42, 73-74
Butler, Samuel, 109
Byam, Milton, 108

Cabello de elote, 99
Cachuchas, 140, 168
Caciques (bosses), 85, 97, 141, 168
Calder-Marshall, Arthur, 55, 101
Calderón de la Barca, Marquise Fanny, 120n19
California, 74, 80n26, 163
Call of the Wild, the, 31
Call to Socialism, 25
Callado dolor de los Tzotiles, el, 110, 140
Calles, Plutarco Elias, President, 41-42, 84, 99
Caloca, Colonel Manuel, 96
Campeche, 87
Campobello, Nellie, 100

Canada, 28, 41, 160
Canaima, 143
Cananea Copper mine strike, 38, 90
Canasta de Cuentos Mexicanos, una, book, 45, 115
Canasta de Cuentos Mexicanos, una, film, 47, 134, 147-148
Cancúc uprising, 37, 95
Candelaria, Maria, 95
Cándido, 109
Canek, 99
Cannes Film Festival, 149
Canessi, Federico, 48, 143
Caoba-Zyklus, viii, 27, 84, 92-93, 143, 162, 168
Capitaine Paul-Lemerle, 125
Capitanchik, Maurice, 77
Capouta, Emile, 114
Carballido, Ermilio, 149
Cárdenas Lázaro, President, 44, 87, 89, 96, 98-100, 105, 125, 142
Cargo system, 85
Carmelita, 150
Carranza, Venustiano, 39-40, 72, 105, 141
Carreta, the, 29, 43-45, 49, 95, 102-104, 129
Carretero, 103, 168
Cart Wheel, the, 114
Carta y el recuerdo, la, 142
Cartano, Tony, 130
Cartucho, 100
Casa Del Obrero Mundial, 15-16, 39, 72, 168
Casa Romano, 106
Casanova, Pablo González, 143

Casement, Roger Sir, 120n30
Cashew Park, 42, 120n25, 172
Casi el paraíso, 17n3
Castaneda, Carlos, 136
Castellanos, Manuel, 142
Castellanos, Rosario, 110, 120n28, 142
Castle, the, 42, 60
Catalan, 1,
Cattle Drive, the, 75, 93
Céline, Louis-Ferdinand, 60, 79n16, 80n17
Celso, 86, 95
Central Intelligence Agency (CIA), 48
Cerruto, Oscar, 56
Chacala, 144
Chamberlain, John, 69
Chamula, 85-87, 95, 109, 118n4, 118n5, 142
Chandler, Raymond, 79n9
Changing Times, 88
Chankin, Donald, x, 4
Chaos and Dancing Star, viii-ix, 243
Chapingo Chapel Murals, 129, 138
Chaplin, Ralph, 107
Chapultepec Castle, 96, 119n14, 137
Charlot, Jean, 139
Chatto & Windus, 55
Chaucer, Geoffrey, 65-66, 68-69
Chauvet, Elizabeth Guadalupe, 150
Checheb, Augustina Gomes, 95
Chemnitz, 7
Cheuse, Alan, 110, 112, 114
Cheyenne Autumn, 78n9

Chiapas, 18n15, 20n30, 29, 35, 37, 39, 42, 47, 49, 72, 83-88, 91, 93, 96, 102, 107, 111, 118n3, 120n33, 129, 132, 135, 142, 150, 154, 160, 164
Chiapas Expedition (1926), 9, 42
Chicago, 4-7, 20n28, 35, 49, 106, 160
Chihuahua, 100
Children of Light, the, 146
Chinese, 1, 42
Choice, 61, 66, 102, 110, 112, 114
Christ, 105
Christensen, Bodil, 127
Christensen, Peter, 70-71
Christian Science Monitor, the, 69
Churchill, Sir Winston S., 123
Cicora, Mary A., ix
Cinquemani, Frank, 102
Cipriano, 74
Ciudad Juárez, 4, 9, 38, 119n17
Ciudad Real, 99, 195
Clasas Films Mundiales, 149-150
Cobb, Lee J., 157n5
Cody, 80n27
Coffin on the Top of the Bus, the, 48, 50n4, 117-118
Colcord, Lincoln, 54
Collins, Mr., 34, 89, 91-92
Cologne, 28, 40, 124
Colombia, 110
Colorados, 169
Columbia, 135
Columbus, Christopher, 84

Comitán, 142
Committee for the Inquiry into the Moscow Trials and the Defense of Free Opinion in the Revolution, 128, 131
Commonweal, 109
Communist Party, the, 34, 78n9, 89, 98-99, 132, 134-135, 137, 140, 142-143, 156n4
Compadre Mendoza, el, 99, 169
Condor Oil Company, 89
Confidence-Man, the, 58-59
Connolly, Cyril, 104
Conrad, Joseph, 34, 53-54, 70, 72-73
Conversion of Some Indians, 75
Cooper, James Fennimore Cooper, 79n13
Cordan, Wolfgang, 42, 93-94, 129
Cornford, John, 18n16
Cortéz, Hernando, 32, 77, 130
Cosmos Science Fiction and Fantasy, 80n29
Cotton Pickers, the, 11, 16, 41, 47-49, 62-68, 72, 75, 131, 133, 162
Council of Adult Education, Victoria, vii, xin1
Count Ten, 164
Counter-Attack, 135
Coutiño, César Belarus, 142
Covarrubias, Miguel, 139, 145, 148
Covarrubias, Rosa, 139
Crane, Stephen, 34, 78n5
Cranwell, Doc, 144
Crazy February, 118n5

Creacíon, la, 141
Creation of the Sun and Moon, the, book and play, 44, 48, 104, 140, 152
Creighton, Basil, 43-44, 49, 67, 101-103, 129
Crevenna, Alfred, 147
Crimmitschau, 38
Cristero uprising, 41, 169
Croves, Dorothy, 6, 38, 49
Croves, Hal, 2-6, 8-9, 18n7, 27, 38, 45, 47, 49, 50n2, 71, 93, 105, 117, 129, 132, 135-136, 139, 145, 147-148, 152, 156, 156n3, 159, 161-162, 165n1
Cuauhtémoc, 52, 169
Cuban Revolution, 47
Cucaracha, la, 141
Cuernavaca, archive, 133, 136, 155
Cumulative Book Review Index, 1966-1985, 121n34
Curtin, 68, 70, 162
Czech, 1, 104, 126, 147
Czechoslovakia, 1, 15, 40, 126

D-Day landings, 45
D. W. Griffiths' Awards, 145
DADA, 124
Dachau concentration camp, 43
Dahlhaus, Carl, 35n4
Daily Telegraph, the, 70
Dana, Richard Henry, 34
Danish, 1, 22, 127
Dante, *Inferno*, x
Danzig, 7, 38-39

Dark as the Grave Wherein my Friend is Laid, 130
Davidson, Donald, J., 49, 88
Davis, Joseph A., 61-62, 153
Daybooks, 131
De Bourba, Ursula Beckmann, 11
De Bourba, Wladislac, 11
De Cordoba, Arturo, 148
De Droog, Fallen Ernst, 11
De Fuentes, Fernando, 99-100
De Lara, Lázaro Gutiérrez, 90
De Leon, Hazera Lydia, 92
Death, 69, 77, 113-114
Death of Artemio Cruz, the, 140-141
Death on the Installment Plan, 79n16
Death Ship, The, book, vii-viii, 1, 3, 9, 12, 14, 18n15, 19n21, 22, 26-28, 31, 35, 41, 43-45, 47, 51-64, 66, 68, 77, 79n10, 80n21, 93, 109-110, 112, 124-125, 127, 136-137, 153, 161
Death Ship, the, films, 2, 27, 47, 63, 137, 148, 150, 159
Death Ship, the, play, 151-152
Death Ship Letters, the, 137
Death Songs of Hyotamore of Kyrene, 20n26, 118
Deathridge, John, 35n4
Deceivers, the, 7
Denied a Country, 22, 26
Denmark, 123
Dennoch eine Mutter, 46, 149
Desierto de la Soledad, el, 106
Desorejamiento, 109
Dewey, John, 128
Día de los muertos, el, 114, 130, 169
Diaries, 60
Díaz, Porfirio, President, 31, 37-38, 85, 90, 92-95, 100, 105, 116, 119n15, 160
Dickens, Charles, 63
Dictionary of American Slang, 119n9
Dictionary of Sea Terms, 119n9
Diplomat, the, 94, 114, 116
Dobbs, 68, 70, 162
Doerflinger, William, 54
Doescher, Karl, 3
Doheny, L., 89-90
Domínguez, Luis Felipe, General, 111
Domitilo aspires to Congress, 97
Don Jacinto, 88
Don Juan Matus, 136
Don Segundo Sombra, 93, 119n12
Dorados, 100, 169
Dörwald, Rudolf, 42, 88
Dos Passos, John R., 33-34, 43, 65
Dostoevski, Fyodor Mikhailovich, 78n2
Dreiser, Theodore, 34, 78n5
Duff, Charles, 46, 107, 109
Durant, Jack, 73
Düsseldorf, 7, 39
Dutch, 1, 3, 9, 59, 126
Dynamite, 115

Eagle and the Serpent, the, 99
Earth Oppressed, the, 129
Earth Underfoot, 143

Echeverría, Luis, President, 49, 123
Eckhart, Dietrich, 62
Ecuador, 100, 120n30
Edberg, George, 68
Edge of the Storm, the, 141
Edifico Zamora, 128
Edward VII, King, 19n20
Edwardian Romance, 129
Effective Medicine, 74-75, 115
Einstein, Albert, 123, 138
Einzige, der, (the ego) 22-23, 70
Eisenstein, Sergei Mikhailovich, 103, 119n18, 132, 151
Eisler, Hanns, 123
Eisner, Kurt, 39-40, 78n1
Ejidos, 106, 169
El angel exterminator, 151
El Día, 140, 157n6
El Gringo, 159
El Machete, 139
El Norte, 149
El Paso, 97
El Paso Del Norte, 97
Ellison, Harlan, 19n21, 113, 136
Elmer Gantry, 78n9
Emerson, Ralph Waldo, vii, 33, 136
Empress of Madagascar, 60-61, 148
Engell, John, 71
Engels, Friedrich, 22, 35n2
English as a Second Language (ESOL), 152
Eritrea: Even the Stones are Burning, 243
Eritrean liberation, x, 156-157n6

Erlebensträger, 11-12, 170
Erzberger, Mathias, 27
Escandón, Fernando Mijares, 106
Essen, 7, 38
Estonian, 1
Estrellita, 104
Everest, Wesley, 107
Excelsior, 1
Eyeless in Gaza, 87

Fallacy of Origins, ix
Fanal, 26
Fanon, Franz, 106
Fantastic, 113, 120n31
Farewell to Arms, a, 42
Fascism, 17n1, 56, 67, 77
Faulkner, William, 141
Favali, Lyda, 243
Federal Bureau of Investigation (FBI), 9
Federales, 146, 170
Feige, Adolf R., 37
Feige, Otto H. A., 7-9, 37-38, 41, 160-163
Félix, Maria, 148
Femgericht (FEME), 27, 36n9, 170
Ferguson, Otis, 78
Fernandez, Ermilio, 147
Ferocious Chieftain, the, 99
Feuerbach, Ludwig, 35n2
Fievre monte a el pao, la, 151
Fight Club, 80n21
Figueroa, Antonio, 142
Figueroa, Gabriel, 100, 142, 147-148, 150
Film Daily, 145
Finnish, 1
Firefly, the, 97
Fitzgerald, Scott, 52

Flandrau, Charles, 120n19
Flandrau, Grace, 76-78, 81n32
Flantz, Richard, 27
Flemish, 1
Fling, 118
Flores, Magón Enrique, 16
Flores, Magón Jesús, 16, 38
Flores, Magón Ricardo, 16, 38, 40-41, 94, 100, 133, 142
Flying Dutchman, the, 58, 137
Flying Eagle Publications Inc., 115
Fontamara, 67
Ford, John, 148
Foreign Correspondent (A Truly Bloody Story), 115
4th International, 127
42nd Parallel, 33, 43, 65
Fourier, Charles, 33, 119n13, 131
Franco, Generalissimo, 44, 132
Franziska, 30
Fraser, Carol Hoorn, 137
Fraser, John, viii, 27, 53, 79n11, 136-137
Frederick III, 12
Free Spirit, 65-66
Freedom, vii
Freemasonry, 79n16, 30, 105
Freiburg, University of, 10
Freien, die, 35n2
Freikorps, 36n9
French, vii, ix, 1, 111, 130
Friendship, 75, 151
Frey, Charles, 18n15
Frustration, film, 149
Frustration, story, 46, 75, 114, 116

Frýd, Norbert, 126
Fuentes, Carlos, 92, 140
Fugitive, the, 148
Fulano, Elizabeth, 121n33
Full Measure, 164

Galbraith, U.S. Consul, 90
Gale, Johann, C.F., 18n8
Gale, Linn, A.E., 15
Gale's International Monthly, 15
Gales, Gerard (Gerry), 14, 18n12, 26, 28, 31, 35, 53-72, 78n8, 79n12, 133, 144, 148, 150, 161-162, 165n2
Gallegos, Rómulo, 148
Galvadón, Robert, 149
Gamekeeper's Gazette, the, 78n10
Garfield, John Julie, 135, 157n5
Gas, 30
Gauguin, Paul, 138
Gegensatz, der, 30, 118
Geismar, Maxwell, 108-109
Geller, Stephen, 65
"General", 112, 143
General from the Jungle, the, 17n1, 44-46, 48-49, 95, 111-112, 151
Georg, Egon, 117
Georg (e), Manfred, 3
German, vii, xi, xn2, 1, 3-5, 11-14, 19n9, 43, 50n1, 53-54, 56-57, 59, 67, 83, 89, 107, 109, 112, 117-118, 150, 161, 163
German Democratic Republic (DDR), 49, 126, 128
Germinal, 93, 119n13

Germination, 129
Gesell, Silvio, 27
Gide, André, ix
Gilet, Louis, 138
Glossary, ix, 167-174
Godfather, the, 113
Godfather Death, 113
Goering, Herman, 54
Gold, Mike (Iztok Isaac Granich), 132
Golden Globe Award, 145
Goldman, Emma, 16
Goldwasser, James; Marut Archive, 154
Goldwyn, Samuel, 78n9
Gómez, Ermilo Abreu, 99
González, 65
Good Soldier Svejk, the, 63
Goodbye Mr. Chips, 69
Goodway, David, vii
Goss, Robert, viii,
Government, 43-44, 46, 49, 101-102, 105, 126, 129
Graf, Oskar Maria, 14, 20n25
Graumulus, 117
Graves, Robert, 10
Great Traven Hunt, the, 152
Greed, 145
Greek, 1
Green Mansions, 93
Green, William C., 90
Greene, Graham, 72, 86-87, 118n7, 148, 153
Grimm Brothers, the, 113
Große Their, das, 117
Grosz, George, 43, 124, 156n1
Guadalajara, 164
Guard, the, 115
Guatemala, 42, 88, 95, 102, 106, 164
Guayamas, 164

Gubn-May, Helmut, 117
Guevara, Ernesto Che, 106
Guillory, Daniel, 57
Güiraldes, Ricardo, 93
Guiteras-Holmes, Calixta, 86
Gulf Stream, the, 138
Gunn, Drewey Wayne, 119n16, 131
Guthke, Karl, viii, 3, 8, 11-13, 28, 50n1, 89, 117, 133, 161
Gutting of Couffignal, the, 61
Guzmán y Franco, Martin Luís, 99

Habermas, Jürgen, 24
Haden-Guest, David, 18n16
Hageman, E. R., viii, 10, 118n2, 134, 154
Hairy Ape, the, 35
Hale, Edward Everett, 58
Hallinan, Charles, 129
Halperin, Maurice (M.H.), 67, 91
Hamburg, 9, 148
Hamlet, 57, 78n6, 79n13, 145
Hammett, Dashiell, 61, 79n9
Hamsun, Knut, 26, 80n17
Hangers on, the, 97, 172
Hanley, James, 53
Hansen, H. C., 123
Hanson, George S., 153
Hanson, Pere Albin, 127
Hard Times, 63
Harvard University, 63, 74
Hăsek, Jaroslav, 62-63
Hauptmann, Gerhardt, 29-30
Hawthorne, Nathaniel, 33
Hays, H.R., 34
Haywood, Big Bill, 65
Healer, the, 113
Hearst, W. R., 14, 90
Heart of Darkness, 53

Hebrew, 1
Hegel, G.W.F., 23, 35n2
Hegre, 4
Heidemann, Gerd, 12, 48, 152
Heidelberg University, 25
Heifetz, Jascha, 44, 132
Heinrich Heine Klub, 144
Hemingway, Ernest, 42, 52, 59, 66
Henestrosa, Alfa, 119n16
Henestrosa, Andrés, 119n16
Hergesheimer, Joseph, 65
Hermosillo, 164
Hernández, General José, 20n30
Herndon, James, 84, 106
Herrera, Pedro, 16
Herwegh, Georg, 35n2
Hess, Moses, 35n2
Hesse, Herman, 129
Hewitt, Lonnie Burstein, 152
Hicks, Granville, 57, 68, 76-77
Hill, Joe (Joseph Hillstron), 16, 28-29
Hill, Lawrence, 2-3, 5, 13, 49
Hill & Wang, 110
Hilton, James, 69-70, 80n26
Hirschfield, Al, 134
Hiroshima, 45
History Workshop Conference, viii
Hitler, Adolf, 15, 36n11, 54
Hoffman, Abby, 136
Holland, 40, 126
Hollinghurst, Alan, 66-67
Hölmstrom, Arne, 126, 149
Hölmstrom, Axel, 44, 126-127,
Holy Grail, the, 31
Homer, Winslow, 137
Homosexuality, 12, 26, 165n2

Hoover Institution, the, 132, 155
Hornsey, 108
Horst Vessel song, 26
Hot and Cold Cultures, 84
Hotel Prado, 148
House, Roy Temple (R.T.H.), 91
House Un-American Activities Committee (HUAAC), 123, 129, 134-135
How the West was Won, 78n9
How to Tame Them, 117
Howard, 32, 68-69, 118, 145
Howard, Peter, 117, 155
Howe, James Wong, 134-135, 149
Howe, Soñora Babb, 135
Huasipungo, 100, 110
Huasteca Petroleum Company, 89
Hud, 135
Hudson, William Henry, 93
Huerta, Victoriano, 39, 41, 80n28, 100
Hughes, Langston, 79n9
Huichole, 72, 80n28
Hulton, Clara, 105
Humphrey, Charles, viii, 152
Hungarian, 1
Hungarian Soviet, 40
Hungary, 12, 14
Hunger, 26, 80n17
Hunter, Clyde, 67
Huston, John, 5-6, 17n5, 34, 45-46, 71, 78n5, 81n27, 144-146, 149, 154, 159-160, 162
Huston, Walter, 17n5, 18n7, 145, 151
Huxley, Aldous, 87, 153

I-Thou, 27
Ibáñez, Vicente Blasco, 78n2
Ibsen, Henrik, 25, 29
Icaza, Jorge, 100, 110
Icelandic, 1, 127
Id, the, 70
Idiot, der, 39
Im Tropischen Busch, 41
Immovable Pilgrims, the, 98
In Dubious Battle, 34-35, 110
In the Fog, 7
In the Freest State in the World, 114, 156
Indian Dance in the Jungle, 114
Indianische Kunst, 88
Indian's Legacy, the, 118
Indigenista, 98-99, 138, 170
Indio, el, 98, 110, 170
Indo-China, 9, 18n13, 142
Industrial Workers of the World (I.W.W.), 1, 15, 20n28, 65, 80n24, 85, 107, 154, 160
Infernal Paradise, 153
Insurgent Mexico, 33
Intelligence Corps, 243
Intentional fallacy, ix
International Brigades, 16, 18n16, 133
Internationale, the, 26
Iron Cross, 10
Iron Heel, the, 31
Irsfield, John, 153
Isle of Man, 10
Israel, 138, 142
Italian, ix, 1, 20n28, 108, 148
Italy, 21-22, 56
Ivan Dee, 106

Jacoby, Hans, 148

Jalisco, 96, 141
Jannach, Hubert, 13-14, 19n22, 88, 116-117
Japanese, 1, 43
Jenkins, Phillip, viii, 64
Jennie Gerhardt, 34, 78n5
John Barleycorn, 31
Johnny Got His Gun, film and book, 134-135
Johnson, Eywind, 127
Johnson, Samuel, Dr. x
Johnson, William Weber, viii, 5, 77, 102, 154
Johnston, Ben, 133
Joyce, James, 70
Jonathan Cape, 55
Jones, Earle K., 110
Juan Pérez Jolote, 85
Juárez, President Benito, 37, 103, 105
Judas, 74; candlestick, 80n30
Jugend, 51
Junapeo, 144
Jungen, die, 25
Jungle, the, 35
Jurado, Katy, 150

Kafka, Franz, 41-42, 60, 80n18
Kafka, Hans, 10
Kahlo, Frida, 80n30, 127, 131, 133, 139-140, 168
Kaiser, Georg, 30
Kalltallgemeinschaft, 124
Kauders, Hans, 46, 113
Kaufmann, Walter, 24
Kazan, Elia, 157n5
Kazin, Alfred, 75-76
Kennedy, President John F, 48
Kenya, 108, 120n26

Kerouac, Jack, 136
Keyes, Evelyn, 5, 8
Khundar, 33, 118
Kidder, Frederick, 73
Kidnapped Saint and Other Stories, the, 7, 49, 75, 78n4, 114-116
Kierkegaard, Søren, 36n8
Kind of Thing That Can Happen in France, the, 7
King Lear, 63
Kirkus Reports, 115
Klein, Herbert Arthur (Arthur Heller), viii, 5, 7, 44, 49, 51-52, 57, 114-116. 134-135, 152, 154
Klein, Mina, viii. 5, 7, 49, 114-116, 134, 154
Knight, Alan, 93
Knopf, Alfred A., 13, 43-44, 52, 55, 67, 79n9, 109, 129
Kohn, José, 147-148
Kohner, Francisco (Pancho), 150
Kohner, Paul, 144-145, 150, 154
Kommunistiche Partei Deutschlands (KPD), 43, 124, 126, 156n1
Korean War, 46
Kostakowsky, Lisa, 91
Kreig, 125
Kreisky, Brunno Chancellor, 123
Kronos Quartet, 133
Kronstadt uprising, 40, 138
Kropotkin, Prince Pyotr Alexeivich, 24
Kun, Béla, 40
Kunst der Indianer, 46

Kutt, Inge, 13

La Farge, Oliver, 85
La Follette, Suzanne, 128
Lacandón, 85, 93, 106, 118n3, 120n24, 143
Lacaud, 70
Ladinos, 101, 120n27, 171
Lady Chatterley's Lover, 78n10
Lamz Duret Prize, 140
Land and Wind, 98
Land Bewitched, a, 125
Land des Frühlings, vii, 42, 46, 52, 83-88, 90-91, 95, 116
Landauer, Gustav, 25-26, 40, 58, 124
Langford, Walter M., 92
LAPD SWAT, 156n3
Lardner, Ring, jr., 156n4
Last Grain Race, the, 78n7
Last of the Mohicans, the, 79n13
Latvian, 1
Laughing Boy, 85
Lawrence, D. H., 78n10, 87, 103-104, 118n8, 138, 153
Laxness, Kilijan Halldor, 127
Leader's Shadow, the, 99
Leaves of Grass, 32
Lebanon, 127
Left Book Club, the, 78n2
Legend of Huehuetonoc, a, 74
Lehman, A., 111
Leipzig, 123, 128
Lenin, V. I., 11, 41
Let's Go with Pancho Villa! 100
Levi, Primo, 63
Lévi-Strauss, Claude, 84, 125

Leviathan, 154
Leviné, Dr. Eugene, 26-27
Lewis, Oscar, 118n6
Lewis, Sinclair, 34
Liberty, 32
Library Journal, the, 73, 88, 102
Library Review, 105
Liebknecht, Karl, 40, 124, 128
Life, 120n33, 159
Life and Letters, 103
Life in a Mexican Village, 118n6
Liga pro Cultura Alemana, 124
Lima, 164
Lira, Nicholás, 140
Listener, the, 73
Lithuanian, 1
London, 3, 9, 43-44, 47-49, 53, 88, 104, 129, 160
London, Jack, 22, 31-32, 54, 73, 78n2, 119n10
London Mercury, 103
Lonesome Traveler, 136
Lopez, Juan, 29
López y Fuentes, Gregorio, 96, 98, 110, 120n18
Lord Jim, 53
Los Angeles, 5, 93, 100, 127-128, 133-135, 150, 154, 163
Lost Horizon, 69
Lottery Ticket, the, 72
Love, Justice and a Bomb, 116
Love of the Fatherland, 29
Lowry, Malcolm, 130, 147, 153
Lübeck, 4, 18n8
Lübbe, Peter, 117

Lucha en Muchos Frentes, una, 156n6
Luján, Rosa Elena, 2-3, 5, 7, 12, 17, 17n2, 27, 44, 46-49, 50n1, 72, 86, 105, 107, 116, 118, 128, 132, 136, 147, 152, 165n1, 168
Lürbke, Anna, 125
Luto humano, el, 140
Luxemburg, Rosa, 28, 40
Lynn, D., 56-57

M.G.M., 78n9, 147
McAlpine, William, 10
McCarthy, Joseph Senator, 61, 134, 139, 147
McCord, Ted, 145
MacDougall, Robert, 68
MacDougall, Stuart, 70
McGrossen, George, 154
Mackay, John Henry, 22
McKinley, President William, 33
Maclean, Alistair, 110
MacNamarra, Desmond, 73
McTeague, 145
Macario (The Third Guest), book, 46-47, 74-75, 77, 113-14, 141, 162
Macario, film, 47, 113, 136, 149
Macías, Demetrio, 96
Made in U. S. A., 163
Madero, President Francisco I., 39, 89, 95-96, 100, 140
Madrid, 43-44
Magdaleno, Mauricio, 96, 98
Magee, Elizabeth, 70n13
Maggie, a Girl of the Streets, 34

Magic Mountain, the, 162
Mair, John, 57, 76
Mala Yerba, 97
Malet, Dora, 154
Maltz, Albert, 134-135, 150
Man without a Country, the, 58-59
Mañana, 17n3
Manges, Dayle, 88
Manhunt, 115
Mann, Anthony, 146
Mann, Thomas, 42, 162
Mano, D. Keith, 110
Man's Hope, 21
Mansur, Carole, 110
Maoz, Igal, 138
March to Caobaland, 43, 47, 49, 105
March to the Montería, 49, 105
Marcuse, Ludwig, 23
Marine Firemen, Oilers and Water Tenders Union, 65
Marks, John, 77
Marryat, Captain Frederick, 58
Marsh, Fred, 68, 70
Marshall, Peter, 23-24
Martell, Christine, 149
Martello, il, 128
Martínez, Maria de la Luz, 4-5, 42, 45, 130
Marut, Helene, 9, 12, 37
Marut, Ret, 2-3, 8-9, 11-12, 14-15, 18n12, 22, 26-29, 33, 35, 36n10, 37-41, 49-50, 54, 56, 62, 75, 78n6, 83, 105, 114, 117, 125, 129, 142, 154-156, 160, 163
Marut, Ret (rock star), 126
Marut, William, 9, 37
Marutendorf, 13
Marx Brothers, the, 59
Marx, Karl, 22, 35n2, 119n14
Marxism, 98-99, 104, 124
Marxistische Arbeiter Schule, 155
Masken, 7, 39
Mateos, President Adolfo López, 47, 96, 147
Mateos, Esperanza López, 44-46, 50n1, 56, 67, 74, 76, 88, 96, 101-102, 107, 109, 114, 116, 135, 141-143, 147, 161-162
Mathis, Peter Henry, 124
Mau Mau, 108, 120n26
Maurhut, Richard, 7, 10, 39, 75, 160
May, Carl, 35, 36n11
Mayan, 85, 87-88, 120n23, 142
Mazatalán, 9, 39, 164
Mazzini, Giuseppe, 21-22
Medina, Julián General, 96
Melville, Herman, 34, 53, 58-59, 64, 78n8
Memorial to Richard Wagner, 124
Memorias de Pancho Villa, 99
Mendez, General Juan, 143
Mercador, Rámon Del Rio, 127
Mercedes Ortega Lazona, 149
Merida, 42, 139, 164
Mermet, Irene (Mennet), 14, 39-41, 47, 50n3, 154
Mestizo, 87, 95, 98, 119n15, 120n18, 171

Mexicali, 38, 164
Mexican, the, 31
Mexico City, 2-6, 15, 17,
 17n3, 39, 41-42, 44-
 49, 52, 64, 74, 89,
 97, 104, 128, 132,
 134, 137, 142, 152
Mexico National University,
 42, 127
Mezo, Richard, 30
*Mi caballo, mi perro y mi
 rifle*, 100
¡*Mi general*!, 98
"Michael Field", 159
Michigan State University,
 154
Michoacán, 16, 83, 99, 126
Midnight Call, story and
 screen play, 75, 116,
 150-151
Mientras la muerta ilega, 140
Milewski, Waclaw, 27
Miller, Bill, 16, 18n9, 132-
 133
Miller, Charles, 18n9, 80n19,
 127, 133-134, 150,
 154
MilPaso Dam, 150
Moby Dick, 53-54, 78n5,
 78n8
Moctezuma, Carlos Lopez,
 147
Modest Proposal, a, x, xin3
Modotti, Tina, 128-129, 142,
 156n2, 161
Monat, der, 11
Monteath, Peter, 84
Montellanos, 108
Monterías, 94, 101-102, 106,
 111, 172
Montevideo, 111
Montseny, Frederica, 20n29

Mooney, Tom, 139
Moravia, 30
Mordida, la, 130, 172
Moreau, Clement, 124
Morelia, 126
Morelos, 39, 98,
Morgan, John Pierpont, 90
Moscow, 151
Mother Beleke, 7, 79n13
Movement for a People's
 Theatre, 25
Mühsam, Erich, 10, 26, 36n7,
 40, 43, 124
Mühsam, Zenl, 36n7
Munich, 14-15, 39-41, 91,
 125
Muñoz, Rafael Felipe, 99
Murals, 92, 94, 104, 119n14,
 129, 132, 137-139
Murphy, Patrick, 23
Mussolini, Benito, 40
*My Visit to the Writer
 Pguwlhkschrj
 Rnfajbzxlquy*, 7, 144
Mystery of B. Traven, the, 11

Nabokov, Vladimir, 55
Naked Spur, the, 146
Nancarrow, Annette, 133
Nancarrow, Canclon, 133
Nation, the, 114
National Board of Review,
 145
National Farmer's Union, 243
Nationalism and Culture, 27
Native American Indians,
 79n13, 84, 93-94.
 101-102, 109, 112,
 132, 136, 140, 143
Nautical Magazine, 79n10
Navajo, 85
Navarro, Shiela, 30, 153

Nave Morte, la, 148
Nazarin, 149, 151
Nazis and Nazi Party, 40-41, 43-44, 51-52, 54-55, 79n16, 106, 108, 124, 147
Neruda, Pablo, 129
Neue Behne, touring company, 38
New Bourgeoisie, the, 97
New English Weekly, 103
New God Was Born, a, 75
New Masses, the, 56, 76, 79n9, 125, 132
New Republic, the, 110
New Statesman, 76
New York, 9-11, 26, 28, 42-45, 47-49, 67, 73, 79n9, 114, 118, 129, 132, 137-138, 145, 154, 169
New York Film Critics Award, 145-146
New York Herald Tribune Books, 76
New York Times, the, 76, 102, 145
New York Times Book Review, the, 55, 112, 114
New Yorker, the, 54, 77, 109
Newby, Eric, 78n7
Newman, Ernest, 24, 106
Newsweek, 108
Neyman, Mark, 66, 106
Nicaragua, 42, 143, 163
Nietzsche, Friedrich Wilhelm, 23-25, 31, 35n3, 35n5
Night of the Iguana, 147
Night Visitor, the, 29, 46, 48, 61, 63-64, 72-74, 113, 115, 133, 144
Nihilism, 126
Noble Prize for Literature, 42, 127
Noble Savage, 79n14, 84
Nolan, Robert, 114
Nordhausen, Frank, 54
Norris, Frank, 90-91, 119n10, 145
Norway, 127
Norwegian, 1, 57
Nostromo, 71, 73
Novela de la selva hispanoamericana, la, 93
Nukanen, Ernest Jr., 110

O'Henry Prize, 113
O'Neill, Eugene G., 35
O'Reilly, Pete, 90
Obregón, Alfaro, 39-40, 72, 105
Ocosingo de Traven, 86
Octopus, the, 90, 119n10
Ode to Fourier, 131
Odets, Clifford, 157n5
Official Secrets Act, the, 120n26
Ohly, Götz, 36n10
Ohrdorf, 38
Oil, 35, 90
Oil, nationalization, 87
Okies, 66, 172
Olafson, Robert, 35, 57, 65, 74, 152
Olivados, los, 150
Oliver, Garcia, 20n29
Olivier, Lord Lawrence, 145
Olschewsky, Reinhold, 149
On the Road, 136
Onyeama, Dillibe, 66
Oranienburg Prison, 26

Originality, 144
Orozco, José Clemente, 104, 119n14, 132, 138-139
Orozco, General Pascual, 100
Ortigoza, Carlos, 147
Orwell, George, 130
Oso Negro hotel, 18n7, 145
Osterle, Heinz, 112
Otomi, 98
Over determinism, ix
Owl of Minerva, the, 125

Painter, George, 110
Palacio Nacional, 119
Palenque, 85-86, 120n24
Palo Alto, 155
Palmer Raids, 40
Pankhurst, Sylvia, 129
Paramount Studios, 78n9
Parque Caché, el, 42, 120n25, 172
Pardoner's Tale, The, 65-66, 68-69, 80n23
Paris, 28, 43, 80n16, 131, 150
Parmenter, Ross, 105
Parsifal, 30-31
Partch, Harry (Slim), 133
Partido Communista Mexicana (PCM), 139, 172
Partido Nacional Revoluciónario (PNR), 42, 172
Pateman, Carole, viii
Pateman, Roy, 30, 156n6, 164, 243
Payne, K., 72
Pearl, the, 34-35, 148
Pearl Harbor, 45
Pearson, Sheryl, M.S., 104, 153

Peck, Gregory, 150
Pedro Páramo, 141
Pehlke, Heinz, 148
Peiro, Juan, 20n29
Penal Colony, the, 60
Peonage, 103
Péret, Benjamin, 131
Peru, 163
Phantom of the Opera, the, 108
Phantom Ship, the, 58
Picture Post, 10
Pilgrim, the, 34
Pilgrim's Progress, the, 63
Pineda, General, 86
Pintacuda, Teresa, 148
Pipip, 78n8
Piscator, Erwin, 26
Pit, the, 92, 119n10
Pity the Tyrant, 163
Plan of Ayala, 39
Plomer, William, 69, 103
Plumed Serpent, the, 103
Poland, 8, 26, 44, 56, 130, 161
Polish, 1, 27, 60
Polonsky, Abraham, 135
Pomerania, 38
Poniatowska, Elena, 128
Ponick, Terrence, 31, 50n2, 77, 92, 148, 153
Pope Paul III, 94
Popocić, Jovan, 146
Porfiriato, 94, 140
Porter, Katherine Anne, 58, 132
Portuguese, 1
Posen (Poznan), 8, 38
Post hoc ergo propter hoc fallacy, ix
Post modernism, 24, 35n4, 144

Postgate, Raymond, 129
Powell, Lawrence Clark, viii, 134, 154
Power and the Glory, the, 87, 148
Pozas, Ricardo, 85, 118n5
Prague, 43
Pratt, Mr., 66
Preczang, Ernst (Ben Spoer), 41, 51, 83, 148
Preparatory Commission for the Formation of the Revolutionary Tribunal, 15
Preparatory School Murals, 104, 132, 139
Princeton University, vii, 243
Prison, 4, 6, 8, 12, 16n7, 26, 101, 103
Prisonero trece, el, 100
Prisoners All, 20n25
Pritchett, V.S., 67
Professor, 108
Proletarian Writing, x, 60-61, 68-69, 71-72, 76
Proudhon, Pierre-Joseph, 19n24, 21-23, 119n14
Prussia, 7, 38, 160
Publishers' Weekly, 66, 77, 102, 105-107, 115
Puerte, Felipe Camarillo, 139
Pulitzer Prize, 85
Punch, 55, 73, 110
Putumayo, 120n30
Pygmalion, 70

Quarter, the, 118
Qué Viva México!, 132, 152
Quetzalcoatl, 104, 173
Quintana Roo, 87

Räderscheidt, Anton, 28

Radio City Mural, 138
Rameau, Emil, 10
Ramparts, 6
Raskin, Jonah, 9, 17n2, 18n7, 35, 101, 116, 132, 136, 143
Rathenau, Walter, 27, 40
Reasons of State, 26
Rebellion of the Hanged, the, book, 9, 44, 46, 86, 93, 107-111, 124, 126, 132
Rebellion of the Hanged, the, film, 9, 46, 132, 134, 146
Rebellion of the Hanged, the, play, 126, 152
Recuerdo que visions aisladas de la Revolución, 100
Recknagel, Rolf, viii, 5, 10-11, 18n8, 29, 35n3, 64, 117, 121n35, 128
Red Badge of Courage, the, 78n5
Red Battalions, 72, 168
Red Poppy, the, 18n10
Redfield, Robert, 86, 118n6
Reed, Alma, 139
Reed, John, 11, 33-34, 154
Reeves, Keanu, 156n3
Reforma Hotel, 17
Regeneración, 38
Regler, Gustave, 125
Regler, James, 15
Reibentanz, Curt, 42, 67, 83
Reichstag, the, 37, 43
Reilly, John, 61
Reinecke, Helmut, 35
Remarque, Erich Maria, 10
Renn, Ludwig (Arnold Vieth Von Golssenau), 125-126

Residual Uncertainty, 243
Reviving the Dead, 114
Revolt of the Fishermen, the, 125
Révolution Surréaliste, la, 31
Revueltas, José, 140
Rexroth, Kenneth, 1
Rhine, the River, 30
Ring, der, 30
Rio de Janeiro, 9
Rio Grande, 119n17
Rio Usumacinta, 94, 111
Risser, Lynn, K., 118n5, 154
Ritter, Wilhelm, 44, 56
Rivas, Geoffroy Pedro, 91, 111
Rivera, Diego, 47, 81n30, 96, 119n14, 127, 129, 133, 137-138, 145, 152, 168
Rivera, José Eustacio, 110-111, 120n29
Road to Wigan Pier, the, 130
Robbery under Law, 87
Robinson, Charles, 150
Rockefeller, John D., 90
Rocker, Rudolf, 27-28, 47, 160
Rodríguez, Antonio, 3, 142
Rollins, Herb, 152
Roman Catholic Church, criticism, 10, 23, 30, 33, 42, 69, 87, 97, 103, 105, 111, 151
Romania, 126
Romanian, 1
Romano and Co., 120n24
Rome, 40, 148
Romero, José Rubén, 100
Roosevelt, President Franklin D., 89, 138
Rose Tattoo, the, 135

Rosenberg, Ethel and Julius, 47
Rosmer, Alfred, 128
ossen, Robert, 134
Rote Sprachrohr, das, 123
Rotterdam, 9, 40, 59
Rubin, Martin, 146
Rubin, Ramón, 110, 140
Ruge, Arnold, 35n2
Rühle, Otto, 128
Ruiz, Miguel, 100
Rulfo, Juan, 141
Rurales, 94, 173
Rus, Jan, 85
Russell, William Clark, *the Death Ship*, 58
Russian, 1, 55
Rutgers University, 152
Rutherford, John, 140
Ryan, John D., 90
Ryder, Albert Pinkham, 137

Sacco, Nicola, 26, 57-58, 127, 156n1
Saigon, 142
St. Louis, 10, 37
San Antonio, 43, 45-47, 93, 159, 164
San Cristóbal de la Casas (Ciudad Real), 37, 95, 106, 142
San Diego, 152
San Francisco, 9, 37, 39, 139, 160
San Francisco Chronicle, the, 9, 17n6
San Francisco Earthquake and fire, 9, 38, 160
San Francisco Examiner, the, 90
San José, 152
San Quentin, 156n4

San Quintín, 94
Sánchez, Luis Alberto, 92
Sandino, Augusto, 129, 143
Sandoiz, Alba, 140
Sano, Seki, 152
Santa Clara camp, 111
Santa Fe, 154
Santa Margarita camp, 111
Sassoon, Siegfried, 10
Saturday Review of Literature, the, 54
Schleswig-Holstein, 13
Schmid, Max (Gerard Gale), 19n17
Schöffler, Julius, 117
Scholl, Hans, 91, 119n11
Scholl, Sophie, 91, 119n11
Schönherr, Johannes, 117
School of Corpses, the, 79n16
Schopenhauer, Arthur, 18n12, 25, 30
Schürer, Ernst, viii
Schwarz, Harry, 5
Schweibus (Zwiebodzin), 8, 37, 130
Screen Writers Guild, 134, 145
Se llevaron el canon para bachimba, 100
Sea and the Jungle, the, 93
Sea Wolf, the, 31-32
Sealsfield, Charles (Karl Postl), 30-31
Secret of the Sierra Madre, the, 152
Seghers, Anna (Netty Reiling), 124-125
Seiwert, Franz Wilhelm, 39, 118, 124
Selected Writings, 117
Selser, Gregorio, 143
Selva encantada, la, 140, 143, 173

Serbo Croat, 1, 146
Serendipity Books, 155
Serge, Victor, 125
Seymour, Jim, 64
Shadow Line, the, 73
Shakespeare, William, 25, 57, 63, 75, 78n6, 79n13, 145
Shanghai, 43
Shaw, G.B., 70
Shelley, Percy Bysshe, 22, 33
Shine, Mr., 66
Ship of Fools, the, 58, 132
Short Stories, 114, 117
Si me han de matar mañana, 99
Siegfried, 33, 79n13
Siempre!, 138
Silcock, Peter, 49, 115
Silence of the Llano, the, 136
Silesia, 38
Silk Scarf, the, 7
Silone, Ignazio, 67, 108
Simiente del corsario, la, 142
Simon, John, 74-75
Simplicissimus, 51
Sinclair, Upton, 35, 55, 78n2, 90
Singapore, 9
Siqueiros, David Alfaro, 48, 90, 94, 119n14, 131-132, 137-138
Sister Carrie, 34
Skipper, 14, 27, 77
Slavery (peonage), x, 85-87, 91, 93, 97-98, 103, 106-107, 111
Slovak, 1
Slovenian, 1
Smith, Bernard, 1, 4-5, 13, 19n21, 43, 55, 67, 69, 76, 79n9, 136
Smythe, Nora, 129

Snyder, Gary, 6
Socialist League, 25
Solipaz, 33, 93, 110, 113
Sommer, Elke, 63, 148
Sommers, Joseph, 110-111
Somoza, President Garcia Anastasio, 143
Song of the Cotton Pickers, 123, 151
Song of the Open Road, 32
Soskin, William, 76
Souchy, Augustin, 127, 155
Soviet Union, 34, 36n7, 42, 44, 56, 79n16, 135, 139
Spade, Sam, 61
Spain, 11, 43, 156n2
Spanish, vii, ix, 1, 5, 28, 48-49, 50n1, 52, 56-57, 68, 74, 76, 84, 88, 91, 99-100, 102, 107, 109-111, 113, 118, 140, 142, 147, 161
Spanish Civil War, 11, 16-17, 18n16, 26, 44, 125-127, 131-133
Spartacist Revolt, 40, 156n1
Special Branch police, 8
Spectator, the, 77
Speed, 156n3
Spell, Jefferson, 97
Spielzeug, das, 88
Spitzegger, Leopold, 10
Spota, Luís, 2, 4, 12, 17n3, 46, 159
S. S. Yorikke, 14, 53, 58, 62, 78n6, 148
Stalin, Joseph, 47, 125, 127-128, 137, 156n1
Standard Oil, 77
Stanford University, 154
Stanislaus, 3, 26, 56, 59-60, 63, 161, 163, 165n2

Steele, Cynthia, 98
Steffens, Lincoln, 134
Steinbeck, John, 34-35, 110, 148
Steinheb, Georg, 118
Steiner, Max, 145
Steppenwolf, 129
Stern 12, 48
Stevenson, Janet, 135
Stevenson, Phillip, 135, 149
Stirner, Max (Johann Caspar Schmidt), 14, 22-25, 33, 36n8, 109
Stockholm, 44, 111
Stoker, the, 60
Stone, I.F. (Izzy), 17n6
Stone, Judy, 2, 5, 11-12, 17n6, 48, 56, 112, 115-117
Stone, Robert, 146
Stories by the Man Nobody Knows, 47, 75, 113, 115-116, 136
Storm, Hans Otto, 120n29, 163-164
Story of a Bomb, the, 114
Story of G. I. Joe, the, 135
Story of a Millionaire, the, 117
Story of a Nun, the, 7
Submission, film, 62, 148
Submission (The Tigress), story, 62, 75, 114, 117
Suhlendorf, 38
Sullivan, Mary, 73
Sunburst, 98
Superego, 70
Sutton, Eric, 43, 55
Sutton, Marilyn, 68-69
Sweden, 127, 149
Swedish, 1, 3, 5, 44, 46, 50n1, 112, 126-127

Swift, Jonathan, *A Modest Proposal*, x, xin3
Switzerland, 4, 40, 51, 106, 147, 162
Sydney, 9
Sylvester, Harry, 109
Syndicate of Revolutionary Painters, Sculptors and Engravers of Mexico, 138-139
Syndikalist, der, 127

Tabasco, 72, 87, 101
Tages-Anzeiger, 19n17
Taiwan, 1
Tamaulipas, 41, 43
Taming of the Shrew, the, 75
Tampico, 15, 41, 51, 65, 132, 143, 160
Tampico, 65
Tannenbaum, Frank, 84-85, 95
Tanner, Michael, ix
Tapachula, 164
Tapia, Primo, 16, 41
Tapio, Helen, 156
Tarascan, 16
Tarso, Ignacio López, 149
Tasker, Robert, 156n3
Tat Gruppe, 26
Tax, Sol, 86
10,000 Baskets, 152
Tepoztlán, 118n6
Tercera Guerra Mundial, la, 45
Terminal Beach, the, 130
Teruel, 11, 18n16
Third Guest, the, 113, 149
Thomas, Wendelin, 128
Thompson, Frederick, 154
Thompson, Ralph, 76-77
Thoreau, Henry, D., 18n9, 32-33, 84, 136
Thunder over Mexico, 103, 152
Thuringia, 7
Tierra Grande, la, 99
Tierra Pródiga, la, 141
Tierra y Libertad, 25, 33, 38, 83, 92, 100, 112, 174
Tierras flacas, las, 141
Time, 71, 76-77, 109, 145, 159
Time in the Sun, 152
Times Literary Supplement, the, 73, 76-77
Timón, 16
Tin Can, 75, 115
Tina Modotti ha muerto, 129
Titles, 7
Tlaxcala, 99
To Frame or not to Frame, 117
To the Honorable Miss S., 7, 10, 39, 50, 75, 115
Tobler, Hans Werner, 92
Tojolabal, 118n3
Tokeah, 30-31
Toller, Ernst, 26, 44, 57
Tomlinson, Henry Major, 53-54, 58, 93
Tönnies, Ferdinand, 25
Torch, the, 119n13
Torch of the Prince, the, 142
Torino, 63
Torsvan, Berick Traven, 2, 6, 8-9, 18n12, 27, 38-39, 41-42, 45-47, 49, 56, 71, 93-94, 105, 118n1, 121n34, 135, 159-161, 163
Torsvan, Burton, 6, 38, 49
Tovar, Lupita, 149-150
Travail, 119n13

Trave, River, 3-4; ship, 4
Traven, Jack, 156n3
Traventhal, 13
Travin, P.I. (Sletov), 11
Treasure of the Sierra Madre, the, archive, 80n25, 154
Treasure of the Sierra Madre, the, book, viii, 4, 9, 17n5, 23, 27, 32, 42-44, 46, 52-53, 66-72, 81n25, 98, 124, 129, 145, 152, 162
Treasure of the Sierra Madre, the, film, 4, 6, 17n5, 32, 46, 52-53, 71, 78n5, 81n27, 110, 144-148, 150, 154, 159, 162
Treasure of the Sierra Madre, the, play, 152
Trefny, Charles, 10, 18n15, 37
Trieste, 156n2
Tresca, Carlo, 128
Tressler, Georg, 148
Treverton, Edward, viii, 1, 50n1, 71, 109, 111-112, 117, 134, 148
Trial, the, 41, 60
Trials of a Genteel Family, the, 97
Trinidad, Vitorino (Felipe), 95
Tristan and Isolde, 30
Tropa vieja, 100
Trotsky, Leon, 42, 44-45, 60, 127-128, 131, 137
Trozas, 44, 50, 94, 106-108, 174
Truman, President Harry S., 134

Trumbo, Dalton (Doc), 134-135, 147
Tucker, Benjamin, 24, 32
Tucson, 27, 149
Tulane University, 85
Tully, Jim, 65
Turkish, 1
Turner, Ethel Rose Duffy, 31, 94, 133, 155
Turner, Kenneth, 90, 94, 119n14, 133
Twentieth Century Fox, 147
Two Years before the Mast, 34
Typographische Mitteilungen, 88
Tzara, Tristan, 126
Tzeltal, 85-86, 95, 120n23
Tzotzil, 85-86, 95, 111

UFA, 148
Uncas, 79n3
Uncle Tom's Cabin, 109
Under the Volcano, 147
Underdogs, the, 93, 96-97, 139, 167
Underground: In Pursuit of B. Traven, 136
United Artists, 150
University of Arkansas, 154
University of California Berkeley (UCB), 155
University of California Los Angeles (UCLA), viii, 154, 243
University of California Riverside (UCR), viii, 134, 150-151, 153-154
University of California San Diego (UCSD), 153
University of Southern

California (USC), 90, 146
University of Southern Carolina, 153
University of Maryland, 153
University of Michigan, 153
University of New Mexico, 154
University of Pennsylvania, 153
University of Tennessee, 153
University of Texas, 7, 152, 154
University of Wisconsin, 153
Unknown Soldier, the, 7
Urquizo, General Francisco L., 100
U. S. Highball, 133
USA, 33
U.S.S. Enterprise, 137
U.S.S. Franklin, 137
U.S.S. George Washington, 59
Usigli, Rudolfo, 127
Utah, 29
Utopia, 27, 33, 93, 113, 119n12

Valensi, Frances, 110-111
Vallejo, César, ix
Vampire State, the, 94
Van Derdecken, Captain Cornelius, 58
Van Heijenoort, Jean, 128
Vanzetti, Bartolomeo, 26, 57-58, 127, 156n1
Venezuela, 143
Venice Film Festival, 145, 147
Veracruz, 39, 41-42, 134
Vesey, Desmond, 46, 49, 111
Vienna, 40, 43

Victoria, Queen, 19n20
Vidali, Vittorio, 156n2
Villa, Pancho, 39, 41, 72, 97, 99, 112, 115, 133, 168
Vingt-Cinq Poèmes, 126
Viva Mexico, 120n18
Viva Zapata, 147
Voice of the Slug, 139, 156
Völkisch Movement, 25, 125, 174
Volksbühne, 26
Vom Wesen Der Anarchie, 117
Von Gagern, Friedrich, 30
Von Sternwaldt, Frau, 12-13
Von Stroheim, Erich, 145
Vortex, the, 110
Vorwärts, 18n10, 41, 51, 64, 75-76, 78n1, 97
Voyage au bord de la Nuit, 60, 80n17

Wagner Richard, vii, viii, 18n12, 23, 25, 27, 30, 33, 35n4, 35n5, 58, 78n2, 79n13, 80n16, 164
Wain, John, 72-73
Walden, 84
Walker, Ronald Gary, 87, 153
Walking, 32-33
War, First World, 8-10, 21, 26, 36n9, 39, 56, 60, 125-127, 156n1, 163
War, Second World, 18n15, 18n16, 44, 54-55, 81n31, 126
War of the Castes, 37
Warfare, 126
Warner Brothers, 18n7, 144, 146, 154-155

238 Index

Warner, John, 72
Washington, D.C., 13, 61, 63, 137-138
Wasserstrom, Robert, 85
Waugh, Evelyn, 86-87, 153
Wayne State University, 154
Web sites, x, 11, 20n28, 28, 139, 146, 155-156
Weber, die, 29

Wedekind, Frank, 30
Weider, Josef, 3, 46
Weill, Kurt, 43
Weimar Republic, 26-27
Weinstock, Herbert, 52
Welfare Hospital, 115
Well Worn Mantle, the, 164
West, John Anthony, viii, 71
Westdeutscher Rundfunk, 151
Westermann, Horace Clifford, 137
Western Federation of Miners (WFM), 65
Westküste, Die, 10-11
Weston, Edward, 41, 128, 131
Westphalia, 38, 160
What Life Means to Me, 32
When the Priest is not at Home, 74-75, 116
Where the Air is Clear, 141
White Guards, 15, 40
White-Jacket, 34
White Rose, the, book, 2, 11, 34, 42-33, 46, 48-49, 51-52, 88-92, 98-99, 114, 162
White Rose, the, film, 47, 135, 149
White Rose Group, 91
Whitman, Walt, 22, 32, 136
Widmer, Kingsley, 65
Wienecke, Albert, O. M., 8
Wienecke, Hormina, 8, 37

Wilde, Oscar, 113
Wilhelm II, Kaiser, 12, 40
Wilhelmshaven Naval revolt, 40
Wille, Bruno, 25
Williams, Adriana, 148
Wilson, Carter, 118n5
Wilson, Edmund, 163
Wilson, Ambassador Henry Lane, 89
Wilson, Sheilah R., 113
Winnetou, 35
Winthrop, 74
Wobblies, viii, 9, 15-16, 20n28, 65-66
Wobbly, der, 16, 41, 64
Wolf, Eric, 85
Wolf, the, 119n10
Wolfe, Bertram, 132, 140
Womack, John, 95-96
Woman Held Hostage, the, 140
Woman Who Rode Away, the, 104
Woodcock, George, 4, 13-14, 17, 127
Woodworth, Fred, 62
Woyzeck, 29
Wren, Percival Christopher, 69
Writer of Serpentine Shrewdness, a, 7, 144
Writers Guild, 145
Württemberg, 25
Wyatt, Will, 4, 7-9, 11, 36n10, 130, 151, 160, 162

Xochiquetzal, 174

Yáñez, Agustín, 141
Yaqui, 136

Yates, Donald, 68
Yiddish, 1
Young, Hugh, 49
Yucatán, 42, 87, 90, 139

Zapata, Emiliano, 25, 39-40,
    72, 95-96, 98, 108,
    112, 147
Zapatista Uprising (1994),
    20n30, 50, 95-96,
    106-107, 156
Zeitgeist, ix
Ziegelbrenner, der, 11, 14-15,
    19n23, 21-22, 26-27,
    30, 33, 36n10, 39-40,
    62, 68, 83, 124, 161,
    174
Zielke, Elfriede, 38-39
Zielke, Irene, 39
Zimet, Julian (Julian Halevy),
    133, 136
Zinacantan, 87
Zogbaum, Heidi, viii, 19n19,
    50n4, 86, 93, 96,
    119n14
Zola, Emile, 29, 93, 119n13,
    164
Zurich, 3, 19n17, 43-47,
    50n4, 56, 83, 113
Zweig, Arnold, 78n2

Author's Biography

Roy Pateman is Professor Emeritus having retired from the Department of Political Science at UCLA in 2002. Prior to twelve years in Los Angeles he had taught in England, Australia and at Princeton University. His non-academic professional life includes a three year regular engagement in the British Army's Intelligence Corps; work in the Australian Federal Public Service and as an agricultural economist with the National Farmer's Union.

He has published *Chaos and Dancing Star: Wagner's Politics, Wagner's Legacy* and *Residual Uncertainty: Trying to Avoid Intelligence and Policy Mistakes in the Modern World* with University Press of America. Other major books include: *Eritrea: Even the Stones are Burning* (Red Sea Press) and *Blood, Land, and Sex: Legal and Political Pluralism in Eritrea* (Indiana University Press, with Lyda Favali).